Popular Politics and Political Culture

Popular Politics and Political Culture
Urban Scotland, 1918–1939

Malcolm Petrie

EDINBURGH
University Press

Edinburgh University Press is one of the leading university presses in the UK. We publish academic books and journals in our selected subject areas across the humanities and social sciences, combining cutting-edge scholarship with high editorial and production values to produce academic works of lasting importance. For more information visit our website: edinburghuniversitypress.com

Edinburgh University Press Ltd
The Tun – Holyrood Road
12 (2f) Jackson's Entry
Edinburgh EH8 8PJ

First published in hardback by Edinburgh University Press 2018

Typeset in 10.5/13 Sabon by
Servis Filmsetting Ltd, Stockport, Cheshire,
and printed and bound by CPI Group (UK) Ltd, Croydon, CR0 4YY

A CIP record for this book is available from the British Library

ISBN 978 1 4744 2561 2 (hardback)
ISBN 978 1 4744 5220 5 (paperback)
ISBN 978 1 4744 2562 9 (webready PDF)
ISBN 978 1 4744 2563 6 (epub)

Contents

Acknowledgements

The School of History at the University of St Andrews has provided a supportive setting in which to undertake this research. I am especially grateful to be part of the Institute of Scottish Historical Research, first as a postgraduate student, and now as a member of staff, and I would like to thank the recent directors of the Institute, Roger Mason and Katie Stevenson, for their tireless work in creating such a sympathetic research environment. While completing this book I was lucky enough to spend a year at the University of Edinburgh as a Leverhulme early career fellow, before returning to St Andrews: the staff and students at both institutions helped to hone many of the arguments presented here. While the list of those who offered advice is lengthy, if in what follows I say anything of interest then it almost certainly started as a conversation with one or more of Bill Knox, Colin Kidd, Ewen Cameron, Gordon Pentland, Claire Hawes and Andrew Thorpe. The flaws, weaknesses and errors, on the other hand, remain, of course, entirely my own.

I am indebted to the archivists and librarians at the following institutions, who assisted with this research, and, where appropriate, granted permission to cite material held in their collections: the National Library of Scotland; the National Records of Scotland; the Labour History Archive and Study Centre, Manchester; the Marx Memorial Library, London; the Imperial War Museum; Dundee City Archives; the Local History Centre at Dundee Central Library; the Mitchell Library, Glasgow; the Parliamentary Archives; and Aberdeen University's Special Collections department. Additional permissions were generously granted by the Educational Department of the Trades Union Congress, Edinburgh Northern and Leith Constituency Labour Party and the Scottish Fabian Society. I am also grateful to Aberdeen Journals, to the Glasgow Herald & Times, and to The Scotsman Publications Ltd, who kindly granted permission to reproduce images from the *Aberdeen Evening Express*, the *Glasgow Evening Times* and the *Edinburgh Evening Dispatch* respectively. Thanks are due also to the editorial team at Edinburgh University Press for all their assistance.

There are three further, fathomless, debts to be acknowledged. This book would never have been completed without the support of my parents, Joyce and Gordon, nor without the love, kindness and patience of my wife, Fiona.

Abbreviations

AEU	Amalgamated Engineering Union
AUL	Aberdeen University Library
CLC	Central Labour College
Comintern	Communist International
CPGB	Communist Party of Great Britain
DLP	Divisional Labour Party
DPL	Dundee Public Library
ILP	Independent Labour Party
IWM	Imperial War Museum
JFWU	Jute and Flax Workers' Union
LHASC	Labour History Archive and Study Centre
MML	Marx Memorial Library
NCLC	National Council of Labour Colleges
NEC	National Executive Committee
NLS	National Library of Scotland
NRS	National Records of Scotland
NUR	National Union of Railwaymen
NUWCM	National Unemployed Workers' Committee Movement
NUWM	National Unemployed Workers' Movement
PAC	Public Assistance Committee
PLP	Parliamentary Labour Party
SDF	Social Democratic Federation
SEC	Scottish Executive Committee
SLC	Scottish Labour College
SLP	Socialist Labour Party
SPP	Scottish Prohibition Party
SPS	Scottish Painters' Society
STUC	Scottish Trades Union Congress
SWMF	South Wales Miners' Federation
TLC	Trades and Labour Council
TLP	Trades and Labour Party
TUC	Trades Union Congress

UAB	Unemployment Assistance Board
WEA	Workers' Educational Association
WSPU	Women's Social and Political Union
YCL	Young Communist League

Figures

Introduction:
Class, Radicalism and Democracy, 1918–1939

In August 1927, Edinburgh town council invited King George V to preside at the inauguration of a new municipal housing scheme in Prestonfield, in the south-east of the city. Uncomfortable with such displays of deference, and responsible for the direction of the small Labour group on the town council, Edinburgh trades council instructed its members to 'abstain from taking part in any of the functions in connection with the King's visit'. Notwithstanding the evident clarity of this guidance, six Labour council-lors nonetheless elected to attend the opening ceremony, a decision for which they were publicly rebuked by their colleagues; indeed, they only narrowly survived an attempt to proscribe their reselection as Labour candidates.[1]

Outwardly, the disquiet occasioned by the appearance of Labour repre-sentatives alongside royalty belongs to the insular and insignificant gesture politics of the provincial radical left. Certainly, the quarrel was discussed in just such terms by the local press: the *Edinburgh Evening News* felt that the decision to censure the councillors was symptomatic of a movement whose 'sole aim ... appears to be to make a long series of ... protests against anybody and everybody'.[2] In retrospect, however, we should be less dismissive, since in such seemingly trivial moments could be glimpsed the central tensions within Scottish, and indeed British, politics after the democratisation of the franchise in 1918. Underpinning the dispute were two conflicting conceptions of political representation and identity, of the purpose of politics, and of the manner in which it should be conducted. For those who condemned the councillors, politics was at root a contest between two irreconcilable sections of society, and demanded fidelity to a constituency constructed in terms of class and locality. Charles Gibbons, a tutor at Edinburgh labour college, thus upheld a distinction between the interests of a working class that Labour was morally obligated to repre-sent, and those of a middle class who masqueraded under the convenient alias of the 'public'; it was, he reasoned in suggestive terms, impossible to serve both 'God and Mammon'.[3] In contrast, the censured councillors and their supporters advanced a conciliatory vision of politics, one that accorded priority to the national electoral prospects of the Labour Party. Frank Smithies, the trades council's political officer, asserted that the councillors had been right to attend the event: as 'public' representatives, they were required to 'stand by the government as then constituted'. Significant too was Smithies' insinuation, echoed in the local press, that the row had been exacerbated purposely by members of the Communist Party of Great Britain (CPGB): he advised that such 'pettifogging' local disputes should be ignored in favour of 'unity on the principles laid down by the National Party'. Likewise, Dr Drummond Shiels, the Labour member for Edinburgh East, complained that Labour's electoral hopes had once more been 'side-tracked by foolish outbreaks of this kind', which only assisted those keen to portray the party as being motivated class envy and resentment.[4] Antagonistic local expressions of class identity were, it appeared, evidence of a dangerous left-wing radicalism, perhaps even Communism, and were a barrier to success at the polls.

This entwining of class and locality with extremism, and its opposition to a national understanding of Labour politics, provides the underlying theme of *Popular Politics and Political Culture*. While studies of the inter-war political left have, of course, been plentiful, they have, all the same, chosen overwhelmingly to foreground ideological distinctions, principally that between Labour's moderate social democracy and the more aggressive Marxism associated with the CPGB, a divide intensified by international events and the undoubted intellectual and financial dependence of British Communism upon Soviet Russia.[5] Instead, this study uses the fate of the radical left as a point of departure, one that permits an examination of the changing ways in which the public understood and engaged with politics. More precisely, the relationship between the various sections of the Labour movement and the Communist Party in the urban centres of Scotland provides a lens through which the reshaping of political identities in a democratic era, and the importance of where these identities were publicised, can be observed. What follows should not, then, be read as a history of Labour or Communist politics. There is little analysis of the social or economic foundations of party support, nor is there any exhaustive discussion of party membership, finances, or organisation; equally, questions of policy and ideology remain largely untouched. Such information may readily be found elsewhere.[6] Rather, this is an interpretative account of the remodelling of inter-war politics, of the strains between local and national loyalties in an age of mass democratic participation, and, ultimately, of the end of a popular radical tradition bounded by its appeal to confrontational local identities and modes of political participation.

The principal concern here is with popular experience, with perception as much as measurable fact, with capturing a political atmosphere or disposition as disclosed by behaviour and language. What, this examination asks, can we discover from a study of urban Scotland of changing attitudes regarding radical politics, and towards public forms of political engagement? Of the consequences of the new franchise for sectional identities? How were such changes understood by local activists, and how did political parties adjust their rhetoric in response? And, critically, what does this reveal of prevailing conceptions of where politics was conducted, by whom, and for whose benefit? As such, *Popular Politics and Political Culture* presents a particular interpretation of inter-war politics as opposed to a definitive empirical record. It is one that will undoubtedly elicit disagreement; nonetheless, it will, it is hoped, stimulate debate.

CLASS, POLITICS AND THE FRANCHISE

British politics was altered profoundly by the extension of the franchise in 1918, and its equalisation a decade later. At the general election of December 1910 the electorate numbered approximately 7.5 million males, enfranchised by virtue of satisfying the requisite property qualifications. Two decades later, this figure stood at nearly thirty million, with women and the working class in a majority.[7] An exclusive political system, in which the vote was an emblem of citizenship earned, was transformed into a democracy, if one as yet rather rough-hewn; significantly, the categories of public and electorate now overlapped in a way not true prior to 1918.[8] The creation of this new polity coincided with a period of sweeping political realignment, as the Liberal–Conservative duopoly of the long nineteenth century at last fractured, and a volatile three-party contest arrived, with Labour approaching parity with the established parties at the four general elections contested between 1918 and 1924. This was followed by the restoration of a two-party system after 1931, but now with Labour striving to contend with a resurgent Conservatism.[9]

Traditionally, these developments were treated as interlinked, with the reform of the franchise, by providing the working class with a political voice, offering a compelling explanation for Labour's rapid electoral advance, and resulting in the formation of the first and second minority Labour administrations in 1924 and 1929.[10] This interpretation was challenged by those who suggested that the Liberals could have retained the loyalties of the working class, alongside their status as the Edwardian party of progress, had it not been for the impact of the First World War. There remained, nonetheless, a consensus that, by the 1920s if not before, class was the central factor in British politics, a development that assisted Labour, nearly ruined the Liberals, and reshaped Conservatism.[11] And while the assumption that the pre-1918 franchise disproportionately excluded the working classes, and that this constituency was, in any event, naturally inclined towards the Labour Party, has since been queried, analysis of the franchise has centred primarily upon the question of which social groups, and, by implication, which political parties, profited most from the advent of mass democracy.[12]

Less attention has, however, been accorded to the changes wrought by the new franchise on political culture more broadly, and, since it fulfilled the central demand made by radicals for more than a century, on the Labour Party in particular. Indeed, the assumption that the new democratic electoral settlement favoured the political left has ensured that historians of the Conservative Party have paid greater heed to questions of political culture, as they seek to account for the remarkable success of the Conservatives between the wars, when the party spent all but three years in office, either alone or as the dominant partner in a coalition.[13] The historiography of inter-war politics is correspondingly rich in explorations of how under the leadership of Stanley Baldwin the Conservatives were able to adapt their message to appeal to newly enfranchised female and working-class voters.[14] Yet the reformed franchise also had decisive repercussions for Labour's understanding of its place within British political life. In late Victorian and Edwardian Britain the public comprised more than just those entitled to vote; broader still was the category of the people. As such, the measurement of public opinion was not simply a matter of tallying the votes at a general election. After 1918, however, the distinctions between people, public and electorate were elided, and national elections assumed a new authority. If, prior to 1914, Labour could be positioned as the inheritor of the radical tradition, and as the representative of those industrious members of the nation refused a constitutional voice, then by 1928 this position was no longer tenable.[15]

The transition from the sectional to the inclusive, and the resultant suppression of discordant opinions, provided one of the key dynamics within inter-war politics, and it was most pronounced on the political left, where those who believed that their role was to speak for the working class alone found themselves unable to prevail over those keen to adopt an identity and a style of politics capable of attracting the support of this diverse new electorate. This divide became especially marked after 1924, when the first Labour government was forced from office after just nine months following a Commons defeat on the issue of the abandoned prosecution of J. R. Campbell, editor of the Communist *Workers' Weekly*, on charges of sedition. Labour lost the ensuing general election amid the controversy of the forged 'Zinoviev letter', which purported to reveal Communist plans to infiltrate the armed forces. The defeat stemmed in truth from a collapse in Liberal support: the Labour vote actually increased. Still, the outward association between the fall of the government and the Communist Party strengthened Labour's desire to publicise its commitment to the constitution, a concern enhanced by the 1926 general strike; further, there was a growing recognition that, if Labour were to secure a parliamentary majority, it would need to compete for the votes of disaffected Liberals. The Labour leadership, and, crucially, a growing number of local activists, accepted that a politics of opposition, of pitting the 'people' against a corrupt and distant parliamentary elite, could not work within a mass democracy in which political institutions retained the confidence of the electorate. A narrow appeal to class identity, which had little resonance beyond Labour's traditional geographic bases of support (and which even there often excluded female voters), began to be viewed as inadequate; such a change in perspective proved terminal for those whose political identity was predicated upon a sense of exclusion, and who advocated extra-parliamentary forms of political campaigning.

The creation of a national electorate fundamentally changed the basis upon which politics was contested, as parties were forced to engage with a diverse body of voters and elections came, particularly after 1924, to revolve around a contest between competing visions of an undeniably British nation. In such a context, to be identified with a section of the electorate rather than the whole was a liability, a constraint that applied equally across the political spectrum, and throughout the country. Both Labour and the Conservatives aspired to represent the nation, even if the latter proved markedly more successful at doing so; to speak, as those on the radical left claimed to, for those excluded from national politics, or worse, to deny the existence of a harmonious political 'nation', was inexcusable. By placing the study of left-wing politics within this context, we may uncover an explanation for the inability of parties such as the CPGB and the Independent Labour Party (ILP) to secure mass support; but, more than this, we may also appreciate the vital role played by the radical left in providing a negative against which other, more successful, identities could be defined. The reasons for the failure of the radical left reside not just in the unsuitability of their ideology to British social and economic conditions, but also in the political culture in which they campaigned, in the replacement of a welter of sectional regional identities with a single national polity, and in the growing political importance attached to the individual act of casting the ballot.[16]

POPULAR POLITICS, POLITICAL CULTURE AND THE 'NEW' POLITICAL HISTORY

Sceptical of electoral sociology and the depiction of political allegiance as a passive reflection of social or economic status, the 'new' political history came to prominence during the 1980s. Proponents of this methodology have stressed the relative autonomy of the political sphere and the capacity of movements and parties to construct political identities and constituencies of support through the use of language and imagery, offering an analysis of political change that looks beyond class to consider the relationship between agency, activism, and material conditions.[17] In particular, the public spectacle accompanying elections has been explored alongside the consequences of the progressive extension of the franchise for popular modes of political participation.[18] Nevertheless, an approach that treats parties as active participants in the political process, and rhetoric and form as interacting with, rather than arising from, social and economic trends, has focused principally on the period before 1918 and the decades after 1945. With the exception of the work of Jon Lawrence, this debate has inspired little response from those examining the inter-war era, an omission especially disappointing in the context of the radical left, which was notably attached to the physical demonstration of political identity through rallies, marches and demonstrations.[19] Equally, while the practical impact of the expanded electorate on Labour's relationship with the mass media has been outlined deftly by Laura Beers, and Lawrence has described the party's abandonment of a divisive class appeal, such studies focus upon national responses rather than popular experiences.[20] This emphasis is especially marked in recent political histories of inter-war Scotland, which have chiefly considered either the electoral fortunes of the three main parties in general, focused on specific localities, or surveyed relations on the political left from an ideological perspective.[21] The latter two trends have been encouraged by the longstanding debate surrounding the origins and lasting significance of the political and industrial unrest on Clydeside during and immediately after the First World War.[22]

In exploring the changing nature of political engagement in Scotland after 1918, this study examines the competing political identities promoted by Labour, the ILP and the Communist Party across urban Scotland, the locations in which the parties campaigned, the electioneering methods they adopted, and the differing reactions they provoked. To be concerned in this way with rhetoric, imagery and form is not to dismiss the role of social and economic factors in influencing political allegiances, but to suggest that while material conditions provide the broad landscape within which political debate takes place, it remains for parties and individual activists to relate their specific appeals to this milieu. Political movements succeed when they are able to grant coherence to economic and social change; the language and style parties adopt in their campaigning, and the spaces in which they seek support, are an attempt to validate a particular interpretation or world-view. If the 'new' political history has, under the influence of the linguistic turn, stressed the importance of rhetoric, then alongside a concern with language we must consider how and where activists campaigned: where politics happens, and is perceived to happen, matters.[23]

Left-wing activists hoped to harness radical customs of public protest and electioneering alongside a class identity contingent upon a specific perception of where and how politics should be pursued that was weakened progressively after 1918. In their reliance on such traditions, members of the Communist Party and the ILP clashed with a Labour Party concerned increasingly with national electoral respectability. From the perspective of practice rather than theory, the inability of the radical left to achieve significant political success unveils the end of a specific culture of popular radicalism, as national party loyalties came to dominate, and notions of acceptable political conduct shifted dramatically. Yet this should not be construed as a simple narrative of the triumph of party, or of the betrayal of local activists by an autocratic party elite, but rather as denoting a deeper change in where political debate was understood to take place, and where political authority was believed to reside, by both party members and the wider electorate. Similarly, while Scottish politics certainly came to be conducted on a national basis in the twentieth century, national should not be seen uncomplicatedly as a synonym for class, and the nation in question was, so far as politics was concerned, Britain. Indeed, although assuming greater significance in retrospect, the emergence of an overtly political, but electorally marginal, Scottish nationalism between the wars was in truth evidence of the extent to which the Scottish question disappeared from mainstream political debate. As Liberalism declined, and Labour politics focused ever more on attaining power at Westminster, Scottish home rule, an issue which had been a key component of Edwardian radicalism, declined in relevance.[24]

By the close of the 1930s class was, politically at least, an outmoded identity incompatible with mass democracy, whatever its undoubted prevalence in the economic or social spheres: a reappraisal of the fate of the radical left in Scotland illuminates this development. In a narrow sense, then, this study suggests that it is in the changing nature of popular political identity and engagement that historians should seek an explanation for the absence of a mass Communist Party, and for the failure of the ILP to enjoy success after disaffiliating from the Labour Party in 1932. More broadly, however, the impact of the rise of Communism in Europe, and the social and industrial unrest of the immediate post-war years, ensured that class politics came to be associated with Bolshevism, while the affection of the radical left, and especially the CPGB, for the politics of the street further discredited the public traditions of urban radicalism, and fostered a more restrained and self-consciously respectable political culture.

STRUCTURE, METHODOLOGY AND SOURCES

Popular Politics and Political Culture rests upon a detailed consideration of the political left in urban Scotland between 1918 and 1939, with particular attention paid to events in Aberdeen, Dundee, Edinburgh and Glasgow. This approach allows the established historiography surrounding the more familiar events on Clydeside to be addressed within the context of broader trends in Scottish and British politics, and local experiences to be situated within a wider national framework. The campaigns undertaken, the tactics adopted and the testimony of activists, as well as the reactions of the press and the authorities, are used to explore changing understandings of popular politics. A shift in radical political identities from class to nation, and, in the conduct of politics, from local public spaces to the national political arena, is traced. To approach this change solely through Labour or Conservative politics is to tell a story of success, to analyse the varieties of politics that triumphed; a consideration of the broader political left unmasks what was lost, the forms and languages of radicalism shed during the early decades of the twentieth century. The local focus of this study is partly a recognition too that all political identities must in some way be made and sustained locally. It is, however, also a means of investigating the increasing prevalence of national considerations in Labour politics, and of illustrating that the changes described herein were debated and comprehended not just by the party leadership, but also at a provincial level, as popular notions of political participation moved towards an ideal of individual voters engaging with Westminster via the ballot box.

The book is structured in two parts. Part I focuses on identities of class in radical politics, and the tensions which arose between competing local and national political loyalties after 1918. The class identity that developed during the nineteenth century was not uniform, but was embedded within local institutions and understandings of loyalty. These expressions of class were primarily defensive, sustained by a sense of opposition to the state, and it was to such highly specific identities that radical activists hoped to appeal. Chapter 1 outlines the crucial relationship between class identity and provincial understandings of popular democracy, and the change undergone in radical understandings of political representation as a result of the growing authority of the national institutions of the Labour movement. It explores first the increasing centralisation of power within the Labour movement during the 1920s, and the related reduction in the status of provincial trades and labour councils. The ensuing friction between centre and periphery is illustrated via an account of the battles conducted regarding the selection of Labour candidates in this period, most notably at by-elections, as Labour representatives were transformed from class tribunes into party politicians, and local recalcitrance came to be viewed as evidence of Communist sympathies. Chapter 2 shifts focus, concentrating less on institutional conflict than on changing perceptions of the ideal working-class activist, and the importance of traditions of self-sacrifice and education. The manner in which the radical left privileged existing, and often obsolete, local cultures of respectability among the skilled male working class is emphasised. This analysis is thereafter developed by means of an examination of the changing aims, nature and content of independent working-class education, as regional labour colleges abandoned a curriculum intended to provide an oppositional class-based alternative to state education, preferring instead to train activists in the practicalities of electoral politics.

Part II considers the changing form and location of radical politics. The new-found focus on national elections within Labour politics not only altered notions of political representation, marginalising sectional identities; it also hardened the determination of the Labour leadership, and, significantly, growing numbers of local activists, to distance their party from the traditions of popular politics adopted so assiduously by the CPGB and the ILP. This divergence reflected a wider shift in perceptions of acceptable political conduct, as domestic unrest and the rise of extremist politics in Europe made what were once accepted features of urban political life appear threatening.[25] Accordingly, the medium by which political messages were conveyed became increasingly significant, with the form of politics adopted by political parties shaping their image, and denoting their fitness to govern. Public protests and clamorous displays of political allegiance became linked to a divisive politics of class: in a mass democracy, extra-parliamentary attempts to influence government policy lacked legitimacy, and local traditions of political protest lost their importance. For Labour, securing a position as a national party required not just the imposition of a disciplined and coherent national programme, but also the distancing of the party from confrontational forms of public politics, as the Conservatives sought to use the aggressive conduct of left-wing activists to depict Labour as a narrow, masculine, trade union interest group, unable to govern in the interests of the wider public. An attachment to public demonstrations identified the CPGB and ILP with precisely the type of politics with which the Conservative Party hoped to condemn Labour.

Chapter 3 traces this shift through an examination of the unemployed protests held in inter-war Scotland, exploring the changing reactions of the Labour Party, the press and the authorities to such demonstrations, which became increasingly the preserve of the Communists. Reliant on the symbolic occupation of contested public spaces, Communist activists sought to mobilise those customs of direct action, rooted in local political cultures, which fell into disuse during the 1920s. Chapter 4 extends this analysis of the changing political use of public space, and the shifting horizons of those involved in radical politics, via a study of the decline in the public celebration of May Day. This is contrasted with the establishment of Armistice Day, highlighting the replacement of local identities of class with an apparently apolitical national identity, and the transformation of local public space from a contested site to one of national remembrance. Chapter 5 concludes the study by assessing the changing nature of inter-war electioneering, outlining the end of a confrontational culture of campaigning, and the increasing association of rowdyism with political extremism. It demonstrates that Labour, conscious of Conservative attempts to portray the party as a threat to the constitution, largely abandoned traditional forms of local campaigning. This shift, and the decision of the CPGB after 1928 to disrupt Labour meetings, was crucial in allowing Labour to appear as a potential party of government.

Radical proclamations of class identity were thus countered by the shared focus of Labour and Conservative politicians on the nationwide electorate; in conventional political discourse class became a pejorative term, one deployed in order to discredit opponents. The mass democracy established between 1918 and 1928 could only function on the assumption that all participants were equal; the radical left, by highlighting conflicts internal to the nation, could not be accommodated within national politics. For Labour, refuting similar accusations of sectionalism demanded a transformation in how and where the party pursued its politics, in the language it used, and in the identities to which it appealed. The failure of the inter-war radical left should be understood as but one aspect of a wider decline in class identities, and in the primarily local forms through which these identities had been expressed. The radical left, and especially the

CPGB, was, at a local level, less ideologically driven and less revolutionary than it has appeared. Rather, it was the manifestation of a defensive, oppositional political identity and a form of politics rendered outdated by the democratic culture that emerged after 1918. It is this story that this book seeks to clarify, and to tell.

NOTES

1. NLS Acc. 11177/56: Edinburgh TLC Political Committee Minutes, 1 Jun. and 13 Jul. 1927; NLS Acc. 11177/22: Edinburgh TLC Minutes, 3 Jun., 1 Jul., 12 and 23 Aug. 1927. The Labour group comprised fourteen of the seventy-one councillors on Edinburgh town council.
2. *Edinburgh Evening News*, 18 Aug. 1927.
3. *Edinburgh Labour Standard*, 27 Aug. 1927.
4. *Edinburgh Evening News*, 17 Aug. 1927; *Edinburgh Labour Standard*, 3 Sept. 1927.
5. Jupp, *The Radical Left in Britain*; Pimlott, *Labour and the Left in the 1930s*; Corthorn, *In the Shadow of the Dictators*; Corthorn and Davis (eds), *The British Labour Party and the Wider World*. On the CPGB, see: Thorpe, *The British Communist Party and Moscow*; Worley, *Class Against Class*.
6. See, for example: McKibbin, *The Evolution of the Labour Party*; Knox (ed.), *Scottish Labour Leaders 1918–1939*; Knox, *Industrial Nation*; McKinlay and Morris (eds), *The ILP on Clydeside*; MacDonald, *The Radical Thread*; Smyth, *Labour in Glasgow*; Howell, *MacDonald's Party*.
7. With comparatively minor qualifications, the 1918 Representation of the People Act granted the vote to men over the age of twenty-one, and women over the age of thirty who either were, or were married to, a householder, increasing the size of the electorate to 20 million. The equalisation of the male and female franchise in 1928 ensured that over 90 per cent of the adult population were enfranchised. In 1910 roughly two-thirds of adult men, and no women, had the vote.
8. Thompson, *British Political Culture and the Idea of 'Public Opinion'*.
9. Cowling, *The Impact of Labour*; McKibbin, *Parties and People*.
10. Matthew, McKibbin and Kay, 'The Franchise Factor in the Rise of the Labour Party'; Dyer, *Capable Citizens and Improvident Democrats*.
11. Cowling, *The Impact of Labour*; Clarke, *Lancashire and the New Liberalism* and 'Electoral Sociology of Modern Britain'; Matthew, 'Rhetoric and Politics in Britain'.
12. Duncan Tanner suggested the bias was against women and young men of all classes. A summary can be found in Laybourn, 'The Rise of Labour and the Decline of Liberalism'. A detailed account is in Tanner, 'The Parliamentary Electoral System, the "Fourth" Reform Act and the Rise of Labour in England and Wales' and 'Elections, Statistics, and the Rise of the Labour Party'. For a reassertion of the importance of the franchise, see: Smyth, 'Resisting Labour'.

13. See: McCarthy, 'Whose Democracy? Histories of British Political Culture between the Wars'. Perhaps surprisingly, this success was replicated in Scotland, where, under the Unionist label, the party dominated electoral politics after 1931: Hutchison, 'Unionism between the Two World Wars'.

14. McKibbin, 'Class and Conventional Wisdom'; Jarvis, 'Mrs. Maggs and Betty' and 'British Conservatism and Class Politics in the 1920s'; Francis and Zweiniger-Bargielowska (eds), *The Conservatives and British Society*; Williamson, *Stanley Baldwin*; Ball and Holliday (eds), *Mass Conservatism*.

15. As James Vernon has suggested, the contest over the boundaries of the constitution provided the 'master-narrative' of nineteenth-century politics: Vernon, *Politics and the People* and Vernon (ed.), *Re-reading the Constitution*.

16. McKibbin, 'Why Was There No Marxism in Great Britain?'

17. The best exposition of the 'new' political history remains that found in: Lawrence, *Speaking for the People*, pp. 1–69.

18. O'Gorman, 'Campaign Rituals and Ceremonies'; Joyce, *Visions of the People*; Vernon, *Politics and the People*; Lawrence, *Speaking for the People*; Thompson, 'Pictorial Lies?'; Black, *The Political Culture of the Left in Affluent Britain*.

19. Lawrence, 'Fascist Violence and the Politics of Public Order in Inter-War Britain' and 'The Transformation of British Public Politics'.

20. Beers, *Your Britain*; Lawrence, 'Labour and the Politics of Class'. Helen McCarthy has persuasively suggested that the inter-war decades saw a rise in non-partisan political activism: McCarthy, 'Parties, Voluntary Associations and Democratic Politics in Interwar Britain' and *The British People and the League of Nations*.

21. Hutchison, *Scottish Politics in the Twentieth Century*; MacDonald, *The Radical Thread*; Smyth, *Labour in Glasgow*; Kenefick, *Red Scotland*.

22. McLean, *Legend of Red Clydeside*; Melling, 'Whatever Happened to Red Clydeside?'.

23. On the importance of language, see: Stedman Jones, 'Rethinking Chartism'.

24. The Scottish National Party was founded in 1934, a result of a merger of the radical National Party of Scotland, established in 1928, and the centre-right Scottish Party, launched in 1932. See: Finlay, *Independent and Free*. On the central place of home rule in the Scottish radical tradition, see: Knox (ed.), *Scottish Labour Leaders*, pp. 41–6.

25. Lawrence, 'Forging a Peaceable Kingdom'.

PART I

Identities of Class

1

Nation, Locality and Radical Identity

In March 1929, as a general election approached, a short story entitled 'The Candidate' appeared in *The Worker*. Founded as the newspaper of the wartime Clyde Workers' Committee, since 1924 *The Worker* had been allied to the National Minority Movement, a Communist pressure group within the trade unions. Narrating the selection of a Labour candidate in an unnamed, fictional constituency, the story opens at a fundraiser held by the local party. Present is Mr Davitt, a solicitor who, having joined the party only in 1927, has now started to play a more conspicuous role in local Labour politics, dispensing free legal advice, and allowing his plush 'west end' home to be used as a venue for party events. Yet Davitt's commitment to Labour politics and to socialism appears recent, and even shallow: he was, we are told, a vocal supporter of war in 1914, and the initial focus of his legal work had been the prosecution of striking workers. Observing events are Dave Raynon, the secretary of the local branch of the Labour Party, and his friend Bill. Raynon is presented as a heroic figure, and in obvious contrast to Davitt: a committed trade unionist, he had been imprisoned during the pre-war labour unrest; an anti-war campaigner, he had been beaten by a jingo mob. Yet Raynon nonetheless welcomes Davitt's conversion to the Labour cause, seeing the attraction of such middle-class recruits as evidence of the tremendous progress made by the party since 1918. Bill, in contrast, is more concerned, and compares the sedate decorum of the new Labour politics unfavourably with the vitality of the party's early years, 'when the crowd used to howl us down', and politics had 'more in it than now, somehow'.

It is assumed that, as branch secretary, Raynon will be selected to contest the seat at the forthcoming election. At the subsequent selection meeting, however, Davitt is glimpsed 'chatting affably' to a representative from Labour's national executive, who thereafter opens proceedings by reminding those present that the party has 'passed the day when it engaged in purely propaganda struggles. Every seat we now contest we are seriously out to win'. As such, Labour must 'ensure that our candidates are men who . . . can command the respect of the community whom it is the party's purpose to serve'. The official then praises Davitt for his 'generous assistance', before concluding by once more stressing the 'place of the party in the national life and its duty to the community'. In response, Davitt intimates that, if nominated, he could contribute to the financing of the election campaign. Appalled by such naked manoeuvring, Bill interjects and proposes Raynon, who has missed the meeting owing to his trade union obligations. Backtracking, the official suggests that a shortlist be submitted to the national executive, since the 'choice of candidates is an extremely important matter', one that requires 'close attention'. The final act takes place a year later, with Davitt, having eventually been awarded the nomination, renouncing politics in favour of a lucrative professional opportunity. Raynon, who accepted the decision in the interests of maintaining unity, finds himself being chided by Bill, who concludes acidly that this has proved to be no more than the 'unity of the executive against the desires of the local people'.[1]

'The Candidate' is, of course, fictional. Appearing at a time when British Communists had, at the prompting of Comintern, forsaken their earlier policy of seeking unity on the political left and instead now denounced Labour as the 'third capitalist party', it offers a crude depiction of a once-proud party reduced to the status of career choice for middle-class carpetbaggers that scarcely surprises.[2] All the same, the story raises questions of political identity central to an understanding of inter-war politics. At heart, 'The Candidate' is, as captured by Bill's yearning for the rough and tumble of the old street politics, a lament for a direct form of political participation and a specific model of working-class representation believed to have been enfeebled by the professionalisation of the Labour Party. For all that it was intended to function as propaganda, the story offers no rousing final victory; instead, it is suffused with an overriding sense of loss. Two further themes are pervasive. First, the belief that the reforms undertaken in 1918, which allowed individuals to join the Labour Party without being members of an affiliated trade union or socialist society, had allowed middle-class careerists, with no roots in the Labour movement and little real understanding of socialism, to dominate Labour politics. Second, the story evokes a sense of provincial exclusion, a suspicion that local activists were being treated with contempt by their leaders. These misgivings met in accusations of an alliance between middle-class recruits and national officials: vital to the tale is the evident collusion between Davitt and the official from the national executive.

This local, defensive understanding of politics was essential to the radical left, and especially to British Communism. Although the CPGB was undoubtedly reliant upon Moscow, the party aspired to represent those disheartened by Labour's construction of a more inclusive, cross-class appeal, who regarded the idea that class tensions could be resolved within a democracy with scepticism. British Communists spoke a language which was inseparable from an attachment to place, and which ridiculed the notion of a single, harmonious polity: class was a tangible local identity, the nation a disingenuous construct; there were, for Communists, 'two nations in Britain. One of them rules . . . the other nation works.'[3] Or, to take an alternative definition offered by *The Worker* in 1930, the 'nation' was 'not composed of people who draw doles or wages. The nation goes to Ascot, is "presented" at Buckingham Palace, and entertains Mr Thomas and others at posh dinners.'[4]

When British Communists spoke of class, then, the term carried a broader meaning than could be conveyed by any narrow, materialist reading of Marxism. Class and locality were indivisible, with local trade unionists considered to be the vanguard of the working class. In part, this veneration of the provincial was a simple question of location: the physical proximity of local activists and institutions to working-class life was felt to ensure that they were more attuned to the needs of their supporters. But there was also a moral aspect to such attitudes, one that drew upon an enduring radical belief that national politics was a corrupt, and corrupting, environment. Working-class representatives who appeared too eager to enter this seedy network of patronage, or who seemed to place the attainment of office ahead of voicing the concerns of their community, were viewed with suspicion: national ambitions were evidence of weakness, a precursor to betrayal. Such a prejudice was apparent in assertions that the post-war centralisation of the Labour movement had, in the opinion of the *Communist Review* in 1923, created a new caste of 'luxurious officials', who, preoccupied with their career prospects and 'doped with capitalist comforts', acted as a check on the militant instincts of their members: they were a 'dangerous parasitic growth upon the workers' movement'.[5] This distrust of the Labour leadership was given a founding myth by the events of April 1921, when, on what came on the left to be referred to as 'Black Friday', the transport and railway unions failed to uphold the so-called 'triple alliance', declining to take industrial action in support of the striking miners. For Communists, this failure could be explained only by the cowardice of 'yellow trade union and parliamentary leaders', who sought nothing more than a 'comfortable parliamentary career'.[6]

This conflation of class, radicalism and locality, and its opposition to a national understanding of political representation, shaped relations on the political left after 1918. Following its foundation in 1920, the CPGB pursued a policy of seeking affiliation to the Labour Party on a similar basis to that enjoyed by the ILP.[7] Yet this 'united front' was only ever envisaged as operating locally, as a means of defending a class identity threatened by the depredations of both the state and the Labour leadership. Although the CPGB claimed to want left-wing unity, the party press could, in 1922, maintain that the '*real* conspiracy' facing the working class was that fomented by the 'trade union leaders themselves', who had 'systematically and successfully undermined every instinctive attempt of the rank and file to put up a fighting resistance against the employing class'.[8] The following year, the Communist *Workers' Weekly* could be found accusing the 'official machine' of the Labour Party of attempting to 'break up local unity'.[9]

This localism was reinforced by political practicalities. In the immediate aftermath of the First World War, trades and labour councils, local bodies composed of delegates nominated by affiliated trade union branches and socialist societies that had emerged during the second half of the nineteenth century, still played a crucial role in Labour politics, especially in Scotland, where the regionalised nature of economic development had hindered the growth of national unions.[10] Indeed, in urban areas such bodies functioned, in effect, as the local branch of the Labour Party, retaining until 1938 official responsibility for the selection of candidates at municipal and parliamentary elections.[11] Further, since industrial delegates to trades councils were nominated by local trade union branches, it remained relatively straightforward for individual Communists to exploit this route into Labour politics. But the perception that there existed a relationship between Communism and local expressions of class identity encouraged the Labour leadership to curb the autonomy previously enjoyed by provincial trades councils: the loophole regarding industrial delegates had been closed, officially at least, by the end of the 1920s.[12] What was, on the surface, an ideological conflict became a contest between opposing conceptions of political identity, representation and engagement, reducible to a question asked with equal force by left and right: who did Labour really represent, the working class or the nation? And if this query was answered firmly with the adoption in 1928 of the *Labour and the Nation* programme, the local debate that preceded this outcome, and the frustration it created among a vocal minority, should not be ignored.[13]

The tensions between these competing models of radicalism are the focus of this chapter. The question of whether Labour was to be a class or a community party was one of location as much as policy, the contest between Labour and the CPGB one of the centre against the periphery as much as social democracy versus Bolshevism. It was moulded too by divergent assessments of the merits of parliamentary democracy. The localism so characteristic of British Communism owed much to a domestic tradition of syndicalism and anti-parliamentarianism inherited almost wholesale from the Socialist Labour Party.[14] Although the CPGB contested elections from its inception, this policy was adopted only after a personal appeal from Lenin, and little effort was made to conceal the contempt with which the party viewed those who believed that the interests of the working class could be furthered through parliamentary representation: as *The Communist* cautioned in 1922, the chief political danger facing the working class lay in placing any faith in the 'stupefying torpor of parliamentary procedure and make-believe'.[15] Yet this dismissal of parliament's value could not be shared by those convinced that the extension of the franchise had, by enfranchising the working class, transformed British politics, and rendered Labour the true party of the nation.[16] This was, then, a dispute about the past and the future, about the content and form of the radical tradition inherited by Labour, and how, if it all, it should be renewed in an era of mass democracy. The mutual incomprehension this debate provoked could be discerned in 1924, when Herbert Morrison, the leading Labour figure in London politics, mocked British Communists for their preoccupation with local autonomy rather than national organisation; they were, he charged, advocating 'a type of organisation more appropriate to the middle of the nineteenth century'.[17]

Focusing principally on the years between 1924 and 1929, which separated the first and second minority Labour administrations, this chapter traces the rise of a modernised, national vision of Labour politics. It considers first the reworking of understandings of sovereignty and democracy within the Labour movement, and especially the growing authority exercised by the national leadership, as the freedom previously enjoyed by trades councils was circumscribed, and local notions of Labour as a confederation of working-class bodies were replaced by a more hierarchical, national model. The electoral consequences of this changing perspective are then assessed, as greater central control began to be exercised over the selection of parliamentary candidates and the conduct of election campaigns. This is not to offer a binary opposition between local militancy and national timidity, or to suggest that the Labour leadership were guilty of suppressing the radical sentiments of their members. Rather, electoral defeat in 1924, and the subsequent debacle of the general strike, encouraged local activists to share the outlook of their leaders, and to prioritise the attainment of national office. This chapter presents, then, a study of the changing horizons of the political left in inter-war Scotland, exploring two opposing understandings of radical politics. One of these, victorious, privileged electoral success; the other, defeated, remained suspicious of national politics, preferring direct local participation. Above all, it is an analysis of the declining importance of locality in the construction of political identities, as the traditions of provincial radicalism proved difficult to sustain after the extension of the franchise.

TRADES COUNCILS, COMMUNISTS AND THE QUESTION OF POLITICAL SOVEREIGNTY

The initial attempts of the CPGB to affiliate to the Labour Party were rebuffed by the latter's national executive in 1920, a ruling confirmed by successive party conference decisions between 1922 and 1924.[18] Nonetheless, this institutional proscription could not be extended unproblematically to encompass individual Communists, and it remained possible for members of the CPGB to be nominated by their trade union to serve on trades and labour councils, and, thereafter, as delegates to the Labour conference, and even as municipal and parliamentary candidates. In 1922, the Labour conference had ruled that candidates must accept the constitution and rules of the Labour Party; further, they could not be members of any party that had run candidates in opposition to Labour nominees, a measure clearly directed at the CPGB, which had contested the August 1921 Caerphilly by-election, won by the Labour candidate Morgan Jones. These restrictions proved, however, near-impossible to enforce in practice, as they required interrogating the political motivations of individuals whose involvement in Labour politics stemmed from their standing within their trade union. The prohibition on dual membership was duly abandoned, and Communists were able to run as locally sanctioned Labour candidates in a number of constituencies. In Scotland, such candidacies were most evident in the industrial west, where the CPGB benefited from the legacy of the shop stewards' committee movement, from which many of the party's early leadership emerged. In Greenock, Alec Geddes of the CPGB ran as the *de facto* Labour candidate in 1922 and 1923; Aitken Ferguson was accorded similar status in Glasgow Kelvingrove. Most conspicuous were events in Motherwell, where J. T. Walton Newbold was nominated by the local trades and labour council despite the opposition of the national executive. Running openly as a Communist, Newbold secured victory in 1922 in a four-cornered contest that featured a Liberal, a National Liberal and an independent Unionist.[19]

Tolerance of such local alliances on the political left, however, failed to survive the collapse of the first Labour government in October 1924, following a Commons defeat on the question of the party's alleged relationship with the CPGB. If Labour's national vote held firm, the result made it clear that perceptions of an association between the party and Bolshevism were driving erstwhile Liberals into the Conservative fold. Indeed, the defeat had been foreshadowed at the May 1924 Glasgow Kelvingrove by-election, when the Communist Aitken Ferguson had once again been nominated by the local Labour Party. Although Ferguson maintained the share of the vote secured by Labour at the 1923 general election, the Unionist candidate Walter Elliot, a future Secretary of State for Scotland, seized two-thirds of the votes received by the Liberals six months earlier, winning a three-way contest with over 50 per cent of the vote.[20] It was becoming apparent that the nomination of Communists as Labour candidates placed a ceiling on the party's potential support, defining Labour as a vehicle for narrow, sectional interests, and as a party for the organised working class only; worse, it exposed Labour to charges that it was a threat to the constitution, a trope deployed relentlessly by the Conservatives. At the 1924 Labour Party conference, the selection of Communists as Labour candidates was at last prohibited outright, and a further resolution proscribing dual membership was also passed. But the exclusion of individual trade unionists on political grounds challenged deep-seated notions of local democracy; moreover, since similar measures had not been taken against individuals with Liberal or Conservative sympathies, the ban could easily be depicted by the CPGB as an attack on the left wing of the Labour movement, and as further evidence that Labour was abandoning its traditional class basis. Notably, while delegates rejected the CPGB's application for affiliation by an overwhelming majority, the bar on individual membership passed by a much narrower margin. If there was little sympathy for the CPGB as a rival party, there nonetheless remained a willingness to view individual Communist activists as allies in the wider working-class movement.[21]

The conviction of the Labour leadership that any involvement with the CPGB was electorally toxic was deepened by the experience of the general strike. Previously, local boundaries on the political left had been blurred; after 1926, they were redrawn according to national demarcations, and the scope for local discretion disappeared. In early 1927, the general council of the TUC withdrew recognition from trades councils affiliated to the National Minority Movement; similarly, the joint council established by the TUC and the Communist-aligned National Unemployed Workers' Committee Movement was abolished.[22] The Labour Party undertook parallel measures, disaffiliating divisional Labour parties with links to the National Left-Wing Movement, yet another Communist-inspired body.[23] Individual trade unions also moved to expel Communists. Finally, in 1928 the Labour conference endorsed a new two-part qualification for delegates, drafted by the national executive, which excluded anyone who had stood in opposition to an official Labour candidate, and any member of a political party ineligible for affiliation to the Labour Party.[24] Yet if this positioning of Labour as a coherent, clearly-defined party, as opposed to a broad coalition of socialist and left-wing groups, was uncomplicated at a national level, where administrative edicts could be applied readily, then locally the issue remained complex. Here the exclusion of Communists, and, later, the disaffiliation of the ILP, necessitated a more fundamental change in understandings of political authority, one that reshaped how individual activists comprehended their relationship with national political institutions, and brought national politics closer to the locality. In Scotland, this shift ensured that trades and labour councils, manifestations of a provincial class identity that pre-dated both the enfranchisement of the working class and the foundation of the Labour Party, ceased to provide a forum for the political left in all its factional variety, and became, in effect, subordinate branches of the Labour Party, expected to conform to national decisions.[25]

The disquiet that this transfer of political sovereignty from the locality to the national institutions of the Labour movement generated is key to understanding the divisions that emerged on the left during the 1920s. Although ridiculous in hindsight, the CPGB posed as the defender of local autonomy and individual liberty, in opposition to an unsympathetic and autocratic leadership interested only in dampening the initiative of local activists. In Communist propaganda, trades and labour councils were not subsidiary to the Labour national executive or TUC general council, but rather embodied a distinctive local identity, acting as repositories of a vital militancy, peopled by activists not yet reduced to 'mere voting cattle'.[26] In May 1927, as the disaffiliation of wayward trades councils began, Harry Pollitt, then the leader of the National Minority Movement but soon to be appointed general secretary of the CPGB, bemoaned the fact that such institutions were being reduced to little more than 'information and distribution centres', beholden to national direction. This silencing of local opinion would, Pollitt suggested, 'create a centralised movement which would be like a head without a body'.[27] The following year, J. R. Campbell argued that the attempt to prohibit individual Communists from acting as delegates to trades councils was

> a denial not only of rights to individual Communists but of the rights to the rank and file members of the unions to elect whom they may please to official positions. It means that instead of the unions controlling the Labour Party, the Labour Party bureaucracy attempts to define and limit the political activities and opinions of trade unionists.[28]

It was on this ground that Communists hoped to appeal to those disenchanted with the path followed by Labour after 1918.

In the early 1920s, Labour and radical politics were, throughout urban Scotland, characterised by a striking degree of co-operation, as trades councils chose to flout the national decisions prohibiting relations with the Communist Party in favour of local alliances. In Edinburgh, for example, where Communist activists assisted with Labour election campaigns, the situation was of such concern that in early 1923 the national executive felt it necessary to issue a reminder that pacts with the CPGB were forbidden.[29] Later that year, Ben Shaw, the Labour Party's Scottish secretary, addressed a meeting of the trades council, emphasising that collaboration with the CPGB was barred, and that the national executive remained 'the only authority for the interpretation of the rules' regarding such matters. Shaw's intervention made little impact: the trades council decided, rather creatively, that advocating support for Communist candidates at municipal elections was acceptable so long as they were not running against Labour nominees, a scenario that it was, not coincidentally, within the power of the trades council to bring about.[30] Likewise, when, in 1925, Labour's Scottish executive reiterated the official ban on working with the CPGB, and alleged that Communists had been responsible for causing disruption within the Labour movement, the trades council demanded to know on what authority the letter had been issued, and requested proof of the alleged disruption, since 'no such thing' existed in Edinburgh.[31] The trades council continued to campaign for Communist affiliation to the Labour Party, and, in contravention of national rulings, granted voting rights to delegates from the local unemployed workers' committees, organisations known to be linked to the CPGB.[32]

In Aberdeen too the trades council had declined to enforce the conference decisions regarding co-operation with the CPGB prior to 1926. William Morrison, a delegate from the local Painters' Society and a member of the city's branch of the Communist Party, served on the executive committee of the trades council throughout 1925 and early 1926; it was only when Arthur Henderson, national chairman of the Labour Party, underlined the non-negotiable nature of the regulations that it was agreed to exclude Communists from official positions. Yet even this was done resentfully, and the trades council contacted both the STUC and the TUC on Morrison's behalf, demanding to know whether they had approved this 'interference with trade union rights'.[33] A similar appeal to precedent was made in Glasgow, where in 1922 the trades council declared that it would ignore the rulings barring Communists from standing as Labour candidates unless the national executive could provide a 'definite reply' as to the grounds on which members of the Communist Party could be 'disbarred' if they had been nominated by an affiliated trade union.[34] By 1924, the trades council executive in Glasgow was willing to concede that Communists could no longer be Labour candidates, but there remained a refusal to accept that individual trade unionists could be prevented from serving as delegates to the trades council, or on local Labour ward committees.[35] This sense of a local class identity, which embraced the political, social and industrial, and which could cut across national party loyalties, was also visible in Dundee, where, during the 1924 municipal elections, the local Labour Party had endorsed James Hodgson of the CPGB as a candidate in the city's sixth ward. Ordered to withdraw the endorsement by the national executive, Nicholas Marra, a member of the trades council's executive committee, made clear that he was opposed to the national rulings, and regretted that he had been forced to implement them, stressing that he did not 'want to create any ill-feeling or friction between what he looked upon as two sections of the Labour Party'.[36]

It was in the distance between such local sentiments and the national desire to avoid any association with the taint of Bolshevism that Communist rhetoric could enjoy some purchase. For the CPGB, the true value of the Labour movement was to be found in its local institutions, which remained free from the tawdry place-seeking and wearisome bureaucracy of national politics. And while this stance was obviously motivated by the desire to discredit the Labour Party, suspicion of central authority was so ingrained within British Communism that party members could, despite the demands of democratic centralism, display similar sentiments towards their own leadership: for Communists, national politics of whatever stripe was always corrosive of political integrity.[37] When, in line with the requirements of the 'united front', the CPGB decided not to contest seats at the 1922 general election where an existing Labour candidate was in place, the move was received with incredulity in Scotland, where it was interpreted as symptomatic of 'a drift towards the Labour Party' in London. There was, according to Bob Stewart, the leading party figure in Dundee, 'throughout Scotland [a] lack of confidence in the central power'.[38] As Andrew Thorpe has observed, the shift to openly attacking Labour as part of the policy of 'class against class', adopted officially in 1929, proved most popular in Scotland and the north of England precisely because in these areas it had long been felt that the executive in London had been too obliging towards the Labour leadership.[39] In their mistrust of the centre, Communists simultaneously channelled an earlier provincial radicalism, which Patrick Joyce has described as a North British 'crusade against privilege', and foreshadowed the allegations of an 'aristocratic embrace' that followed the collapse of the second Labour government in 1931.[40] Looking back, Helen Crawfurd, a pre-war suffragette who left the ILP for the CPGB in 1921, criticised her former Labour colleagues who left Glasgow for the 'House of Commons, trade union headquarters, or other national roles', and in the process reduced their supporters to passive, 'respectable, law abiding citizens', who could only hope 'for great things from the brilliant people leading the national movements from London'.[41]

Yet if Communist appeals to local loyalties received a sympathetic hearing in the early 1920s, after the general strike the willingness of trades councils to embrace delegates and candidates who were members of the CPGB declined. In November 1926, Dundee trades council moved to expel Communists from its executive committee. The decision was condemned by the local branch of the National Union of Railwaymen (NUR), whose delegate, Robert Clark, had fallen foul of the new ruling. The NUR maintained that, as Clark was an industrial rather than a political delegate, his party affiliation was irrelevant. Clark was backed by Duncan Laburn, another Communist delegate, who railed that he did not recognise the authority of 'Eccleston Square', and suggested instead that 'the last say' in such matters lay with the local Labour movement.[42] But such a perspective was naive, and the old appeals to local sovereignty failed. As well as ousting individual Communists from official positions, the trades council agreed to apply the rulings of the national executive barring co-operation with the CPGB, a decision reaffirmed in early 1927. The following year the position of individual Communists was again under question, with a definitive ruling issued preventing any member of the CPGB or its subsidiaries from acting as a political delegate to the trades council.[43] The *Free Press*, the newspaper of the Dundee Labour movement, had once been a radical voice, sympathetic to the ILP left. By 1928, however, it too had swung behind the attitude of the national executive, and responded to the local debate by devoting a front page to reporting the Communist 'menace', and demanding that an end be brought to the toleration of known Communists in Labour ward committees; the *Free Press* even called for Communists to be prevented from serving as industrial delegates. The trades council responded by requesting that individual Labour members affirm their loyalty in writing. Clark protested once more, arguing that he had been an exemplary delegate since 1924, and continued to have the full support of his union branch.[44] But national pressure was also exerted: the National Union of General and Municipal Workers ordered its Dundee branch to withdraw from the trades council, and suspended both local delegates, who, it transpired, had previously been members of the CPGB.[45]

In the aftermath, all affiliated unions were instructed to refrain from electing Communists as industrial delegates to the trades council. This new uncompromising stance was encapsulated by the membership clause adopted by the Dundee and District Jute and Flax Workers' Union (JFWU), the largest and most influential union in the city. Each member of the JFWU's executive committee was now required to sign, in the presence of a notary, a declaration that they were not at present a member of the CPGB, and that they would resign their position if they joined the CPGB in future. There were instances of dissent, particularly from those unions who saw their delegates rejected: both the Boilermakers' Society and the Calender Workers' Union, whose delegates were affected, refused to comply with the new regime on this basis. Even so, what is striking is the degree of compliance: of the thirty-two union branches affiliated to the trades council, twenty-seven implemented the new rules without protest, indicating the degree to which local Labour opinion had shifted since 1924.[46]

Elsewhere the pattern was similar. Glasgow trades council was restructured in late 1927, with Communist delegates being barred from council meetings; such was the ill feeling generated that credential cards were issued to identify legitimate delegates, and the police were summoned to ensure that CPGB members did not disrupt proceedings.[47] In Edinburgh, the prohibition on Communists serving as trades council delegates was enforced in 1927, and the privileges granted to the local unemployed committees rescinded. The response of the local Communist Party was to run candidates in opposition to the Labour Party in two wards at the November 1928 municipal elections, a decision that provoked the trades council to at last expel all political delegates who were members of the CPGB. As in Dundee, this was opposed, to no end, by those who claimed that the right to select delegates rested with local branches.[48] As soon as the general strike had ended, three trades council delegates in Aberdeen were blocked from standing for election to the executive committee; their pleas that their mandates derived from the local membership and not the national executive were ignored.[49] The exclusion of Communists as delegates was enforced in Aberdeen in late 1927, and by late 1928 all delegates belonging to the CPGB had been expelled.[50]

Of course, such moves stemmed partly from the increased pressure exerted by the national leadership of the Labour movement. The failure of the general strike, however, did more than convince those at the top of the party that the bar on Communists needed to be enforced: it also encouraged growing numbers of local activists to reach similar conclusions, and to implement national decisions with a rigour and enthusiasm not apparent earlier in the decade. The isolation of the Communist Party after 1926 was not just a consequence of the stance adopted by the Labour Party, or the victimisation of individual Communists by employers and the state, real as these phenomena were. The events of May 1926, and especially the establishment by trades councils of 'councils of action', tested to destruction the belief that a separate working-class political sphere, opposed to the state, could be constructed at a local level.[51] The strike marked, for a majority of the Labour movement at least, the terminus for a political tradition rooted in local class identities and experienced through a constellation of socialist and radical organisations; equally, the experience made clear the necessity of achieving and retaining parliamentary power, which in turn required the creation of a political identity capable of appealing beyond the industrial working class. As Arthur Woodburn, active in the Edinburgh Labour movement during the 1920s and from 1932 secretary of the Labour Party in Scotland, reflected, after 1926 'hope swung over to politics as the way of progress'.[52] A growing number of local Labour activists now considered themselves to be representatives of a distinct, national political party, an understanding of politics wholly different from the fluid, local alliances previously characteristic of the political left.

REPRESENTING LABOUR: CANDIDATE SELECTION AND POLITICAL IDENTITY

The expulsion of Communist delegates signalled that Labour was no longer a coalition of left-wing groupings, but was, in the words of Herbert Morrison, 'evolving from an extremely loose federation to an organised political party'.[53] Such internal, structural transformations were accompanied by attempts to ensure that Labour's electoral appeal was not limited to the ranks of the political left, or the organised working class; crucial in this respect was the issue of the candidates who stood under the Labour banner. The failure in the May 1924 Kelvingrove by-election had made clear the limitations that any association with Communism placed upon Labour's electoral support. In the wake of Aitken Ferguson's defeat, *Forward*, the newspaper of the Glasgow Labour movement, suggested that the defeat had been the result of the 'incubus' of Communist 'oratory and assistance' that accompanied the campaign. Similarly, John McLure, secretary of the Glasgow ILP, argued that the result had offered the Labour movement a 'very severe lesson' regarding the threat posed by 'obviously counterfeit' candidatures like Ferguson's.[54] The outcome was that, when the October 1924 general election arrived, there was no willingness to repeat the experience. Ferguson's efforts to secure the Labour nomination were blocked, despite his accusations of 'cunning and treachery'.[55] Similarly, in Greenock, the local trades council was threatened with disaffiliation by the national executive if it chose to again nominate Alec Geddes of the CPGB as the prospective Labour candidate.[56]

These debates over who should represent Labour gathered importance after 1926, with the March 1927 by-election in Leith proving a pivotal moment.[57] The contest was caused by the decision of Captain Wedgwood Benn, since 1918 the Liberal MP for Leith, to transfer his political allegiance to the Labour Party.[58] Benn's conversion was hailed within the parliamentary party: Philip Snowden, the then Shadow Chancellor, wrote to Benn, informing him that the news had been met with delight on the Labour benches, and predicting that there would be 'few, if any, questions upon which you and I will not see eye to eye'.[59] Snowden's prophecy of political compatibility was well-founded, and Benn would later serve as Secretary of State for India in the ill-fated second Labour government. In Leith, however, there was no echo of the enthusiasm witnessed at Westminster. At no time had Benn contacted either the divisional party or Edinburgh trades council; in response they refused to select him at the resultant by-election, instead nominating once more Robert Wilson, who had opposed Benn at the three general elections between 1922 and 1924, during which time he had increased Labour's share of the vote from 27 to 40 per cent.[60] Even Benn was conscious of the lack of support he enjoyed from local Labour figures, noting in hindsight that, after he switched parties, they had 'less respect' for him than his 'late Liberal associates'.[61] Despite their shared interest in Leith, Wilson and Benn promoted fundamentally different brands of politics. Although originally from the northwest of England, Wilson had long been resident in the constituency, where he ran a small newsagent's: he was, in effect, a local candidate.[62] Benn's focus, in contrast, was Westminster, where, prior to standing down, he had been a trenchant critic of Lloyd George and a prominent member of the Radical Liberal group. Wilson's local credentials were combined with an explicit appeal to left-wing sentiment: he began the by-election campaign by declaring his admiration for Soviet Russia, and his support for nationalisation without compensation. He then denounced the British Empire as an enormous 'slave plantation', and praised those boards of guardians removed by the Conservative government after issuing unauthorised scales relief to striking miners and their families during the lockout that followed the general strike. These actions he commended as an 'object lesson as to what the working classes could do if they took an interest in their own affairs'.[63] Wilson was, the *Manchester Guardian* concluded, 'the most unreal politician one has met for a considerable period', a 'socialist *à outrance*'.[64]

Wilson's rather individual brand of radicalism did not impress the Labour leadership, and it was speculated that his disregard for official policy had caused a 'pretty quarrel' between the local party and the national executive.[65] Certainly, the leading figures of the parliamentary party were notably absent during the campaign.[66] At one rally the mere mention of the Labour leader Ramsay MacDonald prompted calls of 'twister', with the audience demanding to hear instead of James Maxton, figurehead of the ILP left, suggesting a degree of local disenchantment with the Labour leadership. Indeed, such was the dissonance between the local campaign and Labour's national efforts to refute accusations of extremism that there were claims that Wilson must be a Communist.[67] The contention was not baseless: local Communists campaigned on Wilson's behalf, and he was applauded in the Communist press for having kept 'the class issue clearly before the electorate'.[68] But Wilson was not a Communist, and to dismiss his campaign in such terms only disguised the essential questions his candidacy raised: who did Labour candidates seek to represent, local activists, or the electorate as a whole? And did their mandate come from the local Labour movement or from the national executive?

During the campaign, Wilson received grudging support in the pages of the Labour *Daily Herald*; after his defeat by the Liberal candidate Ernest Brown by just 111 votes, doubts were expressed about the conduct of the campaign.[69] The national executive reacted in similar fashion, attributing the failure to wrest Leith from the Liberals to the local rejection of Benn. Egerton Wake, Labour's national election agent, firmly blamed Wilson for the defeat, arguing that there was 'little doubt' that Benn 'would have held the seat for Labour easily'. Wilson's intemperate outbursts had, he suggested, not only failed to convince undecided voters, but had even managed to alienate many traditional Labour supporters.[70] Such criticism was perhaps harsh: it is clear from the election results preceding and following that it was the intervention of the Unionists in 1927 that allowed Labour to come so close to victory; at the 1929 general election, in which the Unionists stood aside as they had in 1923 and 1924, the Liberal majority was restored. Nevertheless, Herbert Morrison asserted that Benn 'would have made an excellent and almost certainly successful candidate' and attributed the selection of Wilson to 'local egotisms', which had 'failed to subordinate themselves to the wider welfare of the party'. He suggested that the greatest danger to Labour's prospects lay in the 'foolish statements and unwise associations on the part of those thoughtless elements who are either Communists or humorously consider themselves to be "on the left"'. Their conduct only alienated potential voters, especially among the middle classes.[71]

Concerns over the wider implications of the failure in Leith triggered an acrimonious contest between the local Labour Party, which remained loyal to Wilson, and the Scottish and national executives, who were no longer willing to tolerate divergent local candidates. When, in August 1927, the Leith divisional party attempted to have Wilson confirmed as the prospective parliamentary candidate, the Scottish executive refused, and suggested that Wake and Henderson would need to be consulted. The local party declined to arrange a meeting; in response, the Scottish executive demanded a written undertaking that Wilson would 'accept the programme and policy of the party without equivocation', a request rejected angrily by the local party.[72] The impasse continued throughout 1928, and, although Wilson agreed to provide a written pledge on the condition that all Labour candidates be required to do likewise, it was made clear that he merited individual consideration. Henderson declared that victory in Leith had been 'thrown away' by Wilson's campaign: the national executive had, he noted, 'deferred to the local people' when it came to speakers and campaign literature, a mistake he would not repeat. The 'greatest blunder', Henderson determined, had been the refusal to allow Benn to participate in the Labour campaign. That this had been opposed by Labour activists who had spent almost a decade canvassing against Benn was irrelevant. Ben Shaw, responsible for the Labour Party in Scotland, summarised the dangers posed by candidates of Wilson's temperament: 'the national conference', he stated, 'laid down the policy of the party, and if the candidates were not to conform to it we would become a mere rabble'.[73] Endorsement continued to be withheld, and by 1929, as a general election approached, the constituency remained without an official candidate.[74] Wilson's exile was such that in April 1929, despite being elected as a delegate, he was refused entry to Labour's Scottish conference.[75] Although the Labour leadership dismissed any internal criticism as the work of Communists, Wilson's marginalisation suggests that also critical were concerns that contradictory local campaigns would undermine Labour's electoral ambitions, felt to depend upon the projection of a unified national appeal and an image of administrative competence.

The tendency to treat local defiance as synonymous with Communism was, to an extent, self-fulfilling, since the refusal to accept candidates with local support seemed, at least to those inclined to see it, to confirm that Labour was abandoning its working-class heritage. The Communist *Workers' Life* warned working-class activists in Leith that the 'bureaucratic discipline' being demanded by the national executive under the guise of 'unity and discipline' would ultimately hand 'the Labour movement over to the capitalist class'.[76] These efforts to ally the CPGB with Wilson and his supporters were assisted by the record of co-operation which existed on the local political left: indeed, in February 1927, Ben Shaw had been in contact with Edinburgh trades council regarding relations with the CPGB in Leith.[77] But to see the dispute in Leith as evidence of Communist disruption would be to view events from the wrong perspective. The belief that Labour had betrayed its roots was shared by others besides the insignificant official membership of the CPGB. The post-1926 official Labour policy of 'Industrial Peace' provoked calls for a 'socialist revival' from the miners' leader A. J. Cook and James Maxton of the ILP. The Cook–Maxton campaign was supported by the *Edinburgh Labour Standard*, the newspaper of the local Labour movement, which expressed disbelief at being asked to accept that Labour was 'no longer a working-class party but a party representing all sections of the community'.[78] It was this sentiment that drove events in Leith, and which sustained the belief that local identities alone remained in harmony with Labour's working-class origins: at an ill-tempered meeting with the Scottish executive in June 1930, Wilson declared that 'no candidate ... acceptable to the Scottish and national executives would be acceptable' in Leith.[79] In truth, sympathy for Communism reflected the limited resonance that a political language of localism could enjoy during specific instances of conflict between local and national institutions. Equally, the transition from the 'united front' to 'class against class' during late 1928 and early 1929 made little practical difference, since both privileged local opinion. Certainly, support for the CPGB increased in Leith during the dispute: circulars were issued by a 'left-wing committee', and, despite the official position adopted by the CPGB, there were joint Labour and Communist meetings in the summer of 1929.[80]

But this was, all the same, a minority response. The discord caused by the 1927 by-election, and the national pressures it generated, motivated Edinburgh trades council, responsible for the Leith divisional party, to implement the decisions of the national executive barring relations with the CPGB.[81] When, in 1930, the divisional party in Leith refused to adhere to the municipal manifesto produced by the local Labour movement, the trades council chose to run official Labour candidates in Leith without local backing.[82] The trades council further endorsed the decision of the Scottish executive to disaffiliate the Leith branch, assisting in the founding of a new body and ensuring that only 'loyal' delegates were nominated to the restructured party.[83] The settlement of the question of the Labour candidature in Leith followed, with Arthur Woodburn receiving the endorsement of the Scottish executive. Woodburn was defeated at the 1931 general election; a year later he was appointed Scottish secretary of the Labour Party. His replacement as candidate in Leith was Agnes

Dollan, wife of Patrick Dollan, the dominant Labour figure in the west of Scotland after the disaffiliation of the ILP, and later Lord Provost of Glasgow.[84] In the event Dollan did not stand, and the constituency was not won for Labour until 1945. In an important sense, however, since 1927 this had been a secondary concern: what mattered was that Leith had been brought into the mainstream of Labour politics, and would be contested by a candidate capable of articulating and defending the national outlook of the Labour Party. Crucially, by the late 1920s this was, as revealed by the position adopted by Edinburgh trades council, a perspective shared by a majority of party activists.

A similar transformation was apparent in Glasgow, where Aitken Ferguson, despite being blocked from running in Kelvingrove at the 1924 general election, continued to exercise influence at a local level. The question of relations on the political left was, however, resolved in 1927; once more it was the tensions raised by Communists running as Labour candidates that proved decisive. This time the contest was at the municipal level: a vacancy arose in the city's Anderston ward, located within the Kelvingrove constituency, after the death of the sitting Labour councillor William Kerr. Pleading time constraints, the trades council executive moved to nominate a candidate for the subsequent by-election without engaging in a full selection process; as a result, Joseph McClounie of the NUR was selected. Immediately, Ferguson, who had retained the support of the Kelvingrove divisional party, alleged that there had been foul play, and chalked notices began to appear in Anderston proclaiming that Ferguson was the 'official' Labour candidate. Curiously, eight of the nineteen members of the trades council executive committee, while denying they were Communists, then issued a statement withdrawing their support for McClounie's candidacy, and alleging that his selection had been the result of an 'undemocratic policy of intrigue and jobbery'. They urged Labour supporters to instead back Ferguson, who had decided to stand as a Communist. McClounie's nomination was, nonetheless, supported by both Ben Shaw and George Shepherd, Labour's assistant national election agent.[85] The result was, predictably enough, a split in the Labour vote, and the loss of the election to the Moderates, who took the ward with a minority of the vote.[86]

Despite its rather marginal status, it is evident that both sides saw the by-election as a crucial moment in determining the future of the Labour Party in the city. As an unnamed trades council official informed *The Scotsman*, Ferguson and his allies were set on using the contest to 'force an open fight for the acceptance of Communists as members of the Labour Party': in the changed atmosphere of 1927 the executive had, he concluded, been left with 'no alternative but to take up the challenge'.[87] The disagreement continued after the election, with the Communists being blamed for the Moderate victory: as the headline in *Forward* stated, 'That's the United Front: Communist candidate wins seat for Capitalist'.[88] Yet beyond such partisan abuse, underpinning the dispute were two divergent conceptions of the purpose of Labour politics. Ferguson couched his claim to the candidacy in terms that prioritised the wishes of local party members: Labour complaints that his campaign had done 'nothing but pour forth a cataract of ignorant abuse of Labour Party leaders and officials, national and local' exposed Ferguson's reliance on the established localism of Communist rhetoric. Ferguson claimed that he would have been willing to support McClounie, but only if the executive had secured the backing of the divisional party in Kelvingrove, and if McClounie had had his candidacy endorsed by a full meeting of the trades council. Candidates nominated without this wider local legitimacy were, Ferguson asserted, 'interlopers and disruptionists'. Who, he demanded to know, had 'made McClounie the official candidate?'. The answer was the 'reactionary bureaucrats' at the head of the Labour Party, who had 'persisted in foisting a candidature in Anderston', with no consideration of the wishes of either the local Labour movement or the trades council. This, Ferguson resolved, might be his opponents' idea of democracy, but it was not his.[89]

The response of the Labour movement to events in Anderston was, however, to expel those trades council delegates who had supported Ferguson's campaign, including Ferguson himself, who represented the Boilermakers' Society, and the eight members of the executive who backed his candidacy. At a trades council meeting in September, these delegates were ordered to leave: the meeting ended in chaos, as Ferguson and his supporters refused to depart, until the lights in the building were switched off and proceedings were brought to an early close.[90] Subsequent meetings were suspended, as the trades council moved to eradicate Communist influence; in November, the trades council reconvened in order to fill the vacant seats on the executive, and to hold an inquiry 'with a view to expelling all members who in any way supported the Communist campaign'. It was further reiterated that all delegates nominated to the trades council had to be loyal to the Labour Party, and that any organisation that nominated a Communist would be disaffiliated.[91] And although the ruling led to confrontations between Labour and Communist supporters as the latter were denied entry to trades council meetings, by early 1928 it was clear that the supporters of the national stance of the Labour Party had been successful in excluding those attached to local, cross-party models of left-wing politics.[92]

If Benn's conversion to the Labour cause had been suggestive of the changing nature of Labour's appeal after 1926, then the expulsion of

Ferguson, and the disaffiliation of the divisional parties in Leith and Kelvingrove, offered evidence of the determination of the party to ensure that Labour presented a coherent, disciplined, and moderate image to the public, both locally and nationally. Fittingly, Benn and Ferguson received an opportunity to test their respective political visions at the Aberdeen North by-election in August 1928. The contest arose from the death of Frank Rose, who had held the seat for Labour since the 1918 general election.[93] An engineer before enjoying success as a journalist and drama- tist, Rose was the opposite of candidates such as Wilson and Ferguson, having been imposed upon a local party from above. Rose received the Labour nomination just two weeks before polling in 1918, when it was decided that the original nominee, John Paton of the Aberdeen ILP, would struggle given his prominent opposition to the war. Rose promptly con- ducted a virulently anti-German and pro-war campaign, and refused any assistance from Paton and the local political left.[94] Rose proved deeply unpopular with the Labour movement in Aberdeen almost immediately. An isolated figure within the Labour Party, he was a vocal critic of indus- trial action, and despite repeating his electoral success in 1922, by the following year Aberdeen trades council was, in a reverse of the demands later made of Wilson, requesting that Rose provide a guarantee as to his future conduct. Although the disagreement was defused by the intervention of the Amalgamated Engineering Union (AEU), which sponsored Rose and subsidised his election expenses, in May 1924 the discord between Rose and the trades council resurfaced.[95] Rose had announced that he supported compulsory arbitration in industrial disputes: the trades council responded by resolving that, although bound by the national executive's ruling that all sitting MPs were to be granted automatic reselection, it considered Rose incapable 'of defending the interests of Labour', and requested permission to nominate an alternative candidate.[96]

Yet whatever the strength of feeling Rose's statements provoked locally, the national executive had no intention of allowing him to be deselected.[97] Local animosity was, however, reflected in the Communist press, where the tolerance extended to a right-wing malcontent like Rose could be accom- modated easily within an established critique of the Labour leadership as having betrayed the ideals of the party's founding generation, one which had gathered force with the election of the first Labour administration: by 1924, the leading Communist William Gallacher was accusing members of the Labour cabinet of succumbing to the 'glitter and pomp of decadent government'.[98] Such accusations gathered strength from the appearance of Labour ministers in court dress; Labour members were supposed to represent their working-class constituents, not be distracted by parliamentary tradition, and in this regard form and spectacle were as important as policy.[99] As the Communist lecturer and journalist T. A. Jackson suggested acerbically, by kissing the King's 'sacrosanct hand', Labour had exchanged the simple attire of radicalism for a 'neat frock coat and unimpeachable silk hat'.[100] Writing in *The Worker*, J. R. Campbell aligned the CPGB with Rose's opponents, publishing a letter from Rose to his election agent, in which the former had declared his intention of 'shattering the last remnants of the extremist movement' in Aberdeen.[101] Clearly there was an element of political calculation to Campbell's actions. Nevertheless, this should not detract from the sincerity with which many Communists defended local political identities. Indeed, Campbell found his own intervention was criticised by the Aberdeen branch of the CPGB, which insisted that it should have been consulted beforehand.[102]

In one sense, of course, this was all crude anti-Labour propaganda. Nevertheless, the language deployed was instructive, informed as it was by the recurring themes of loss, marginalisation and exclusion. The story related in 1924 by the Oxford-educated Communist theorist Rajani Palme Dutt of the aged Labour supporter who had confessed wearily that it had taken thirty years to build the Labour Party only to see it now destroyed by the likes of MacDonald and Snowden was likely apocryphal, but it is significant that it was this nostalgic persona that Communists chose to conjure.[103] Similarly, such a perspective exposed the extent to which the policy of the 'united front' was local in its focus. British Communists articulated a desire to reconstruct the Labour Party from below, to return to an earlier form of political engagement, purer in its motivations, free from the grubby compromises required to secure national electoral success. As Campbell argued, if all that mattered were elections then all that need be done was to find candidates willing to tell the electorate what it wanted to hear: but surely no 'serious' working-class party would be willing to simply 'adapt itself to the prejudices implanted in the workers' minds by capitalism'.[104]

The link between local identities and radicalism was, however, a device open not just to the CPGB. Rose happily attributed any criticism of his behaviour to Communist machinations, using such charges to secure the support of the national executive. When, in October 1925, the trades council finally severed ties with Rose, and renominated, by a margin of eighty-one to five, John Paton, the national executive simply ignored the decision.[105] Instead, in a ruling that lent credibility to Rose's accusations of a Communist smear campaign, Egerton Wake intimated that a full ballot of all affiliated organisations in Aberdeen would be held.[106] The reluctance of the national executive to endorse Paton had three causes: firstly, Rose had won four consecutive elections, increasing his majority from barely 200 in 1918 to almost 5,000 by 1924; secondly, he retained the political and financial backing of the AEU; lastly, although Rose's pronouncements were in conflict with official Labour policy, they were not delivered from the political left.[107] Rose was thus able to define his local opponents as Communists, effectively rendering them voiceless in national Labour politics. In the context of the mid-1920s, his electoral success offered a contrast to the dangers of identification with left-wing extremism. There were, then, differing types of ill discipline; for those with national financial support and a record of electoral success, there was greater leeway.

It is unclear whether Rose believed his claims or whether he deliberately exaggerated the Communist presence in Aberdeen; in any event, such allegations allowed him to exploit the language of nation, community and electorate employed by the Labour leadership.[108] In May 1926, Rose advised Wake that he cared for neither the opinion of the trades council nor the planned ballot: for Rose, the only ballot that mattered was the last general election.[109] At a moment when Labour was keen to stress its commitment to the constitution, and refute accusations of class interest, this was a powerful appeal to electoral legitimacy. Wake delayed the ballot until September 1926; even then the result was withheld.[110] The national executive clearly hoped that the local animosity towards Rose would eventually dissipate: Paton recalled that after being nominated he was pressured to withdraw. It was only in December 1926, when Rose threatened to run as an independent if his antagonists were not expelled, that Paton was finally endorsed.[111] That this decision had been forced upon a reluctant national executive by Rose's actions was revealed by Wake and Arthur Henderson's confession that the ratification of Paton's selection had been deliberately delayed, only for the local ballot to deliver what were coyly termed 'unsatisfactory results'.[112] Yet even then the national executive refused to abandon Rose completely. When Paton withdrew as the nominee in March 1927 following his election to national office in the ILP, Wake and Henderson sought to engineer a reconciliation between Rose and the local Labour movement.[113] This continued willingness to indulge Rose was motivated by national electoral considerations: addressing the trades council in January 1928, Henderson pleaded with the assembled delegates to consider the general election he expected to be held that year, and the detrimental impact that any dispute in Aberdeen could have 'elsewhere'.[114]

Henderson's intervention initiated a local debate regarding the function of Labour representatives. Rose understood his duty to be to the electorate rather than the local Labour movement. For this he was praised in the local Unionist press: the *Aberdeen Evening Express* applauded his 'adherence to the doctrine that a Member of Parliament is responsible to his constituents, and not to an organisation which is purely sectional'. Mirroring Communist claims to be the inheritors of the original ethos of the Labour Party, Rose's opponents were depicted as those who clung to the 'crude theories of the tub-thumpers [and] early apostles of socialism'. Rose's stance, it was felt, only echoed the Labour leadership's efforts to counter accusations of political extremism; it was the local Labour movement which was allied with Communist sentiment, and which clung to the outdated class doctrines of pre-war socialism.[115] This conception of political representation was challenged by those who emphasised the primary loyalty of Labour representatives to the working class.[116] Writing in the *Aberdeen Citizen*, James Leatham, then a councillor in rural Aberdeenshire but a socialist activist since the 1880s, suggested that it was 'absurd' to call Rose a Labour MP, and defended those accused of harbouring Communist sympathies, arguing that the rejection of industrial delegates on political grounds was 'pure inquisitorial intolerance'. He likened the position of Communist delegates to his own decades before, when he had been the only socialist on a trades council still Liberal in loyalty: now, as then, Labour was 'too anxious about "respectability"'.[117] The fundamental issue was expressed with clarity by James Younie, an ILP activist and labour college lecturer, who contended that the conflict with Rose was only symbolic of the larger question of whether Labour was to be 'a "class" or a "community" party'. It was, Younie reasoned, 'idiotic to think that the Labour Party . . . may fit itself into the existing political machine, while at the same time fulfilling the historic mission of the working class'.[118]

The quarrel was only resolved by Rose's death in July 1928.[119] The resultant by-election exposed the conflicting local and national visions of Labour politics. Wedgwood Benn, late of Leith, received the Labour nomination after being released from his prospective candidacy in West Renfrewshire. He was manoeuvred into place by the national executive, who ordered the trades council to refrain from any decision 'pending consideration by the national office'. Wake informed the national executive that Benn was willing to stand if he received local backing; he also indicated that Ben Shaw was in Aberdeen 'representing' the national viewpoint, and was in 'consultation' with the trades council; it was, then, little surprise when Benn secured the nomination.[120] Benn's selection was welcomed by the local press, which lauded him as a 'versatile politician and parliamentary hand', and commended Labour for realising that the party's candidate should 'not only be a moderate, but a man of weight, with something of a name and a national reputation'.[121] Yet the appearance of an erstwhile Liberal standing under the Labour banner was not universally welcomed.

Bob Cooney, later the Communist Party organiser for the north-east of Scotland, was in 1928 a member of the ILP. It was Benn's selection which convinced Cooney to support Aitken Ferguson, selected by the CPGB, a decision which resulted in his expulsion from the Labour Party; for Cooney, Benn simply 'wasn't a socialist'.[122]

Although Ferguson was not a local candidate, his campaign identified the CPGB with those who had opposed Rose; according to reports in *Forward*, the CPGB had 'jumped in early, and played upon the quarrels between Frank Rose and the local Labour Party'.[123] Ferguson accentuated his working-class and trade union credentials, and accused Labour of becoming just another Liberal Party. The Labour candidate was, in Ferguson's words, 'an ex-Liberal . . . connected with the Liberal Party until 1927 . . . When one looks at the programme which Mr Benn stands for one can easily see why . . . It is a Liberal programme.' The veteran socialist Tom Mann, who had contested Aberdeen North as an Independent Labour candidate in 1896, entered the fray on Ferguson's behalf, highlighting that only the Communist candidate was a member of a trade union.[124] The CPGB attempted to make the contest a referendum on the decision to expel individual Communists from the Labour Party, and to disaffiliate trades councils and divisional Labour parties that refused to sever their ties with the Communist Party. *Workers' Life*, in a rather pointed reference to Benn, contrasted this edict with the admission of 'a monstrous crew of ex-colonels, captains, [and] Liberal lawyers'.[125] It was proudly claimed that, disgusted at Benn's selection, the Labour ward committees in the working-class areas of St Machar, Greyfriars and St Clement's had joined the Communist campaign en masse, as had both local branches of Ferguson's union, the Boilermakers' Society.[126]

Benn made perfunctory attempts to contest the Communists' claim that they alone spoke for the working class, but it was clear that the Labour campaign targeted a broader audience.[127] Whereas Ferguson and his supporters saw in Benn's Liberal past a weakness, Benn appealed directly to disaffected Liberal voters, contending that Labour had inherited 'all that was best in the old Radical Party', a category which included, we may assume, himself.[128] In this, ironically, both parties were in agreement: when Shapurji Saklatvala, Communist MP for Battersea North, declared during the campaign that Labour was 'not a working-class party . . . but a national party', he was saying no more than official Labour propaganda.[129] If anything, Labour welcomed such attacks, since they gave support to the party's denials of sectionalism. The *Daily Herald*'s correspondent in Aberdeen reproached one Unionist voter for accusing Labour of fomenting 'class hatred': it was, he pointed out, 'precisely because it will not stand for the doctrine of class hatred that the Labour Party is so bitterly assailed by the Communists'.[130] Likewise, the Labour correspondent for the *Evening Express* suggested that the 'Red propaganda' had made clear the gulf between the two parties.[131]

Benn held the seat for Labour by a comfortable margin, although Ferguson did not perform poorly in the context of his party's wider electoral record, polling a quarter of the Labour vote and forcing the Liberal candidate into fourth place. Both Labour and Communist commentators interpreted the result positively. William Joss, Ferguson's campaign manager, highlighted the support the Communists had secured in the working-class areas of the constituency; according to Joss, Greyfriars had been added to the list of Britain's 'Little Moscows' on account of 'the enthusiasm and display of red flags in the ward', and some fifty workers had joined the CPGB during the campaign.[132] Dutt, the party's leading intellectual, went further, extrapolating from the result to predict a nationwide Communist vote of one million.[133] For Labour, meanwhile, Benn's decisive victory offered confirmation that future success lay in broadening the party's appeal to encompass former Liberal voters, and suggested that the electoral rewards of such a course would more than compensate for any votes lost to the CPGB. Communist opposition freed Labour from accusations of class interest, achieving the clear distinction that the leadership had long sought. Dutt's accusations that Labour had presented a united front alongside the Unionists and Liberals in opposition to the Communist campaign in Aberdeen, and that Benn had echoed the language used by the government during the general strike when he spoke of Labour representing 'the public', were perhaps perceptive, but were nonetheless immaterial.[134]

Communist accusations of class treachery were the reflection of Labour's appeal to the nation, and it was the latter which proved more powerful. The size of the Communist vote in Aberdeen North suggested a degree of disillusionment with Labour's trajectory, but such disaffection was a reaction limited to those on the political margins. If local activists were forced to choose, then a majority found the model of Labour politics promoted by the leadership, that of a party rising to national office via electoral success, more convincing than any appeal to working-class exceptionalism, especially when combined with established ties of loyalty to the institutions of the Labour movement; those trades council delegates who had supported Ferguson's campaign were expelled.[135] In tandem with this shift came an acceptance that Labour MPs received their mandate from the electorate as a whole, and on the basis of their party's agreed national policy; in this they were no different from their Tory and Liberal contemporaries. For the Labour leadership, this was a source of pride, not shame; that the middle classes could be won for socialism was proof of the strength of Labour's case, not of betrayal. The growing importance of national concerns in Labour politics was an indicator of progress, and was vindicated by the return of the second Labour government in 1929. It was the Communists and, at times, the ILP who continued to stress the primacy of local political loyalties, and in this they were largely alone.

CONCLUSION

Just weeks before the general strike, *The Labour Organiser*, the periodical of the party's election agents, offered an opinion that was perhaps, given the background of oncoming industrial conflict, oddly shorn of any explicit sense of class identity. Instead, it was noted that, since 1918, a 'new and strictly non-party body of electors had been brought into the field'. Here was an awareness that mass democracy would not operate automatically to Labour's benefit, that the post-war recipients of the vote were not predestined to be Labour supporters merely because they were overwhelmingly working-class in social and economic terms. These were, it was emphasised with some disquiet, electors 'without the tradition of loyalty to any fixed ... principles of political action', an 'apparently unorganisable mass'. Labour was faced now with 'problems of political engineering' that required the forging of a political identity capable of appealing to those who were beyond the influence of the 'continual contacts and associations' provided by the Labour movement.[136] Three months later, as the Labour movement came to terms with the failure of the general strike, J. R. Clynes, the Labour MP for Manchester Platting and the party leader between 1921 and 1922, offered a different, more optimistic, interpretation of the extension of the franchise. Writing in *The Labour Magazine*, Clynes argued that the mass franchise was an instrument of 'priceless value' to the Labour Party, and had obviated the need for extra-parliamentary tactics such as the general strike. For Clynes, it had taken 'generations to win for the masses the electoral power' they now held; and although they were still learning how best to use this new influence, they 'need never again think of a governing class apart from themselves. As soon as they want to be the governing class they can be.'[137]

Together, these two responses, as refracted through the experiences of 1924 and 1926, reshaped perceptions on the political left, and altered how the Labour Party understood its role within British politics. The sheer scale of the new electorate acted as an incentive to ensure that Labour campaigned more efficiently, and did so armed with a message that could attract those without formal connections to the Labour movement; appeals to class, trade and place gave way to a focus on issues of consumption that could transcend class and regional boundaries.[138] This necessitated, of course, a restructuring of the party, and the granting of greater authority to those at the centre. At the same time, the sense that the post-war mass electorate represented the triumph of the radical tradition was widespread, discrediting the view, still prevalent in the ranks of the CPGB and the ILP, that it was possible, and certainly desirable, to pursue a separate, working-class, political path.[139] Class, in a political sense at least, had been dissolved in the new franchise: the working class had been admitted, finally, to the ranks of the nation. How, in this new climate, was it possible to deny the legitimacy of parliamentary elections, and, by extension, the state? As Arthur Henderson declared when addressing the annual Scottish Council of the Labour Party in April 1928, Labour had to show the electorate that it had 'grown up': party members should not be 'ashamed to tell the people we are a constitutional party'.[140]

Significantly, this was a new political culture: national success did not necessarily reflect the sum of local enthusiasm, or the securing of positions of influence within local party branches. This insight eluded British Communists; it also thwarted the post-disaffiliation ILP, which, although entrenched in its redoubts in Glasgow and provincial England, was unable to reach beyond the locality.[141] When, in 1927, the Communist journalist Robin Page Arnot ventured to predict the future of the Labour Party, he chose to base his deductions on a survey of local institutions. Here he claimed to have found a movement 'nearer to an epoch of decay and disruption than at any time in the last forty years'. This he attributed, unsurprisingly, to the strictures imposed by the national leadership that prevented local co-operation between Labour and Communist activists. But politics did not operate in the way that Arnot assumed; as many within the Labour Party understood, a committed membership and vigorous branch life were no substitute for a coherent national political appeal and an ability to speak for a wide cross-section of the electorate. It was, indeed, the national 'façade', of which Arnot spoke with such contempt, that was decisive.[142] And while class identities could survive in certain localities, and provide a basis for Communist support, these could not prosper when confronted with the determination of the national executive to minimise any threat to Labour's electoral hopes, and the growing backing such an uncompromising stance had secured from party members by the late 1920s.

Labour's return as the largest party in the Commons in 1929 justified such an approach. Yet this national perspective, while triumphant, could from a provincial perspective appear largely devoid of overt ideological content. Instead, it represented a victory for hierarchy, for structure, for form. When George Shepherd, who succeeded Egerton Wake as Labour's national election agent, attended a meeting of the Scottish executive in late 1931 to discuss the campaign to recruit one million new individual members, matters of policy and political principle were left unspoken. Shepherd preferred to offer advice on the conduct of meetings, the distribution of reports and preparation of agendas, and effective organisation in municipal wards.[143] Such political appeals as were to be made would be delivered nationally; this required a clear institutional hierarchy in which local opinion was subordinate to electoral realities and national decisions. When, in the late 1930s, the question of Labour co-operating with Communists and the ILP in a united or popular front resurfaced, a neat summary of how the relationship between national and local institutions operated was offered by Arthur Woodburn. Local bodies, he stated, were to 'propagate in the localities, the policy and programme agreed upon by their organisations'; in turn, it was the responsibility of 'national authorities . . . to ensure that branches do not, by a contrary policy in the localities, prejudice the general policy of the organisation'.[144] Or, put more bluntly, local sentiment was of no importance in such matters.

By the 1930s, then, Labour representatives were no longer perceived, as the post-war Clydeside ILP MPs had been, as local tribunes, sent to parliament to voice the discontent of the people, but were instead vested with an authority which stemmed from their support among the wider electorate and their national party.[145] Woodburn's later rebuke of Maxton for remaining a 'great evangelical orator' rather than becoming a 'practical statesman' reflected the importance of this shift.[146] A political identity emerged which favoured national cohesion over local radicalism, and which was willing to countenance compromise in order to secure electoral success. For those whose political appeal was dependent upon the notion of a separate working-class political sphere, incompatible with and antagonistic to Westminster politics, this was a fatal development. In appealing to provincial traditions of radicalism, British Communists found themselves mining a depleted political resource, speaking to and for an ever-decreasing stratum of the polity. And if there were those who felt betrayed by Labour's rejection of an exclusive class identity, and who longed for a return to an oppositional politics, they were outnumbered by those willing to accept the new political settlement, something apparent in the failure of either the CPGB or the ILP to profit from the collapse of the second Labour government in 1931. As the constitution came to embrace the entire political nation, faith in working-class political exceptionalism declined. This was a change with far-reaching consequences for the practice of politics, and one to which Labour responded with greater nous than the CPGB. Even Harry Pollitt, surveying Labour's triumph in a number of suburban constituencies in 1929, was forced to admit that the party's manifesto, *Labour and the Nation*, 'designed to catch the middle-class voter, has succeeded in a way that has certainly surpassed the expectations even of MacDonald'.[147] But British Communists were convinced this renunciation of class identity would, in time, engender an apathy that would be ruinous for the Labour Party: they were wrong.

NOTES

1. *The Worker*, 29 Mar. 1929.
2. On the change in policy, see: Thorpe, *The British Communist Party and Moscow*, pp. 117–91; Worley, *Class Against Class*, pp. 27–51.
3. *Communism is Commonsense* (London, 1928), p. 5.
4. *The Worker*, 27 Jun. 1930. The reference is to J. H. Thomas (1874–1949), the Labour MP for Derby between 1920 and 1936, and the then Secretary of State for the Dominions in the second Labour government. Thomas was a favourite target for Communist criticism, both for his position on the Labour right and his alleged fondness for the perks of office.
5. *Communist Review*, vol. 4(1) (May 1923), p. 158.
6. *Communist Review*, vol. 1(5) (Sept. 1921), p. 4.
7. Thorpe, *The British Communist Party and Moscow*, pp. 19–34.
8. *Communist Review*, vol. 3(3) (Jul. 1922), p. 119.
9. *Workers' Weekly*, 10 Mar. 1923.
10. Fraser, 'Trades Councils in the Labour Movement', pp. 1–28; Kenefick, *Red Scotland*, pp. 9–13. In Scotland, trades councils were represented directly at the STUC; they received no equivalent treatment at the British TUC.
11. Knox, *Industrial Nation*, pp. 241–2. On the history of trades councils in general, see: Clinton, *Trade Union Rank and File*.
12. Howell, *MacDonald's Party*, pp. 218–19.
13. *Labour and the Nation* (London, 1928).
14. On the SLP, see: Kendall, *The Revolutionary Movement in Britain*; Challinor, *The Origins of British Bolshevism*. On the prevalence of localism in British syndicalism, see: Price, 'Contextualising British Syndicalism', pp. 266–9; Morgan, *Bolshevism and the British Left Part 3*, pp. 23–63.
15. *The Communist*, 9 Dec. 1922. On the acceptance of electoral action, see: Klugmann, *History of the CPGB, Volume 1*, pp. 41–8.
16. On the spectrum of Labour attitudes to parliament, see: Toye, 'Perfectly Parliamentary'.
17. Quoted in Clinton, *Trade Union Rank and File*, p. 53.
18. For an overview of Communist attempts to affiliate to the Labour Party in the early 1920s, see: Howell, *MacDonald's Party*, pp. 380–403.

19. Newbold lost the seat at the 1923 general election. See: Duncan, 'Motherwell for Moscow'.
20. The Unionist vote increased from 43 to 55 per cent compared to in the 1923 general election; the Liberal vote collapsed from 18 to 5 per cent: LHASC Labour Party NEC: E. Wake, *Kelvingrove By-Election Report*, 13 and 28 May 1924; Howell, *MacDonald's Party*, pp. 390–4.
21. Affiliation was rejected by 3,185,000 votes to 193,000; the ban on individual membership passed by a margin of 1,804,000 to 1,540,000: Howell, *MacDonald's Party*, pp. 394–5.
22. Clinton, *Trade Union Rank and File*, p. 148; Worley, *Class Against Class*, pp. 62–6.
23. Thorpe, *The British Communist Party and Moscow*, pp. 107–8.
24. Martin, *Communism and the Trade Unions*, pp. 78–101; Howell, *MacDonald's Party*, pp. 399–402.
25. The trades council in Glasgow was founded in 1858, with Edinburgh following no later than 1859. Similar bodies followed in Dundee (1861) and Aberdeen (1868).
26. *Communist Review*, vol. 3(3) (Jul. 1922), p. 120.
27. *The Worker*, 27 May 1927.
28. J. R. Campbell, *Red Politics in the Trade Unions: Who Are the Disrupters?* (London, 1928), p. 15.
29. NLS Acc. 11177/19 and 20: Edinburgh TLC Minutes, 22 and 31 Oct. 1922, 3 Apr. 1923.
30. NLS Acc. 11177/20: Edinburgh TLC Minutes, 11, 18 and 26 Sept. 1923.
31. NLS Acc. 11177/21: Edinburgh TLC Minutes, 14 and 21 Apr. 1925.
32. NLS Acc. 11177/21: Edinburgh TLC Minutes, 13 Oct. and 29 Dec. 1925.
33. AUL MS 2270/3/1/13: Aberdeen TLC Minutes, 18 Feb. and 15 Apr. 1925, 31 Mar, 14 and 28 Apr. 1926.
34. ML: Glasgow TLC Minutes, 27 Sept. 1922.
35. ML: Glasgow TLC Minutes, 23 Nov. 1922.
36. *Dundee Advertiser*, 6 Nov. 1924.
37. Such concerns were shared by many in the ILP, which, in 1923, voted narrowly to request MPs to refuse invitations to non-Labour social events: Owen, 'MacDonald's Parties', pp. 9–10.
38. LHASC CP/LOC/SCOT/01/01: Meeting of the Scottish Central Committee CPGB, 15 Aug. 1922.
39. Thorpe, *The British Communist Party and Moscow*, pp. 156–7.
40. Joyce, *Visions of the People*, pp. 329–31; Owen, 'MacDonald's Parties'.
41. LHASC CP/IND/MISC/10/1: Crawfurd Papers, TS Unpublished Autobiography, p. 153.
42. *Dundee Free Press*, 6 Nov. 1926 and 14 Jan. 1927. Eccleston Square was the location of the Labour Party headquarters in London.
43. *Dundee Free Press*, 25 Feb. and 25 Mar. 1927, 13 Jan. 1928.
44. *Dundee Free Press*, 2 and 9 Mar. 1928.

45. *Dundee Free Press*, 23 Mar. 1928; LHASC CP/SCOT/LOC/01/09: Dundee Branch Records 1925–26, 23 Nov. 1925.

46. *Dundee Free Press*, 6 Apr., 4 and 11 May, 15 Jun. 1928; Dundee City Archives GD/JF/1/13: DDJFWU Management Committee Minutes, 28 Oct. 1928.

47. *Dundee Evening Telegraph*, 17 Oct. and 17 Nov. 1928, 19 Jan. 1928; *The Scotsman*, 18 Oct. 1927.

48. NLS Acc. 11177/22: Edinburgh TLC Minutes, 27 Mar. and 27 Nov. 1927, 10 and 19 Oct., 9, 12 and 21 Nov., 7 and 11 Dec. 1928.

49. *The Worker*, 22 May 1926.

50. AUL MS 2270/3/1/13: Aberdeen TLC Minutes, 10 Aug. 1927, 5, 12 and 26 Sept., 3, 10 and 17 Oct., 21 Nov. 1928; *Aberdeen Evening Express*, 25 Oct. 1928.

51. Significantly, it was this aspect of the strike that the CPGB chose to celebrate. See: Emile Burns, *The General Strike of 1926: Trades Councils in Action* (London, 1926).

52. NLS Acc. 7656/4/1: Arthur Woodburn Papers, 'Some Recollections' (TS Unpublished Autobiography, n.d.), p. 53.

53. *Forward*, 27 Sept. 1924.

54. *Forward*, 31 May 1924.

55. ML: Glasgow TLC Minutes, 18 Nov. 1924.

56. *Forward*, 25 Oct. 1924.

57. For a discussion of the by-elections in Leith and Aberdeen North, which places these contests within the wider context of Labour's changing approach to electioneering after 1924, see: Petrie, 'Contests of Vital Importance'.

58. On Benn's career, see: Leslie Hale, 'Benn, William Wedgwood, first Viscount Stansgate (1877–1960)', rev. Mark Pottle, *Oxford Dictionary of National Biography*, Oxford: Oxford University Press, 2004; online edn Jan. 2008, http://www.oxforddnb.com/view/article/30705 (last accessed 4 April 2017).

59. Parliamentary Archives, ST/85/2: P. Snowden to W. W. Benn, 5 Feb. 1927.

60. *Daily Herald*, 7, 9 and 10 Feb. 1927.

61. Parliamentary Archives, ST/292/2/1: TS Unpublished Autobiography, Chapter 8 (unpaginated).

62. *Daily Herald*, 7 and 23 Feb. 1927.

63. *Edinburgh Evening Dispatch*, 1 and 12 Mar. 1927.

64. *The Manchester Guardian*, 17 Mar. 1927.

65. *Edinburgh Evening Dispatch*, 15 and 16 Mar. 1927.

66. *Daily Herald*, 1 and 11 Mar. 1927.

67. *Edinburgh Evening Dispatch*, 8 and 16 Mar. 1927.

68. *Edinburgh Evening Dispatch*, 22 Mar. 1927; *Workers' Life*, 25 Mar. 1927.

69. *Daily Herald*, 25 Mar. 1927.

70. LHASC Labour Party NEC: E. Wake, *Leith By-Election Report*, 27 Apr. 1927.

71. H. Morrison, 'When "Left" is "Right" and So Righted Is Wrong: Is British Labour Having a Little Too Much Russia?', *The Labour Magazine*, vol. 6(3) (Jul. 1927), pp. 102–3.
72. LHASC Labour Party SEC: File 2, 15 Aug., 14 Nov. and 12 Dec. 1927, 16 Jan. 1928.
73. LHASC Labour Party SEC: File 2, 13 Feb., 13 Mar. and 14 Apr. 1928.
74. LHASC Labour Party SEC: File 2, 30 Apr. and 20 Aug. 1928. It was eventually contested, unsuccessfully, by A. H. Paton, a local Labour Councillor.
75. *The Labour Party, Scottish Council: Report of the 14th Annual Conference* (1929), p. 32; NLS Acc. 11177/23: Edinburgh TLC Minutes, 2 and 14 Apr. 1929.
76. *Workers' Life*, 27 Apr. 1928.
77. NLS Acc. 11177/21: Edinburgh TLC Minutes, 13 Oct. and 29 Dec. 1925; Acc. 11177/56: Edinburgh TLC Political Committee Minutes, 25 Feb. 1927.
78. *Edinburgh Labour Standard*, 30 Jun. 1928. On the Cook–Maxton campaign, see: Howell, *MacDonald's Party*, pp. 280–1.
79. LHASC Labour Party SEC: File 2, 30 Jun. and 8 Sept. 1930.
80. NLS Acc. 11177/23: Edinburgh TLC Minutes, 12 Apr. 1929. There were also joint Labour and CPGB meetings in Leith in August 1929: *Edinburgh Evening News*, 3 Aug. 1929.
81. NLS Acc. 11177/22: Edinburgh TLC Minutes, 27 Mar., 8 Apr. and 27 Nov. 1927; 10 and 19 Oct., 9, 12 and 21 Nov., 7 Dec. 1928; *Edinburgh Labour Standard*, 15 Dec. 1928.
82. LHASC Labour Party SEC: File 2, 8, 15 and 20 Sept. 1930; NLS Acc. 11177/23: Edinburgh TLC Minutes, 10, 12, 14, 15, 21 and 26 Oct., 7 and 23 Nov., 5 and 9 Dec. 1930, 20 Jan. and 17 Feb. 1931.
83. NLS Acc. 11177/23: Edinburgh TLC Minutes, 14, 15 and 21 Oct., 23 Nov., 19 Dec 1930, 20 Jan. 1931.
84. LHASC Labour Party SEC: File 3, 17 Aug. 1931 and 23 Oct. 1933. On Dollan and Woodburn, see: Knox (ed.), *Scottish Labour Leaders*, pp. 89–92 and 284–9.
85. *Forward*, 3 Sept. 1927.
86. *Forward*, 10 Sept. 1927.
87. *The Scotsman*, 26 Aug. 1927.
88. *Forward*, 10 Sept. 1927.
89. *Forward*, 17 Sept. 1927.
90. *The Scotsman*, 9 Sept. 1927.
91. *Dundee Evening Telegraph*, 17 Oct. 1927; *The Scotsman*, 18 Oct. and 16 Nov. 1927.
92. *Dundee Evening Telegraph*, 17 Nov. 1927 and 19 Jan. 1928; *Dundee Courier and Advertiser*, 20 Jan. 1928.
93. For Rose's career, see the obituary in *The Times*, 11 Jul. 1928.
94. On the 1918 election see: Paton, *Proletarian Pilgrimage*, pp. 311–16.

95. AUL MS 2270/3/1/12: Aberdeen TLC Minutes, 14 and 20 Nov. 1923; *Aberdeen Evening Express*, 19 Nov. 1923.

96. AUL MS 2270/3/1/12: Aberdeen TLC Minutes, 14 May 1924; *The Worker*, 31 May 1924.

97. AUL MS 2270/3/1/12: Aberdeen TLC Minutes, 16 Jul. 1924.

98. *Communist Review*, vol. 1(5) (Sept. 1921), p. 4; *The Worker*, 31 May 1924.

99. On the role of clothing in radical identity in the nineteenth century see: Pickering, 'Class without Words'; Epstein, 'Understanding the Cap of Liberty'.

100. *Workers' Weekly*, 2 May 1924.

101. *The Worker*, 31 May and 7 Jun. 1924.

102. LHASC CP/CENT/PC/01/01: CPGB Political Committee Minutes, 10 Jun. 1924.

103. R. P. Dutt, 'Notes of the Month', *Labour Monthly*, vol. 6(7) (Jul. 1924), p. 387.

104. *The Worker*, 31 May 1924.

105. AUL MS 2270/3/1/13: Aberdeen TLC Minutes, 14 Oct. 1925.

106. AUL MS 2270/3/1/13: Aberdeen TLC Minutes, 28 Apr. 1926.

107. On Rose's anachronistic presence in the PLP see: Howell, *MacDonald's Party*, p. 27.

108. Rose claimed that there were between ten and twelve Communists on the Executive Committee of the TLC. See: Phipps, 'Aberdeen Trades Council and Politics', pp. 150 and 194–204.

109. *Aberdeen Press and Journal*, 20 May 1926.

110. AUL MS 2270/3/1/13: Aberdeen TLC Minutes, 8 Sept., 10 and 17 Nov., 8 Dec. 1926.

111. Paton, *Left Turn*, pp. 271–2; *Aberdeen Citizen*, 15 and 23 Dec. 1926; *Aberdeen Evening Express*, 15 Dec. 1926; LHASC Labour Party SEC: File 2, 17 Jan. 1927.

112. LHASC Labour Party NEC: A. Henderson and E. Wake, *National Agent's Report*, 7 Feb. 1928.

113. *Aberdeen Citizen*, 15 Mar. 1927; AUL MS 2270/3/1/13: Aberdeen TLC Minutes, 6 and 27 Apr., 18 and 25 May 1927.

114. AUL MS 2270/3/1/13: Aberdeen TLC Minutes, 17 Jan. 1928.

115. *Aberdeen Evening Express*, 23 Apr. and 9 Jan. 1928.

116. See the letters contained in the *Aberdeen Citizen*, 23, 27 and 28 Jan. 1928.

117. *Aberdeen Citizen*, 27 Jan. 1928. On Leatham's life see: Duncan, *James Leatham*.

118. *Aberdeen Citizen*, 31 Jan. 1928.

119. *Aberdeen Citizen*, 6 and 13 Jul. 1928; *The Times*, 11 Jul. 1928.

120. LHASC Labour Party NEC: *National Agent's Report* (n.d., Jul. 1928); AUL MS 2270/3/1/13: Aberdeen TLC Minutes, 12, 23, 29 and 30 Jul. 1928; *Aberdeen Evening Express*, 31 Jul. 1928.

121. *Aberdeen Citizen*, 3 Aug. 1928; *Aberdeen Press and Journal*, 31 Jul. 1928; *Aberdeen Evening Express*, 26 Jul. 1928.
122. IWM Acc. 804: Interview with R. Cooney, Reel 1; AUL MS 2270/3/1/13: Aberdeen TLC Minutes, 14 Nov. 1928.
123. *Forward*, 18 Aug. 1928.
124. *Aberdeen Citizen*, 10 Aug. 1928.
125. *Workers' Life*, 20 Jul. 1928.
126. *Aberdeen Evening Express*, 9 Aug. 1928.
127. *Aberdeen Citizen*, 10 Aug. 1928.
128. *Daily Herald*, 4, 8 and 14 Aug. 1928.
129. *Aberdeen Citizen*, 10 Aug. 1928.
130. *Daily Herald*, 11 Aug. 1928.
131. *Aberdeen Evening Express*, 16 Aug. 1928.
132. W. Joss, 'The Lessons of North Aberdeen', *The Communist* 3(9) (Aug.–Sept. 1928), pp. 484–6.
133. R. P. Dutt, 'Notes of the Month: Aberdeen and the Labour Party', *Labour Monthly*, vol. 10(10) (Oct. 1928), pp. 580–3.
134. Dutt, 'Aberdeen and the Labour Party', p. 590.
135. AUL MS 2270/3/1/13: Aberdeen TLC Minutes, 5, 12 and 26 Sept. 1928.
136. *The Labour Organiser*, vol. 63 (Apr. 1926), pp. 62–3.
137. J. R. Clynes, 'The Political Lessons of the Strike', *The Labour Magazine* 5(3) (Jul. 1926), pp. 100–1.
138. Savage, *The Dynamics of Working Class Politics*, pp. 179–80 and 188–200; Tanner, 'Class Voting and Radical Politics'; Lawrence, 'Labour and the Politics of Class', pp. 246–7.
139. Lawrence, 'Labour and the Politics of Class', pp. 243–9.
140. *Aberdeen Citizen*, 16 Apr. 1928.
141. On the ILP, see: Cohen, 'Happy Hunting Ground of the Crank'.
142. *The Communist*, vol. 2(9) (Oct. 1927), p. 106.
143. LHASC Labour Party SEC: File 3, 12 Dec. 1931.
144. NLS Acc. 7656/9/1: Arthur Woodburn Papers, 'Declaration upon Unrecognised Organisations' (n.d. 1937–8).
145. W. W. Knox, 'Ours Is Not an Ordinary Parliamentary Movement', pp. 154–5.
146. Woodburn, 'Some Recollections', p. 73.
147. *Sunday Worker*, 2 Jun. 1929.

2

Radicalism and Respectability in Working-class Political Culture

Speaking in the early 1980s, a distance of more than half a century, Tom Murray reflected on his career as left-wing activist in inter-war Scotland, when he had been successively a member of the ILP, the Labour Party and the Communist Party, and had served in the International Brigades during the Spanish Civil War. The grandson of a Free Church minister and son of a tenant farmer, Murray was born in 1900 in rural Aberdeenshire. A school friend of James Leslie Mitchell, the author of *Sunset Song*, Murray left school at the age of fourteen, spending the next eight years working in agriculture; during this time he became active in the Farm Servants' Union, and also joined both the ILP and the Scottish Home Rule Association. The major focus of his initial political activism was, however, the cause of temperance, and in 1922 he moved to Perth, where he worked as an organiser for the 'No Licence' campaign, which aimed to secure local restrictions on the drink trade under the local ballot scheme introduced by the 1913 Temperance (Scotland) Act. Soon, Murray was a delegate to the trades council in Perth, working on the local strike committee during the general strike. While in Perth, he befriended Joe Fordyce, a cobbler whose workshop hosted what Murray described in retrospect as a 'kind of working-class study group that developed spontaneously . . . Joe was an untutored tutor, a brilliant proletarian activist.' Under Fordyce's influence Murray became an avowed Marxist; he remained, nonetheless, committed to the cause of temperance, and in 1927 he departed for Edinburgh to continue his work for the 'No Licence' movement. It was only in 1930 that Murray joined the Communist Party; alongside his continued participation within the Labour movement, he now found himself distributing literature, addressing open-air meetings and rallies, and organising campaigns on behalf of the unemployed. He also embraced the party's myriad attempts to create a distinctive Communist cultural world, joining the workers' film society, and attempting to learn Esperanto. For the rest of the decade, however, Murray acted as a 'subterranean' party member, retaining his

Labour membership, and even securing election in 1936 as a Labour councillor in Edinburgh, a role he maintained until 1944. The success of this
clandestine Communism was perhaps questionable: certainly, his selection
as the prospective Labour parliamentary candidate in Dundee in the late
1930s was blocked by Arthur Woodburn.[1]

Murray's was, in many respects, a unique career: an elected Labour
representative who served in Spain, he remained a lifelong member of the
CPGB, and was an unrepentant defender of Stalin's legacy. Yet the course
of Murray's political life reveals much of the particular pull of Scottish and
British Communism, and, at the same time, the very limits of that appeal.
His youthful involvement in the temperance movement and his support for
Scottish home rule placed Murray firmly within a radical political tradition
which was indebted to the respectable working-class culture of the nineteenth century, and which drew heavily on a rhetoric of religious dissent.
This culture had informed the ethical socialism of the early ILP, as well as
the more peripheral Marxism of the pre-war Socialist Labour Party (SLP).[2]
In Dundee in particular, temperance had long been central to the tenor
of the city's politics, with Edwin Scrymgeour's Scottish Prohibition Party
enjoying considerable local influence until his eventual electoral demise at
the 1931 general election.[3] Indeed, Bob Stewart, the Communist Party's
Scottish organiser in the early 1920s, and a senior party figure throughout
the inter-war era, began his political career within the Prohibition Party,
and was elected to Dundee town council on a prohibitionist ticket in 1908.[4]
More than this, it was education that inspired Murray's journey from radicalism to Communism, and it was with evident pride that he stated that,
upon joining the CPGB, he found it be an especially 'painstaking political
organisation'. His commitment to self-improvement was motivated by the
conviction that he had been forced to leave school prematurely owing to
financial pressures; aged twenty, he resolved to forgo alcohol, tobacco and
marriage until he rectified this perceived intellectual deficit. Even when he
did finally marry it was to a fellow temperance campaigner, a schoolteacher
from a pious Protestant family who was active in both the Co-operative
Women's Guild and the Socialist Sunday School movement.[5] For Murray,
as for the wider radical tradition, temperance, self-education, and the individual and collective improvement of the working class were interdepend-
ent: intellectual, moral and material progress were within reach, if only the
masses could be convinced of the merits of sobriety and restraint, of dignity
and self-respect.[6]

Nonetheless, late Victorian and Edwardian Scottish radicalism had
important limitations, most notably a strain of moral and intellectual condescension, which restricted popular support for its exponents.[7] In adopting

almost wholesale the overweening elitism of the pre-war radical tradition, particularly as had been embodied in the exclusive outlook of the SLP, the Communist Party inherited these flaws alongside socially conservative notions of working-class respectability.[8] In Scotland, at least, the outcome was the construction of an image of the ideal Communist activist that was reliant upon the figure of the skilled male worker, teetotal and respectable in his appearance and personal life, and, if not actually Protestant, then certainly not Catholic. Tellingly, Murray attributed the paltry membership of the CPGB to the intense physical and intellectual commitment that the party demanded. Thus, when challenged with accounting for the success of John Cormack's reactionary Protestant Action Society in Edinburgh during the 1930s, he simply dismissed the adherents of militant sectarianism as 'nitwits and illiterates', located where the 'poverty was worst'.[9] Here was echoed the proud pre-war claim of the ILP that its newspaper *Forward* was not read in the slums of Glasgow.[10]

This aloofness was in part the product of an entrenched craft tradition and trade union identity concerned chiefly with the defence of the privileged position of the skilled male worker, and which, although not incompatible with a certain brand of militancy and radicalism, acted as a limit on the popular appeal of socialist politics.[11] The radical opposition to the licensed trade, a bequest from austere Presbyterianism, was similarly an electoral liability. In the view of Jim Smyth, prior to the upheavals occasioned by the First World War, the ILP in Glasgow had 'little perception of women or the poor as part of its own constituency'.[12] Iain McLean has gone further, arguing that the wartime industrial unrest on the Clyde was driven by sectional concerns: it was only when this narrow appeal was discarded in the post-war period that Labour was able to widen its constituency and achieve electoral success.[13] Yet in undergoing this evolution, Labour also cast aside many of the tenets of working-class radicalism that it had inherited from Radical Liberalism, most conspicuously the longstanding commitments to temperance and home rule.[14] As the ILP became an increasingly marginal voice in Labour politics during the 1920s, the old, exclusive radical identity, which had fused political fervour and an autodidactic tradition with a profound moral and social conservatism, was inherited by the CPGB.[15] For all that British Communists proclaimed their commitment to building a mass movement, Bolshevik-derived notions of the party as a political vanguard were often simply crudely superimposed upon existing understandings of respectable working-class radicalism.

During the inter-war decades, identities of class were constructed largely with reference to specific localities. But equally important was a sense of the boundaries of this identity, and the obligations it imposed: it did not require just a belief in a discrete working-class political sphere, but also created distinctive spheres within the working class, which distinguished decent, respectable working-class radicals from the 'lumpen', rough masses. The intrinsic elitism of Scottish and British Communism was a crucial and, in certain respects, self-fulfilling factor in constraining the party's influence, just as it had been for the Edwardian socialists. When, at a meeting of the Communist Party's Scottish committee in August 1922, it was noted that the party appeared to 'be a sieve into which you throw masses of people and in the process you are able to divide that which is of use from that which is of no use', it was not meant as a lament.[16]

Class, in the Communist world-view, was not an economic identity granted by the mere collection of the weekly wage packet: it was one earned through conduct, and in this the party stood closer to a moral or ethical stance than its members realised, or, perhaps, cared to admit. Identifying those deserving of class identity was a process conducted not just with reference to political activism and personal conduct, but also, implicitly, with regard to gender and religion. Communists duly sculpted an ideal party member in their own image: a skilled worker, active in the Labour movement, who spent his – and it was nearly always his – free time and spare money not on drink or gambling, or in the company of women, but in study, self-improvement and political engagement. This was, of course, a culture that always attracted only a small minority of the working class.[17] But in the inter-war period this already limited appeal was restricted further, as the rise of mass democracy and mass culture made radical study groups, cycling clubs and rambling trips seem not just the preserve of the politically active few, but also appear hopelessly out of date. This, as William Knox has suggested, eroded the 'cultural underpinnings' of the Scottish Labour movement, and played a crucial role in the decline of the ILP, as the radical tradition was superseded by a national politics which necessitated a less exclusive appeal. The CPGB did not exist outside of this wider context, and was not immune from the changes identified as central to the fate of the ILP in Scotland.[18] British Marxists may have professed to practise a more scientific and less sentimental brand of socialism than their predecessors; but theirs too was an insular and often conceited culture, which, with its distaste for the pub, popular culture and most sports, and reverence for restraint and self-betterment, could alienate those it purported to represent, and which, when faced with the failure of the masses to heed their self-appointed betters, could easily turn to contempt. Drawing on the personal testimony of individual activists and the records of the labour college movement, this chapter charts the social and cultural limits of Communism in Scotland, exploring the party's appeal in terms of activism, religion and gender, and the autodidactic tradition. Despite its Soviet trappings, the CPGB was archaic rather than alien, and its course revealed a wider decline in the potency of a political appeal reliant upon separate, if often idealised, working-class worlds.

TRUE MEMBERS OF THE WORKING CLASS: ACTIVISM AND THE COURTROOM

In July 1930, Duncan Butchart, a 25-year-old member of the Dundee branch of the Communist Party, was arrested near the entrance to the RAF training base at Leuchars in Fife after attempting to distribute copies of a pamphlet entitled *The Soldier's Voice* to servicemen. The leaflet urged members of the armed forces to campaign for political rights, and to refuse to enforce British rule in India. Charged with sedition, Butchart pleaded not guilty, and his trial was held in Cupar Sheriff Court in October 1930. During the proceedings, he displayed no contrition; conducting his own defence, he instead sought to use the trial as a forum in which to promote his political views. The jury, however, required just five minutes to reach a guilty verdict: Butchart was sentenced to five months in prison. At this, he rose, shook the hands of his supporters in the public gallery, smiled, and said simply 'cheerio'.[19]

Butchart's pugnacious courtroom demeanour, and the stoicism with which he accepted his arrest and subsequent imprisonment, was praised by local Communists, who felt that such apparent courage reflected well on their party. His supporters were keen to contrast Butchart's supposed bravery with the failure of Michael Marcus, the Labour MP for Dundee (and a solicitor too), to speak out on behalf of the young activist: for Communists, Butchart had, through his conduct, proved that he was, unlike Marcus, a 'true member of the working class'.[20] By willingly facing incarceration, appealing to pacifist sentiment, and researching and conducting his own defence, he embodied a political commitment at once physical, moral and intellectual.

Butchart's attempt to convert the courtroom into a political space, and demonstrate his contempt for the authority of the state, was, to be sure, motivated by his Communism; yet in doing these things, he was also invoking an established radical tradition, one that, through the exercise of the right of the accused to act in their own defence, viewed criminal trials as a public platform and, by extension, as a political opportunity. There were, no doubt, prominent recent examples to which Butchart could turn for inspiration. John Maclean, the radical schoolteacher and labour college lecturer, had been charged with sedition in 1916 and 1918; during the latter trial, he had declared famously that he appeared not 'as the accused', but as the 'accuser' of a capitalist system 'dripping with blood from head to foot' after four years of war.[21] That this remained a compelling example for those on the radical left throughout the inter-war decades was clear in the regret expressed by William Gallacher at his failure to act with similar conviction at his own sedition trial in 1916. If, Gallacher reflected two decades later during his tenure as the Communist MP for West Fife, by representing himself in court Maclean had 'held high the banner of revolutionary struggle', by agreeing to legal representation he himself, along with his fellow defendants, had

> dragged it, or allowed it to be dragged, in the mire. Even now it is hard to think of it without a feeling of shame . . . The conduct of [the defence] . . . was a disgrace to the movement. If we had made a fight . . . there was a faint possibility that we might have made it difficult for them to sentence us, because of the feeling we could have aroused among the workers . . . But our capitulation simply played into their hands. Weakness and timidity can avail us of nothing in such a situation.[22]

When, in 1925, Gallacher found himself among the twelve leading Communists arrested and tried with incitement to mutiny, care was taken to ensure that such an error was not repeated. It was agreed that some would represent themselves in court while others engaged legal counsel, in order to, as Gallacher phrased it, gain the 'full benefit' of both the 'political and legal arguments'.[23] Equally telling was the opprobrium heaped on J. H. Thomas, the Labour MP for Derby and general secretary of the railwaymen's union, when, after instituting libel proceedings against *The Communist* in 1921, he was alleged to have complained that Arthur MacManus, a member of the Communist Party's executive committee, had called him 'Jimmy' in court. Communist accounts ridiculed Thomas for his pomposity; however, they also juxtaposed Thomas's appeal to the authority of the court with the self-reliance and wit of MacManus, who, of course, had represented himself in court.[24] True working-class radicals did not hide behind courtroom etiquette: they challenged it.

Beyond such recent examples, Butchart's desire to politicise his hearing mimicked a practice of even older provenance, one which had its roots in the sedition and treason trials of the late eighteenth and early nineteenth centuries. As James Epstein has shown, the reaction of the authorities to the domestic agitation for reform during this period, and the legal measures taken to suppress popular discontent, offered radical defendants an opportunity to contest the legitimacy of state action. This was most apparent when the accused chose to represent themselves rather than instruct legal counsel. Such decisions were motivated partly by intellectual pride; but influential too was a mistrust of the privileged legal community, and fears that a lawyer might, shamefully, seek mercy on behalf of their client.[25] Although faced by the full might of the state, by conducting their own defence radicals were, as Epstein notes, able to enter 'into a rather curious dialogue' with the authorities.[26]

This dialogue was also participatory. The presence of a partisan audience in the public gallery, and the appeals made by defendants to the members of the jury, made of such trials a public spectacle; courtroom speeches were often printed, sometimes daily, and distributed to a wider audience. Although there were obvious, and severe, personal consequences resting upon the outcome of any individual trial, in purely political terms the judgement was of less importance than the capacity of the accused to convince the public of their integrity. A guilty verdict accepted stoically, and which could be presented as an affront to popular conceptions of justice, could be as valuable as an acquittal. Crucial was that the accused fulfil the role of the 'citizen-hero', victimised by the state. Indeed, as Patrick Joyce has explained, a conviction, with the attendant dramatic narrative of trial, incarceration and letters from prison, and the eventual redemption of release, could, by making a political martyr of the accused, often be of greater significance.[27] This was certainly the case in Scotland, where the memory of those, such as Thomas Muir, Andrew Hardie and John Baird, who had been imprisoned, transported or executed between the 1790s and the 1820s retained a political cachet in radical circles throughout the nineteenth and early twentieth centuries.[28]

It was the theme of martyrdom that aligned most closely with the politics of the radical left, and especially with the apocalyptic world-view that informed much Communist rhetoric. If Communist activists were, at least in their own opinion, representatives of the working class, they also considered themselves to be superior to their class peers, elevated by their intellect, dedication and moral severity. Party members were, through their commitment and self-sacrifice, expected to offer an example that would inspire a wider audience.[29] By the 1930s, however, it was becoming clear that any appeal that such a stance might once have exercised had faded; the party's efforts to exploit radical traditions of martyrdom were futile. The conviction that the masses would follow the example set by Butchart misjudged the popular mood, and while members of the local CPGB and National Unemployed Workers' Movement (NUWM) branches campaigned on his behalf, the reluctance of Marcus to intervene on his behalf was more closely attuned to the public mood. Nominated as a candidate in Dundee's eighth ward at the 1930 municipal elections while still in prison, Butchart polled less than 4 per cent of the vote.[30] Indeed, if anything, Communist self-importance was mocked by Labour supporters, who dismissed the party's tactics as laughably outdated in an era of professionalised electioneering, and in which Labour had twice been able to hold national office. In a letter to the local Labour press, James Leahy, a disillusioned former member of the NUWM, admonished his erstwhile colleagues, and ridiculed the Communist faith in the positive example of militancy. If, Leahy suggested mordantly, critics of the party would only

> take an unimpassioned look at the Dundee local [CPGB branch] they will find abundant proof of selfless altruism. They will see unceasing, unslacking service of the leadership in raising the rank and file above the snotty, sordid squabbles of policies, finances and such stupidly fatiguing questions as the election of salaried officials. They will see the ordinary member being nursed and guided to a true evaluation and pursuit of the spiritual things in party politics only to be found in carrying platforms and banners, chalking streets, and selling papers – and seeing prisons.[31]

Butchart was, in this reading, not a martyr but simply credulous, misled by a party guilty of tactical ineptitude.

More successful in securing the credibility that the CPGB believed would be conferred by imprisonment was John Gollan, whose trial and detention followed, and largely overshadowed, Butchart's. In May 1931, aged just twenty, Gollan was arrested after he and David Lesslie, a fellow Communist, offered copies of *The Soldier's Voice* to uniformed soldiers in central Edinburgh; he was charged with distributing literature likely to cause sedition or disaffection among members of the armed forces. Given Butchart's conviction the previous year, the ease with which Lesslie evaded arrest, and Gollan's defiant not-guilty plea, it seems almost certain that the spectacle of a trial was the intended outcome. At his trial at Edinburgh Sheriff Court in July 1931, Gollan handled his own defence. He did not dispute the substance of the prosecution case, and confessed freely that he had circulated the pamphlet in question. Instead, in front of a public gallery filled with sympathisers, he took the opportunity presented by the trial to question the prosecution witnesses on the definition of sedition and their knowledge of the Russian revolution, drawing applause from his supporters when he remarked that the charges had been brought not by ordinary soldiers, but by 'higher authorities'. The prosecuting counsel concluded by briefly addressing the jury, submitting only that, since the acts set forth in the indictment had not been contested, the accused was evidently guilty. Gollan addressed the jury for nearly two hours, appealing directly to the memory of the war by declaring that his intention had been only to avert 'anything in the nature of the catastrophe of 1914 to 1918', while outside a crowd of supporters attempted to gain entry to the courtroom. After an hour's deliberation, the jury reached a guilty verdict, albeit one tempered by the request that Gollan be found guilty only of acts likely to cause disaffection and not sedition, suggesting that his semantic and etymological efforts had not been entirely wasted. He received a custodial sentence of six months.[32]

Gollan's arrest, trial and imprisonment provided a focus for Communist propaganda in Edinburgh and further afield, as the image of the principled and youthful pacifist, detained for the peaceful expression of his political beliefs, was exploited for the benefit of the party. Great mileage was extracted from the fact that Gollan had, as a political prisoner, been granted additional privileges, including the right to wear his own clothes and to receive books from outside. Following his conviction extensive fundraising efforts were undertaken to assist his family, with Butchart being enrolled to address public meetings in Edinburgh and Dundee, where he drew the obvious parallels between their cases.[33] In the immediate aftermath of the trial there were clashes between the police and members of the so-called 'Gollan defence committee' outside the home of Sheriff Brown, who had heard the case.[34] Occurring during the 'class against class' period, and while the second Labour government remained in office, the case also offered an opportunity to contrast the militancy of Communists with the willingness of Labour politicians to enforce the law against working-class activists. In the run-up to the trial, a petition calling for the charges against Gollan to be dropped, said to contain 2,000 signatures, was presented to the Lord Advocate Craigie Aitchison, the Labour MP for Kilmarnock.[35] Gollan personally condemned the failure of the Labour Party to intervene on his behalf, and the CPGB secured a minor victory when, in August 1931, they convinced Edinburgh trades council to call for his release, contradicting the sentiments expressed by the Labour MP for Edinburgh Central, William Graham.[36]

Aside from the immediate opportunities to attack the Labour Party that the case presented, Gollan's trial offered the chance to stress the positive moral qualities of individual Communists. Gollan was rendered as the ideal working-class activist made manifest, combining militant self-sacrifice with respectability and intellectual skill. Especial emphasis was placed on the proficiency with which he had conducted his defence: Gollan had, it was claimed in one party pamphlet, 'dealt devastatingly with the prosecution's whole case, rising to a giant's height despite his youthful years and stature'.[37] It was recounted with equal pride that even Sheriff Brown had commended Gollan on the quality of his defence, stating that 'his legal researches have been most laudable'.[38] The depiction of Gollan as selfless and heroic continued after his trial, with the party making it known that the young inmate's 'only real worry' was how his mother was coping in his absence.[39] The contrast between political prisoners and the 'lumpen', criminal element provided a further theme: it was reported with revulsion that Gollan had suffered the indignity of being taken to court 'handcuffed to a man charged with culpable homicide'.[40] This distinction was of importance to Communists: Bob Cooney remembered with pride that, during his own time in prison in Aberdeen in the late 1930s, the governor had, in an 'almost fatherly' manner, told him not to waste his time speaking with the other inmates since they were not of his 'class'.[41]

The image of Gollan as a valiant working-class autodidact was, it should be said, not without foundation. Born in Edinburgh in 1911, he left school before his fourteenth birthday to train as an apprentice painter in his father's business; he was, according to his family, an exemplary worker. Gollan's father Duncan, whom he described as a 'kind of Robert Tressell type', was, despite a weakness for alcohol, a convinced socialist, and early friend of the future Irish republican James Connolly, who spent his spare time studying socialist theory. It was via his father that he developed an interest in politics that was predominantly intellectual: he later cited their political discussions as having been more influential than the inter-war economic depression in shaping his world-view. Asked to explain why, in 1927, he had joined the CPGB rather than Labour, he replied that he had been attracted to Communism because he found it 'intensely satisfying in explaining the world'.[42] While in prison he asked his father to send him works by Keynes, Plato and Marx.[43] Within the insular world of British Communism, Gollan's imprisonment was central to the subsequent course of his career. After his release from prison he was swiftly made editor of the *Young Worker*, newspaper of the Young Communist League (YCL); in 1935, he became general secretary of the YCL. Such early prominence paved the way for his eventual appointment in 1956 as general secretary of the CPGB.[44] In Edinburgh too, Gollan provided local Communists with a heroic example. His younger sister Jessie stressed the role her brother had played in convincing her to join the YCL by encouraging her to read works of history and political theory. Under the guidance of John, Jessie's Communism was similarly academic and moral in nature; she felt she had 'developed more intellectually . . . by knowing the Communist Party' than she had at school.[45] It was thus a moment of great pride when he chose her rather than his father to walk beside him when he left prison.[46]

Jessie's husband, Murdoch Taylor, spoke of John Gollan's influence in similarly appreciative terms. Taylor had been raised in Leith by his politically active mother, and his initial involvement in politics came via his attendance at classes taught by Gollan. Taylor never met his father, and grew up in a house that, after his sister had been dispatched to a convent, contained only him, his mother and various 'itinerant men'. Although his mother was loosely engaged in Communist politics, selling the *Sunday Worker* for the party during the 1920s, it was the ascetic and intellectual radicalism embodied by Gollan that appealed. Indeed, he condemned his mother's lifestyle, as epitomised by her failure to keep a clean house, as 'reprehensible' and 'totally amoral'; while he subsequently admitted that this was not 'terribly important objectively', he was nonetheless 'mortified' when party colleagues visited his home. In contrast, and ignorant of the difficulties presented by their father's alcoholism, he admired the respectable life of the Gollans, considering it to be 'conservative in the best sense of the word . . . it was real, it had values'. He summarised his reasons for joining the party as an 'amalgam of wanting to find a place to go' and, having spoken to 'Johnnie', as being about 'books' in particular.[47]

Despite such endorsements, however, this was a vision of radical respectability that failed to impress outside the ranks of the political left. Clearly, the notoriety that accompanied criminal proceedings could offend less radical understandings of working-class morality. Mary Gollan was humiliated by her son's arrest, and found the demonstrations organised by the so-called 'defence committee', which would assemble outside the family home, a source of embarrassment.[48] Bob Cooney had a similar relationship with his mother, who, he claimed, followed at a distance when he chalked the streets of Aberdeen with Communist slogans, washing his political messages off the pavement before her neighbours could read them.[49] Besides the contested nature of respectability within the working class, the failure of Butchart and Gollan to exploit their individual cases beyond the confines of Communist politics also exposed the extent to which, even among the politically active, the figure of the radical 'hero' had lost its allure. This was apparent in the ostracism of the romantic socialism of James Maxton within the Labour Party, and, in due course, the disaffiliation of the ILP in 1932 under his direction.[50] The dominance of the conciliatory and bureaucratic professionalism of Stanley Baldwin and Neville Chamberlain, and the rejection of the die-hard Unionism of the Edwardian era, arguably reflected a similar shift in Conservative politics. What has, in the context of the nineteenth century, been described as the 'radical ordeal', with its risks of imprisonment, and commitment to an austere lifestyle of temperance and material sacrifice, no longer appeared inspirational but antiquated and, frankly, ridiculous in a mass democracy.[51] More than this, in Scotland traditions of dissent, protest and heroic sacrifice carried deeply divisive historic connotations.

RADICALISM AND THE DISSENTING TRADITION

Recalling his time as Communist Party organiser for the north-east of Scotland, Bob Cooney recounted an incident that took place in the late 1930s, when, in an effort to combat the activities of the local branch of the British Union of Fascists, he travelled north to Peterhead with some colleagues from Aberdeen. Upon arriving, they found that the fascists had erected a platform in the town square; but when the fascist speakers tried to address passers-by, Cooney, assisted by Tommy Stephen, the sole Communist Party member in Peterhead, up-ended the podium: for the following three nights, the party held rallies in the square to celebrate their victory. In Cooney's account, these exploits inspired a sermon by a local Church of Scotland Minister, who 'told his congregation that as I spoke he could see the fanatical light in my eye. "If only we Christians had the same fanatical faith", he said, "the Church would sweep everything before it."' Cooney revelled in this reading, extending the praise to Stephen, who had 'for a long time . . . ploughed a lone furrow'; his was 'the faith of which the local clergyman spoke'.[52]

A similar comparison between the missionary zeal of the Church militant and the commitment of Communists to the emancipation of the working class was drawn by Jessie Gollan. Distraught at the financial and emotional impact of her father's drinking, as a child she had been a devout Christian and advocate of temperance reform; at night, she would fantasise about emigrating to the prohibition-era USA. Influenced by her brother, however, she came to believe that the social transformation Christianity promised could be achieved only through political change. After reading Engels' *Origin of the Family, Private Property and the State*, she came to view Christianity as 'ridiculous', and found herself no longer able to 'believe in things like that'.[53] Where previously she had prayed for her father to cease drinking, she now decided that if she wanted change, she would have 'to work for it'. Aged seventeen she joined the YCL, finding in Communism a practical means of achieving the material improvement in working-class life that had inspired her religious faith. The YCL also replicated the companionship she had found in organisations such as the Girl Guides, offering Sunday rambles in the hills and social evenings as well as political meetings and rallies. Jessie saw few contradictions in this transition: she had believed that 'Christianity offered something', and it was that same 'something' she found in politics. Communism was, then, both an intellectual revelation and a source of moral and spiritual strength; simultaneously a practical doctrine that 'helped people to understand what was going on', and an emotional 'consolation'. Looking back on her political evolution, she felt that she had simply 'wanted everybody to be happy and have a decent standard of living . . . the misery of working-class people, it was just abominable . . . the party satisfied me. I realised then that's what I'd been trying to get out of Christianity.'[54] Politics offered the hope of achieving in the present a change which religion postponed to the future, and the ardour, the commitment to helping others, the belief in temperance, education and self-respect, were all as applicable to her Communism as they had been to her Christianity.

The relationship between Communism and Christianity was, all the same, specific rather than general, and it was with the dissenting Protestant tradition that the CPGB proved to be most compatible. In part, this empathy derived from a populist, democratic reading of British constitutional history, common across the radical left, which treated the Levellers of the 1640s as the precursors of modern socialism, and, in Scotland, celebrated the Covenanting tradition of the seventeenth century as a popular revolt against despotism that served as an inspiration to the Paineite radicals of the 1790s.[55] Upon this had been overlaid a Marxist historical analysis that saw the Reformation and the religious conflicts which ensued as a 'bourgeois revolution', to be followed inevitably by its proletarian equivalent, and which, in this seemingly objective sense, viewed the reformed churches as an advance on Catholic absolutism.[56] Alongside this, however, lay a more essential identification with Protestantism, the strength of which can, in Scotland, be understood only in the context of an endemic popular distrust of Catholicism, derided as a religion of superstition, autocracy and ignorance. During the nineteenth century, this had fused with an antagonism towards Irish immigrants that was still prevalent in the inter-war decades, creating a legacy of economic discrimination that ensured that the skilled industrial working class, the intended audience for Communist propaganda, was largely of Protestant descent.[57] Even Murdoch Taylor dismissed his mother's involvement with Communism as merely 'emotional', something he attributed to her Catholic upbringing.[58]

This historicist reading was deployed by the Communist journalist and labour college lecturer T. A. Jackson, who confessed that he could 'not shake off the conviction that an actual father-to-son organisational descent might be traced', from the Social Democratic Federation and ILP of the Edwardian era, 'back through the Chartists and the English Jacobins, to the . . . Leveller agitators of the New Model Army'. Born in London, Jackson considered this ancestry to be especially pronounced in Scotland, where, he alleged, Marxism had secured a wider audience via the activism of the SLP. This he ascribed partly to the Scottish educational tradition, which in his opinion had fostered a 'popular respect for learning that had no counterpart in England'. However, he also discerned a link between the sectarian purity of the early Marxists and the legacy of Calvinism. As he stated ironically:

> It was said – and not without truth – that [the SLP] resembled herein that sect of ultra-Calvinists whose 'theme-song' was –
> 'We are the pure selected few,
> And all the rest are damned!
> There's room enough in Hell for you!
> We don't want heaven crammed!'[59]

Given the prominence of ex-members of the SLP in the early Communist leadership, it is little surprise that such elitism was a trait of British Communism.

The influence of the nonconformist tradition on British Marxism was highlighted by Raphael Samuel, who noted the Methodist upbringing of many of the leading members of the Communist Historians' Group of the 1950s. Samuel also observed astutely that it was the Marxist sectaries of the CPGB who often better exemplified the missionary ideal than the Christian socialists in the Labour Party.[60] Yet this link is more than a historiographical curio: the affinity between radicalism and dissent gave British Communism its peculiar moralising tone, especially in Scotland, where popular Protestantism formed an essential element in the rhetoric of the radical left.[61]

Helen Crawfurd, the Communist candidate in Aberdeen North at the 1931 general election, was born in Glasgow in 1877 to parents from Scotland and Ulster. Her upbringing was evangelical Protestant in faith and sharply Unionist in politics, and she confessed that, as a child, she had shared her mother's perception of the Catholic Church as a 'bulwark of reaction and superstition', even to the extent of viewing the 'Catholic Irish as sub-human'.[62] After marrying a preacher from her father's Church, she became a committed pacifist and temperance advocate, pursuits which were compatible with her distaste for Catholicism. Her radicalism was interwoven with respectability: in her words, late nineteenth-century Glasgow was a scene of 'sordid, ugly poverty, with an orgy of drunkenness and emotional religion, doping masses of the people'. By the turn of the century her religious interests were partly eclipsed by social and political concerns, particularly the campaign for female suffrage, and she joined the Women's Social and Political Union (WSPU) in 1910. After the outbreak of war in 1914, and the death of her husband that same year, she embraced a more explicit socialism and joined the ILP. In July 1920, she travelled to Moscow to observe the second congress of the Comintern; when the ILP finally rejected affiliation to the Comintern, she became a member of the CPGB, soon securing election to the party's executive committee.[63] Like Jessie Gollan's, Crawfurd's Communism was a means of bringing to the here and now what religion had withheld for the future. It was, she thought, 'wrong that the religious people should be so much concerned about heaven and a future life, and so little concerned with the present'. Yet although her passage from Christian socialism to Communism entailed the outward repudiation of her religious beliefs, Protestantism continued to shape her political rhetoric. As a campaigner for the WSPU her public addresses had been 'punctuated with Biblical quotations', and this, she confessed, remained true of her Communist speeches. Indeed, during the 1920s she and Alec Geddes, the party's parliamentary candidate in Greenock, clashed with the Communist theorist Rajani Palme Dutt over their continued predilection for religious allegory.[64]

The relationship that Crawfurd felt existed between Communism and Protestantism went deeper than just the borrowing of biblical imagery, and extended to how she understood the relation of party members to the state and wider society. The sustained harassment faced by activists, and the ever-present threat of imprisonment, which remained real until at least the middle of the 1930s, encouraged the belief that Communists were a persecuted minority.[65] For those steeped in the Scottish Presbyterian tradition, this echoed the repression of the Covenanters during the seventeenth century. Crawfurd drew on this history: writing of her unsuccessful candidacy in Bothwell in 1929, she likened her campaign to the 1679 Battle of Bothwell Brig, when government troops defeated a Covenanting force. Accepting that she too had been 'routed', she maintained that this 'didn't prove that either the Covenanters or the Communists were wrong'.[66]

A parallel conflation of class, respectability and Presbyterianism was voiced by Tom Bell, who graduated from the pre-war SLP to be become one of the key figures in the early years of British Communism. As an atheist and vegetarian, Bell operated on the radical fringes of Edwardian socialism; even so, he never fully shed his youthful suspicion of Catholicism. He criticised the efforts of John Wheatley, the Labour MP for Glasgow Shettleston and Minister of Health in the first Labour government, to win Catholic voters for Labour through his founding of the Catholic Socialist Society: for Bell, socialism should lead the people away from religion, not compromise with irrational faith. But this commitment to freethinking was suffused with a particular mistrust of the Catholic Church: Bell accused Wheatley of unspecified 'manoeuvres' in luring David Kirkwood from the SLP to the ranks of the ILP; it had been, he suggested pointedly, a curious example of the 'Calvinist succumbing to the Jesuit'.[67] In Bell's world-view, class was linked to respectability, and was incompatible with Catholicism. On this basis, he attacked J. T. Walton Newbold, elected as a Communist MP in Motherwell in 1922, in terms that seemed to suggest that his subsequent departure from the party had been prophesied by both his shabby personal appearance and his alleged willingness to pander to the prejudices of Catholic voters.[68] Bell complained that Newbold 'went about unkempt and unshaven, wearing a dirty collar and clothes, trying to look "proletarian"', and using 'the most vulgar swearwords'. 'Such individuals', he argued, brought shame 'on our movement, for the average workman does not *glorify* the dirt and uniform of his occupation.' He also claimed that in 1923 Newbold had pleaded with the Comintern to intervene in the trial of Orthodox priests in Russia as it was alienating Catholic voters in his constituency.[69]

The portrayal of the Catholic community as a backward element among the Scottish working class, who voted according to the instructions of their clergy, pervaded Communist politics. Although devoid of an overt Presbyterian identity, Communists retained a distrust of a Church they considered corrupt and riven with superstition; they also frequently identified the Irish community with the unskilled, as a 'lumpen' drunken mass lacking the self-respect and discipline necessary for political organisation, and beholden to the political instructions of their priests. John MacArthur, a party member in Fife, alleged that Catholics who joined the CPGB during the general strike soon left under pressure from their priests. Such fickle behaviour was contrasted with those who, as a result of their 'Calvinistic Scots upbringing, and . . . early association with leaders like Bob Stewart and Willie Gallacher who were temperance advocates', proved more dependable. David Proudfoot, another Fife activist, was similarly critical of the Catholic population. During the six-month lockout which followed the general strike, he at first contended that the blacklegs handling coal locally were mere 'lumpen' elements, the 'sons of vomits and dregs . . . the lowest of a low caste'. Later, however, he was convinced that they were 'almost without exception composed of the religious fraternity', a reference unlikely to have been directed at Protestants.[70]

The social conservatism evident in matters of religion extended to Communist perceptions of female involvement in radical politics. The party's understanding of politics, framed in the conventional terms of skilled work and participation in the Labour movement, almost by definition excluded women.[71] Helen Crawfurd felt that, although women were 'encouraged by the executive', individual party members displayed more traditional attitudes.[72] This was certainly true: Mary Docherty, who had joined the party in Fife before moving to Edinburgh, found that when she returned to Cowdenbeath in the early 1930s it was assumed that she would continue her earlier work with the women's and children's sections. She was even helpfully warned by Bob Selkirk, the district organiser, to take care that the former did not deteriorate 'into a gossiping section'.[73] Even Crawfurd, accorded a prominent role in the party hierarchy, and whose experience in the suffrage campaigns ensured that she was in demand as a public speaker and organiser, was, via her involvement in Workers' International Relief, responsible for the humanitarian aspects of Communist politics.[74] In truth, in Communist politics women were, as a result of their relative absence from the ranks of the Labour movement and the CPGB, treated as a threat rather than an opportunity.[75] In a party training manual issued in 1927, Bell, an opponent before 1914 of female suffrage, asserted that there was,

> in the inactive, uninformed and unorganised mass of women workers, a positive hindrance to the working-class struggle. The fight against this danger, which is fortified by the influence of the bourgeois church and bourgeois superstitions, must be intensified to draw more and more women into the working class.[76]

The party would, then, not pander to 'feminist' concerns such as equal suffrage: women were expected to act as 'co-workers in the common struggle of the working class men against capitalism and for Communism'.[77] Such comments undermine assertions that female Communists were treated as equals: whatever the theory, the reality of party life was often less than revolutionary.[78] Even where women were, by virtue of their economic status, objectively working class, they were not truly so until they had been drawn into the largely male world of union and party branches.

The claim of the CPGB, in theory at least, was that it would awaken women to their class status, and involve them in radical political activity. Yet despite this insistence on a productionist version of equality between men and women, there remained a contradictory assumption that there were specific, largely domestic, female issues, a gender distinction that the Communists shared with the ILP.[79] At the Aberdeen North by-election of 1928, the Communist appeal to female voters concentrated on domestic matters and questions of social policy.[80] Moreover, Bell's essentialist fear that women were more susceptible to the appeals of religion and social deference was widely shared, and enhanced suspicion of the Irish community. Worse still was the attitude espoused by Bob Stewart, who, when recalling his candidacy in Dundee in 1929, claimed that both his Unionist and Liberal opponents had been selected on the basis of their looks in an attempt to appeal to newly enfranchised youthful female voters.[81] In the face of such assumptions female activists struggled to find a space in which to engage with Communist politics. Equally, when women did display what could be construed as a class awareness, the response of male activists could be hostile, and the sight of female workers participating in what was still considered a male sphere was not always welcomed.[82] This was most obviously the case in Dundee, where, as a result of the scale of female employment in the jute industry, and the establishment of the local Jute and Flax Workers' Union in 1906, women played a more prominent role in the Labour movement than elsewhere.[83] Yet, notwithstanding the claims of Communists that they sought to awaken female workers to their plight, this was not appreciated by local activists, as revealed by the lack of support received by Mary Brooksbank, a party member, when she founded the Dundee Working Women's Guild.[84]

Exemplary was the attitude displayed by James Littlejohn who, as a member of both the JFWU and the CPGB, attended his union's annual general meeting in Dundee in October 1929. When his motion to lift the prohibition on individual Communists being elected to union office was ruled out of order, the meeting descended into pandemonium as he and his supporters attempted to seize the platform. The obvious division was that between the Communists in the audience and the Labour-aligned platform headed by John Sime, the secretary of the JFWU. But there was also a clear gender divide between the female membership, largely supportive of Sime, and the male Communists, and it was one that Littlejohn highlighted. In a letter to the *Dundee Free Press* Littlejohn gave his version of events, and left no doubt that he found the participation of women in the confrontation unpleasant. Contrasting his own manly restraint with Sime's reliance on female support, Littlejohn suggested that Sime 'must have thought that in view of the opposition I was getting from his women supporters I would be glad to get clear of the hall'. However, in the face of such provocation Littlejohn stood his ground, and 'took the battering from the women, who know no better'.[85] Communist politics was a male pursuit, and in this women were doubly damned: if they did not participate they were dangerously apolitical; if they did, they were 'rough' and undignified, and violated the respectable ideal.

The adoption by the CPGB of a nationalist, radical-democratic reading of Scottish and British history after 1935 has been viewed as simply the ritualistic domestic enactment of the Comintern's decision to pursue a popular front, and the party's populist rhetoric dismissed, according to preference, as either cynical politicking or a betrayal of the revolutionary ideal of 1917.[86] But both critiques rest on the assumption that there had at one time existed a Communism constructed without reference to the radical tradition, and which represented a genuine rupture in the history of the political left. Yet in Scotland, at least, Communists had long been indebted to their radical predecessors. This included an adherence to a populist interpretation of history that positioned the CPGB as the culmination of a tradition of heroism and sacrifice that dated back to the Covenanters. Thus, when, in 1938, Aberdeen Communists staged a pageant of Scottish history, the banner which proclaimed that the Covenanters had waged 'the heroic struggle of the common people' was not simply an attempt to gain popular support, although it was certainly that too. Communists, with their emancipatory understanding of historical progress, treated their party as heir to the Scottish radical tradition. The Covenanters were followed in the pageant by the radical martyrs of the late eighteenth and early nineteenth century, Thomas Muir, John Baird and Andrew Hardie, who in turn begat Keir Hardie, John Maclean and William Gallacher.[87] This lineage was claimed with equal conviction by the ILP.[88]

The contention that the CPGB had broken with existing political and social traditions was embraced for different reasons by both party members and their opponents. The pervasiveness of Protestant assumptions, allegory and imagery indicates, all the same, that inter-war radicalism did not represent a new dawn, but rather a redrawing of old boundaries. In his study of what he termed the 'Labour sects', Eric Hobsbawm suggested that the impact of religion on 'modern' working-class movements was limited to short-lived endeavours such as the Labour Churches, and that, by the twentieth century, the working-class movement was 'purely, if not militantly, secular'.[89] The influence of Christianity on radical politics was restricted to the ethical socialism of the Labour Party. There is, however, an alternative interpretation to Hobsbawm's progressive narrative. It was, in fact, the Christian-inspired ethical socialists of the Labour Party who successfully tempered their religion, and, in consequence, broadened their appeal. More than this, while Hobsbawm's contention that the ILP was a socialist rather than a religious organisation was rightly challenged by later historians who recognised that the ILP was deeply influenced by Protestantism, we should not accept a division between what has been described as the 'eclectic, elitist and Calvinist' ILP and the Marxism of the CPGB.[90] In the narrowness of their social background, and the extreme nature of their political commitment, their similarities outweighed their differences. The ebbing of the radical tradition, central to the decline of the ILP and Labour's shift to a national and statist understanding of politics, was central too to the failure of British Communism.

THE FAILURE OF INDEPENDENT WORKING-CLASS EDUCATION

Attempts to expand the educational opportunities open to the working classes on a systematic basis could be traced at least to the university extension movement of the 1870s. These efforts had been motivated by a liberal humanism that saw little, if anything, to criticise in the content of higher education; reform was, on the contrary, a question of enabling gifted working-class students to access the academic riches taken for granted by the middle and upper classes. A similar ethos had informed the foundation of Ruskin College in 1899. Launched with the support of American philanthropy and operating on a residential basis, Ruskin was, aided by its links with the University of Oxford, designed to offer working-class students an experience akin to higher education, with their attendance assisted by trade union scholarships.[91] Likewise, the Workers' Educational Association (WEA), established in 1903, aimed, through its programme of provincial evening classes, to replicate what was considered the objective atmosphere of a university tutorial; to this end, the WEA employed university-educated tutors, and was willing to accept financial support from local education authorities.[92]

A very different understanding of the purpose of education was voiced by the movement for independent working-class education that began with the Plebs League and Central Labour College (CLC), formed in 1908–9 by students at Ruskin College frustrated by the perceived interference of the University of Oxford in their education, and especially by the absence of Marxist economics from the curriculum. The CLC, which relied on support from the South Wales Miners' Federation and the NUR, and which relocated from Oxford to London in 1911, was intended to promote a distinctive, working-class perspective in the educational field, offering tuition in history and economics from a socialist, Marxian viewpoint. The early labour college movement was thus driven by the conviction that the education provided by schools and universities was intrinsically partial, and offered only intellectual justification for the social and economic status quo.[93] As such, the issue was not access to but rather the content of education, and the political sympathies of those who dispensed it. Indeed, merely increasing access to existing institutions would be dangerous for the working class, and the efforts of the WEA were, as a result, viewed with contempt. Instead, the aim was to create an alternative educational apparatus, one outside the influence of the state, and which would be managed by the working class. Such an outlook was closely allied in ethos with the syndicalism and industrial unionism that had helped to inspire the labour unrest of the Edwardian era.[94] If the trade unions were the embodiment of working-class interests in the economic sphere, and the Labour Party, even if not wholly consistent with the tenets of syndicalism, fulfilled a similar demand for political independence, then the CLC and the Plebs League hoped to encourage a corresponding intellectual autonomy.

Although hampered by the outbreak of war in 1914, the CLC provided a template for others to follow. A Scottish Labour College (SLC) was founded in 1916, an extension of the educational work undertaken in Glasgow and Fife by John Maclean, and by 1920 close to 3,000 students were studying under its auspices.[95] In 1921, the SLC merged with its equivalents elsewhere in Britain to establish the National Council of Labour Colleges (NCLC).[96] In Scotland, the labour college movement embraced the combative class identity that had inspired the foundation of the CLC. In 1920, in an appeal addressed to trades union branches and socialist societies across Scotland, it was declared that the existing educational provision offered by the state was inadequate, since subjects such as history and economics were considered only from the viewpoint of the 'ruling classes'. The SLC would provide a forum in which the working class could attain intellectual independence; aware that such an endeavour would never be supported by those 'privileged in the present society', the SLC issued a plea for financial assistance.[97] Yet, as the 1920s progressed, this vision of working-class autonomy and self-sufficiency, expressed through a distinctive curriculum and supported by a separate set of institutions, would also suffer, as the traditions of the radical left, and especially the hostility towards the state that had underpinned the emergence of the labour college movement, declined.

In June 1922, Edinburgh trades council debated whether to affiliate to the local labour college or to the Edinburgh branch of the WEA; unable to reach an immediate decision, each organisation was asked to outline their case. The submission provided by Edinburgh labour college encapsulated the heady mixture of vaulting ambition and weary cynicism that was typical of the movement. Schools and universities were, it was suggested, 'simply part of the capitalist state's educational machinery', which existed only to 'educate the workers ... for capitalism, that is, to give them the necessary technical skill and the equally necessary pro-capitalist outlook'. The academic approach of the WEA was dismissed in similar terms: the study of the arts was pointless 'hobbyism'; workers needed to study subjects that would help them to overcome their present 'industrial and political difficulties'. In this world-view, class was an overarching category, one that suffused every aspect of life, not just the workplace or electoral politics; it was foolish to treat education as a neutral field, and obvious that the working class needed to be 'as independent in education as they

are in politics'. If, the labour college's submission concluded, 'the capitalist political parties cannot provide for the workers' political needs; if the
capitalist newspapers cannot provide for the workers' informational needs,
neither can the WEA, with its university education, meet the workers'
educational needs'. The labour college operated on the 'same principle
as trade-unionism and Labour political action, namely, the conflict of
interests, hopes, and ambitions between employers and wage-workers'.[98]
The appeal to class identity was successful, and the trades council voted to
affiliate to the labour college by a margin of four to one.[99]

Similar sentiments were expressed elsewhere. In Dundee, the local
labour college issued a circular declaring that it had been founded as a
consequence of the 'opposition of ideas between the owners of capital and
those who own nothing but the power to labour': the college aimed to
make the working class 'conscious of this antagonism for the purpose of
removing it', and believed in the 'independence of Labour – Industrially,
Politically, and Educationally'.[100] Glasgow labour college saw its purpose
in a comparable light, declaring that it planned to ready the workers
for the 'class struggle', and assist them 'in the fight for the abolition of
capitalism'.[101] This confrontational world-view appeared to find a growing
audience in post-war Scotland, and by 1925 fourteen district labour colleges had been formed, delivering nearly 250 classes to approximately
6,000 students, with financial support from over 900 affiliated labour
and socialist societies.[102] The same class-based philosophy was evident in
the classes offered by the regional colleges. At the founding conference of
the SLC in 1916, it was declared that the basis of the curriculum would
be history and economics, taught unambiguously from the 'working-class
point of view'.[103] This emphasis was sustained during the early 1920s. In
Edinburgh, of the twenty-four classes organised by the labour college in
winter 1922, seven were in economics and eight in history; the next year,
sixteen of the thirty-seven classes arranged were in economics, with a
further eleven in history. By 1924, fully twenty-six of the forty-six classes
offered were in economics. In Glasgow, the focus was the same: in the
winter 1923 session, twenty classes were organised, of which seven were in
economics and six in history; in 1924, twelve of the eighteen courses held
were in economics, and the following year this figure reached fifteen from
a total of twenty-two. The only options offered in Aberdeen in the 1923–4
session were in industrial history, political economy, economic geography,
historical materialism and the 'rise of civilisation'.[104]

The labour colleges offered an outlet for a powerful local class identity,
one that drew upon a profoundly political interpretation of history and
economics. Yet the relationship between this belief in a separate working-

class educational sphere and party allegiance was unclear. The movement for independent working-class education encouraged, at least until the mid-1920s, a deep scepticism regarding the capacity of Westminster to meet the needs of the working class, which produced an indifference to electoral politics and national party labels. This was apparent in the prominent role played by individual Communists within the district colleges. Like the trades councils, labour colleges were a curious amalgam, the product of local loyalties and membership, yet part of the broader Labour movement; this ambiguity allowed scope for Communist participation. Moreover, the class basis of the education offered by the colleges clearly chimed with the stance adopted by the early CPGB. In Aberdeen, the openly Communist William Morrison was secretary of the local labour college; in Glasgow, William Joss, Aitken Ferguson, and William Allan, all prominent Communist activists, were tutors at the labour college.[105] The labour college in Edinburgh, founded in 1920, united a variety of disparate Marxist educational schemes that had been operating since before 1914, including those managed by the ILP, the SLP and the local Marxian School of Economics. The Communists William Deas, Fred Douglas, Euphemia Laing, William McKie and Hew Robertson all tutored at the new institution, as did their party colleague Robert Foulis, who was barred from standing as the Labour candidate in Leith in 1922 as a result of his membership of the CPGB.[106] Such was the crossover in membership that, in 1923, the secretary of the miners' lodge in Loanhead complained that 'nearly all' of the Edinburgh college tutors 'were Communists'. This was, however, an exaggeration: Labour and SDF activists were also influential.[107] Arthur Woodburn, for example, tutored in economic history in Edinburgh, and in 1925 was appointed secretary and chairman of the labour college there.[108]

The leadership of the CPGB had initially welcomed the expansion of the labour colleges, seeing it as evidence of a rising class consciousness. The 'bolshevisation' of the party during 1922 and 1923, when the CPGB adopted, under the direction of the Comintern, a more centralised structure, saw this attitude change, however, as a greater degree of control over the education of party members was demanded.[109] A party training department was created in 1923, followed by a central training school; the first British students departed for the International Lenin School in Moscow in 1926.[110] The impact of the general strike, followed by the leftward trend of official Communist politics, encouraged the increased separation of Communist education during the second half of the 1920s. By 1927, the CPGB was denouncing the NCLC as 'a mere educational department of the trade union bureaucracy'.[111] Yet whatever the changes in the official stance of the CPGB, individual Communists continued to work within the labour colleges. In Edinburgh, William Deas continued to act as a tutor throughout the 1920s, as did Robert Foulis. Similarly, William Morrison represented Aberdeen labour college on the national committee of the SLC as late as 1927.[112]

The labour college movement drew upon a tradition of provincial radicalism that could cut across party loyalties. Yet, as we have seen, during the 1920s this political identity, and the autodidactic tradition it inspired, was weakened. It has been suggested that this resulted from the refusal of the CPGB to participate in educational efforts not under party direction, leading to the isolation of party members, who were left reliant on an increasingly arid and doctrinaire Soviet-derived Marxism. Jonathan Rose has even argued that the rigid, prescriptive education offered to members of the CPGB was fundamentally amoral and attracted few but 'cynics and authoritarians'. As a result, for Rose, the British working classes rejected Marxism, and cleaved to the more liberal intellectual tradition embodied by the WEA.[113] The leadership of the CPGB was, to be sure, cynical and authoritarian; all the same, to attribute the collapse of the autodidactic tradition to the sectarian policies they implemented would be to vastly overstate their influence. In any case, party members appear to have continued their involvement with the labour colleges throughout the 1920s. Of far greater importance was the displacing of the traditions of provincial radicalism, and the growing weight attached to electoral politics. Radical politics came to be synonymous with the Labour Party, and, as outlined in the previous chapter, a hierarchical model of political participation came to predominate. The labour colleges were not safe from the consequences of these changes. The appointment of J. P. M. Millar as secretary of the NCLC in 1923 ended the official toleration of Communism within the organisation, which increasingly became a provider of training for trade union officials and aspiring Labour representatives, as Millar competed with the WEA for Labour movement support.[114] This shift had important consequences for both the nature of labour college education and the identity of those providing it.

The initial impact of the general strike was to kindle interest in the labour colleges; nevertheless, by late 1927 the SLC faced falling student numbers, particularly in the mining regions of Fife, Lanarkshire and Stirlingshire, where the local unions were unable to continue to fund evening classes after the six-month lockout that followed the general strike. The financial implications of declining enrolments provided the leadership of the NCLC, and especially Millar and Woodburn, who had long been concerned that the autonomy granted to the district colleges had permitted Communist participation, with the justification they needed to restructure the labour college movement in Scotland. In early 1928 the national committee of the SLC resolved, by ten votes to six, to reorganise the various district colleges into eastern and western divisions, with each division being managed by a full-time organiser, who was to be appointed and paid from the centre. Due to come into operation in July 1928, the scheme was delayed by the local hostility it provoked. The labour college in Glasgow refused to co-operate with Joe Payne, the new organiser in the west of Scotland; the colleges in Lanarkshire, Dunbartonshire, Stirlingshire and Fife withdrew their delegates from the SLC in support.[115] Nevertheless, the SLC persisted with the reforms: a new college was formed in Glasgow in late 1928, a move which deepened the dispute and created dissension among the local Labour movement, with ILP branches in the city refusing to recognise the new institution.[116] By the following year, however, the determination of the SLC proved decisive, and the wayward colleges had returned to the fold.[117]

Crucially, these structural reforms were accompanied by a shift in the education provided by the labour colleges. The traditional emphasis on history and economics continued in the immediate aftermath of the general strike. During the winter 1926 session in Edinburgh, seventeen of the twenty-five classes organised addressed economics; in 1927, fourteen of thirty-six classes were in working-class and industrial history, with a further seven classes in economics. Similarly, in Glasgow half of the twenty-two classes in winter 1926 focused on economic questions. By the end of the decade, however, the focus of the curriculum had shifted. In winter 1929, just two of the twenty-five classes arranged in Edinburgh dealt with economics; a year later this had fallen to just one of twenty-seven; and, astonishingly given the collapse of the second Labour government in August 1931, in the winter 1931 session just three classes from a total of forty-three addressed economic issues. Similarly, the number of classes in history arranged by Edinburgh labour college fell to just one in 1929 and 1930; there was none in 1931. The curriculum offered by the restructured Glasgow college developed along similar lines: in the winter 1932 session, there were no classes in economics in Glasgow, and a mere three in working-class and labour history.[118]

The classes on economics and history, which were rooted in a combative, if simplistic, Marxian analysis, were replaced by courses dealing with the practicalities of Labour politics. In March 1929, as an election loomed, the national committee of the SLC reported approvingly that classes in 'election conduct', including 'chairmanship, canvassing, electoral law [and the] duties of polling agents', were being held in Edinburgh. These classes were also being held in Glasgow, where eight 'good students' were sent to be trained as tutors in election law and chairmanship; only members of organisations affiliated to the Labour Party were eligible to take part.[119] The new courses in electioneering were accompanied by those intended to improve Labour's administrative competence: four classes on the 'Constitution and Problems of Local Government' were held in 1930; classes entitled 'Problems of a Labour Government' arrived in 1928 and 1930. Courses on 'Chairmanship', 'Public Speaking' and 'Business Meeting Procedure' appeared with greater frequency after 1928, as did those in 'English Grammar and Writing'; classes in the 'Art and Practice of Debating' arrived in 1933. Six of the eighteen classes arranged in Glasgow in winter 1932, for example, were concerned with public speaking.[120]

Whereas the labour colleges of the early 1920s existed to challenge the education offered by the state, and to provide an alternative reading of history and economics, a decade later this mission had been replaced by a curriculum that complemented existing academic education by providing practical campaigning and administrative skills for Labour activists. The earlier suspicion of the state, and of university education, began to dissipate, particularly once Labour was established as the official opposition. As Labour competed in the national electoral arena, the old isolation came to appear self-defeating: 'Labour' was but one political identity among many, not an all-encompassing social, economic and intellectual category. Symbolic was the decision of the TUC general council to accept the offer made in 1927 by the University of Oxford to make available a number of two-year scholarships to trade unionists.[121] This new attitude could also be discerned at a local level. In January 1929, at a debate hosted by the Edinburgh Fabian Society, it was T. A. Cairns, chairman of Edinburgh trades council, who spoke in favour of the proposition that the working class could not 'afford to neglect university education in fitting themselves to attain socialism'. It was left to Charles Gibbons, a labour college tutor involved with the Plebs League and the CLC since before 1914, to defend independent working-class education. Cairns' proposition was carried by thirty-four votes to twenty-one.[122]

As the traditions that had sustained local class identities were weakened by the arrival of mass democracy, the NCLC adapted; in doing so, it became an institution of party rather than class. The necessary accompaniment to these changes in the curriculum and ethos of the labour college movement was the removal of those tutors who either had links to the CPGB, or who simply refused to adapt. Robert Wilson, the discarded Labour candidate in Leith, resigned as a tutor in December 1927; William Deas was removed from his position as a tutor in Edinburgh in August 1931 on the grounds that he remained a member of the CPGB.[123] The NCLC was, by the 1930s, the educational department of the Labour

Party, not of the working class; as the changes to the curriculum suggest, this was a very different role.

We may take as instructive the course of James Younie's career as a labour college tutor. A member of the ILP in Lossiemouth, Younie had studied at the CLC during the 1920s; he was also a dogged opponent of the Labour MP for Aberdeen North, Frank Rose. By 1930, he was employed as an organiser by the SLC, in charge of Fife and the north-east of Scotland.[124] In 1931, he transferred to the NCLC head office in London, where he assumed responsibility for the assessment of coursework. Soon, however, Younie was removed from his new position after accusing Millar, still the national secretary of the NCLC, of abusing his position for financial gain. An official enquiry followed, which, after finding that the allegations were based in fact, recommended that Younie be reinstated. The executive, however, upheld his dismissal, and supported Millar. There was, clearly, a very real dispute between Younie and Millar over the latter's management of the NCLC. Yet there was also an underlying contest over the direction that the NCLC had taken under Millar's leadership. An unapologetic Marxist, Younie had clashed with Woodburn in 1931, attacking the latter's *Outline of Finance*, in which Woodburn had supported the retention of the gold standard.[125] Woodburn later supported Younie's removal, alleging that he had been an inadequate tutor. Given the series of promotions he received, however, it seems more likely that it was his radicalism that left him bereft of allies when he clashed with Millar. While it is unclear whether he ever officially made the transition from the ILP to the CPGB, he was certainly present at the open-air rally held at Aberdeen's Castlegate in 1931 to nominate Helen Crawfurd as a 'workers' candidate' in protest at the decision of the trades council to allow Wedgwood Benn to stand for re-election. It was, he declared from the platform, 'better to split the workers' vote than to be represented in Parliament [by Benn] . . . They wished for a real working class representative.'[126]

That the autodidactic tradition largely vanished in inter-war Britain is correct; however, to blame this on the narrow Marxism promoted by the CPGB is to neglect the wider changes that were taking place on the political left. If we delve beneath the national picture, it is evident that the CPGB was as much a casualty of these developments as it was a cause. The Communist leadership may have wished to keep the education of its members under central control, but that does not mean it was able to do so. Certainly, Younie's response to his dismissal was not to retreat into party-approved Marxist isolation, but to lead a rebellion at the labour colleges in Aberdeen and Dundee that saw both institutions fall outside the control of the NCLC until early 1933.[127] But the basic lesson of inter-war radicalism was that local Communist activists and those on the ILP left lacked the wherewithal to challenge the dominance of the national executive politically, and of the reformed NCLC educationally. There was to be no return to the belligerent, emancipatory and deeply political vision of independent working-class education enunciated by the SLC in 1920; the NCLC offered instead vocational training in the technicalities of party politics.

It seems churlish to now criticise the judgement of the Labour leadership; if anything, Labour's achievement in becoming the largest grouping in the Commons in 1929 is even more astonishing when placed in the context of the subsequent struggles of its successors to the status of third party. Yet electoral success, while a triumph for those who constructed Labour's national appeal, came at a cost ultimately borne by local political cultures and radical traditions, as the decline in the numbers attending labour college classes makes clear. Student numbers in Scotland fell from 3,741 in winter 1926 to 1,595 five years later.[128] In Edinburgh, annual student enrolments more than halved between 1922 and 1933, from over 1,000 to less than 400; they had halved again by 1939.[129] The apparent placidity of the working class, and especially the unemployed, during the 1930s, which struck observers then and has detained historians since, undoubtedly had disparate causes.[130] But the decline of a radical autodidactic tradition, founded in local identities of class, surely played a part, as the conviction that the world could be changed by educating the working class in history and economics was replaced by a faith in central government. As Fred Douglas of the Edinburgh CPGB complained in 1935, the NCLC, like so many other elements of the Labour movement, had been 'successfully bureaucratised by the system of staff ... paid and bossed from the top', while the critique of the type of education offered by the WEA, which had once been accused of 'class collaboration', had long since been forgotten.[131]

Politics was not, then, something immediate, to be shaped daily by your behaviour at work and deportment in the street, or found in the books you read; instead, it was a process conducted elsewhere, performed by national figures, who arrived in the locality only at election time. That a certain quiescence resulted should not be surprising; what was significant was that it was welcomed in the Labour Party. In Edinburgh, labour college alumni had been at the forefront of the contest over the direction of the Labour Party, clashing with William Graham, the Labour MP for Edinburgh Central between 1918 and 1931, and Dr Drummond Shiels, who represented Edinburgh East from 1924 until 1931. Both were on the moderate wing of the parliamentary party, and faced vocal local opposition from members of both the ILP and the Communist Party. Significantly, prior to his election Graham had attended the University of Edinburgh, and had been a tutor for the WEA: in 1920 he only just survived an attempt, initiated by the labour college tutor Robert Foulis, to force his deselection.[132] It was only after Woodburn assumed control of Edinburgh labour college in 1925 that such opposition abated. In 1929 Shiels congratulated Woodburn on the transformation he had overseen, noting that the college was now 'a neat co-operating factor' rather than a source of obstruction. By 1932 Shiels was content that the 'sneering critics' produced by the labour college a decade earlier had since been successfully converted into 'useful helpers'.[133]

CONCLUSION

The CPGB, and the local activists who bore the party's message in Scotland, hoped to lay claim to a radical tradition that was simultaneously militant yet respectable, combative yet sober, oppositional yet scholarly. In this the party promoted a particular vision of respectability, one dependent on the conviction that there existed a separate working-class world, with its own rules, expectations, and customs. Equally, in their identification with the persecuted religious and political minorities of the past, their understanding of the criminal justice system as a site of conflict with the state, and their belief in the need for a specific working-class curriculum, Communists understood politics as, in essence, the fight to defend a distinctive working-class way of life. Of course, none of this was to say that this conception of working-class life was harmonious: there were workers who, by failing to show the required bravery, commitment, and respectability, fell below the necessary standard. Communist activists were not alone in this perspective, and their counterparts in the ILP displayed similar sentiments; they suffered, however, alike fates. The belief in a uniquely working-class politics could not be reconciled with the arrival of mass democracy, the rise of the mass media, and the growth of popular culture. Ultimately, it was the Labour Party which adapted successfully to this new political culture, recalibrating both its internal organisation and outward image to appeal to a mass electorate.[134] The exclusivity of the old radical vision of working-class politics became a hindrance; politics was no longer the pursuit only of the active minority, of the skilled male worker. The aspirations expressed in Labour's 1928 manifesto *Labour and the Nation* had on the surface been achieved: Labour now spoke not for a class apart, but was, in Arthur Woodburn's portentous phrase, 'the party of the people, the whole people, and nothing but the people'.[135]

This focus on electoral propriety, which predated, and indeed hastened, the disaffection and ultimate disaffiliation of the ILP left, transformed

Labour's sense of its own place in the polity, and dismantled the separate working-class sphere upon which radical politics was predicated. It was the appeal to the nation that mattered, not that to class. The eventual removal of the difference between 'Labour' and the 'nation', which would come to fruition in 1945, was a triumph for the Labour Party and those who led it between the wars. Yet this process rendered redundant the local political identities that had sustained popular radicalism. Labour was not to be built from the ground up, but directed nationally; the localities were to conform rather than inform, to act as outlets for national policy. More than this, the supremacy granted to national elections had critical consequences not just for political identity, but also for how politics was to be legitimately pursued. When James Littlejohn clashed with John Sime's female supporters at the JFWU annual general meeting in 1929, at stake alongside an exclusively male political and industrial identity was a belief in how politics should be conducted. Littlejohn's intervention resulted from his motion being ruled out of order: his refusal to accept this decision, and subsequent unruly conduct, was criticised by union officials who suggested caustically, and, one imagines, with an eye on the reformed labour college curriculum, that he might choose to 'go in for a study of rules pertaining to motions and standing orders at business meetings'.[136] Here was mirrored the view of *The Labour Organiser*, which just months before had argued that meetings held under Labour auspices were an opportunity to publicise 'the business qualities of the party as displayed in the management of even its simplest affairs'.[137] If Communists believed that conduct was a marker of class identity, their opponents in the Labour Party now considered it a demonstration of a party's fitness for national office; in this regard too, Communist and radical understandings of political engagement collided with the newly defined parameters of inter-war politics. How and where parties conducted their politics became a crucial element in the construction of political identities.

NOTES

1. MacDougall (ed.), *Voices from Work and Home*, pp. 258–72, 292–3 and 309. On the cultural aspects of British Communism in the early 1930s, see: Worley, *Class Against Class*, pp. 194–225.
2. On the role of temperance and home rule in the Scottish radical tradition, see: Knox (ed.), *Scottish Labour Leaders*, pp. 22–46. For a summary of the respectable culture of the Victorian working class, and the historiographical debate which surrounds it, see: Kirk, *Change, Continuity and Class*, pp. 111–40. On the culture of respectability in Scotland, and its links

with Radical Liberalism, see: Smout, *A Century of the Scottish People*, pp. 239–51.

3. Walker, *Juteopolis*, pp. 333–93.
4. Stewart, *Breaking the Fetters*, pp. 42–9; Walker, 'The Scottish Prohibition Party', pp. 361–2.
5. MacDougall (ed.), *Voices from Work and Home*, pp. 269 and 325–7.
6. Knox, *Industrial Nation*, pp. 168–73.
7. Knox (ed.), *Scottish Labour Leaders*, p. 52.
8. For a critical discussion of the similarities between the SLP and the CPGB, see: Kendall, *The Revolutionary Movement in Britain*, esp. pp. 68–72. A more sympathetic portrayal of the SLP is provided in: Challinor, *The Origins of British Bolshevism*.
9. MacDougall (ed.), *Voices from Work and Home*, pp. 302–3.
10. Knox, *Industrial Nation*, p. 170.
11. On this paradoxical relationship, see: Hinton, *The First Shop Stewards' Movement*, esp. pp. 56–100; Morris, 'Skilled Workers and the Politics of the "Red" Clyde'.
12. Smyth, *Labour in Glasgow*, p. 27.
13. The debate surrounding 'red' Clydeside is voluminous, but for McLean's revisionist account see his: *The Legend of Red Clydeside*; and 'Red Clydeside after 25 years'.
14. Knox, *Scottish Labour Leaders*, pp. 22–6 and 43–5.
15. On the marginalisation of the ILP during the second half of the 1920s, see: Howell, *MacDonald's Party*, pp. 264–87.
16. LHASC CP/LOC/SCOT/01/01: CPGB Scottish Central Committee Meeting, 15 Aug. 1922.
17. Hobsbawm, 'The British Communist Party', p. 30; Hoggart, *The Uses of Literacy*, pp. 318–23.
18. Knox, *Industrial Nation*, pp. 202 and 247. In this regard see also: Smout, *A Century of the Scottish People*, pp. 271–5; McKinlay and Morris (eds), *The ILP on Clydeside*.
19. *Dundee Courier and Advertiser*, 22 Jul. and 14 Oct. 1930; *The Scotsman*, 14 Oct. 1930; *Dundee Free Press*, 17 Oct. 1930.
20. *Dundee Free Press*, 7 Nov. 1930.
21. The speech is repr. in: Torrance (ed.), *Great Scottish Speeches*, p. 73.
22. Gallacher, *Revolt on the Clyde*, pp. 119–20.
23. Gallacher, *Rolling of the Thunder*, p. 82.
24. Hyde, 'Please, Sir, he called me "Jimmy!"', pp. 534–9.
25. Epstein, *Radical Expression*, pp. 29–69, and *In Practice*, pp. 59–82. As Epstein notes, the cases during this period drew inspiration from the seventeenth century. I am grateful to Dr Gordon Pentland for his insights on this period.
26. Epstein, *Radical Expression*, p. 33.
27. Epstein, *Radical Expression*, pp. 32–6 and 54–60; Joyce, *Visions of the People*, pp. 45–6.

28. Pentland, 'Betrayed by Infamous Spies?'.
29. Samuel, 'The Lost World of British Communism: part I', p. 43.
30. *Dundee Free Press*, 7 Nov. 1930.
31. *Dundee Free Press*, 26 Dec. 1930.
32. LHASC CP/IND/GOLL/01/02: Gollan Papers, *Lord Advocate v John Gollan* 17 Jul. 1931 (TS account of case, n.d.); *The Scotsman*, 18 Jul. 1931; *Aberdeen Press and Journal*, 18 Jul. 1931.
33. The Gollan Defence Committee and the Edinburgh Friends of the Soviet Union, *The Workers' Voice: Against the Next War for Capitalism, for the Fight – How to Win Socialism* (Edinburgh, 1931), p. 2; *The Scotsman*, 20 Aug. 1931. For the fundraising campaign, see the reports in the *Daily Worker* between May and August 1931.
34. *Daily Worker*, 19 May, 1 Jun. and 28 Jul. 1931.
35. *The Workers' Voice*, p. 1.
36. *Daily Worker*, 18, 19 and 20 Aug. 1931; *The Workers' Voice*, p. 2.
37. *The Workers' Voice*, p. 3.
38. LHASC CP/IND/GOLL/01/02: Gollan Papers, *Lord Advocate v John Gollan*.
39. *The Workers' Voice*, p. 4.
40. *The Workers' Voice*, p. 1.
41. MML Acc. 4530: Cooney, 'Proud Journey' (Unpublished TS, 1944), p. 33.
42. LHASC CP/IND/KETT/06/03: Kettle Papers, Draft TS of Unpublished John Gollan Biography, pp. 1–7; CP/IND/KETT/05/01: Kettle Papers, Further Interview with Jessie Taylor, Apr. 1986; CP/IND/KETT/05/03: Kettle Papers, Interview with John Gollan (n.d.); *The Sunday Times*, 3 Jul. 1966.
43. LHASC CP/IND/GOLL/01/03: Gollan Papers, J. Gollan to D. Gollan, 6 Oct. 1931.
44. LHASC CP/IND/GOLL/01/01: Gollan Papers, Biographical Sketches (n.d.).
45. LHASC CP/IND/KETT/01/01: Kettle Papers, Draft for 'Recollections of a Younger World', Interview with Jessie Taylor (née Gollan), Mar. 1983, pp. 41 and 46.
46. LHASC CP/IND/KETT/05/01: Kettle Papers, Notes of Interview with Jessie Taylor, 8 Apr. 1986.
47. LHASC CP/IND/KETT/01/01: Kettle Papers, Draft for 'Recollections of a Younger World', Interview with Murdoch Taylor, Mar. 1983, pp. 52–6, 59 and 61.
48. LHASC CP/IND/KETT/01/01: Kettle Papers, Draft for 'Recollections of a Younger World', Interview with Jessie Taylor (née Gollan), Mar. 1983, pp. 38–9.
49. Corkill and Rawnsley (eds), *The Road to Spain*, pp. 114–15.
50. Knox, *James Maxton*, pp. 94–106; McKinlay and Smyth, 'The End of the "Agitator Workman"'.
51. Roberts, *Political Movements in Urban England*, pp. 54–8.
52. Cooney, 'Proud Journey', pp. 12–13.

53. See: Engels, *Origin of the Family, Private Property and the State*. Originally published in 1884.
54. LHASC CP/IND/KETT/01/01: Kettle Papers, Draft for 'Recollections of a Younger World', Interview with Jessie Taylor (née Gollan), Mar. 1983, pp. 43–4.
55. Cowan, 'The Covenanting Tradition in Scottish History', p. 126; Brims, 'The Covenanting Tradition and Scottish Radicalism'.
56. See the outline of British history prepared for classes at the Edinburgh Labour College: NLS Acc. 5120/38: Lecture Material, C. L. Gibbons, 1924–5.
57. On attitudes to the Catholic Church between the wars, see: Walker and Gallagher, 'Protestantism and Scottish Politics'; Brown, 'Outside the Covenant'. For the historic context, see: Knox, *Industrial Nation*, pp. 101–3 and 139–43.
58. LHASC CP/IND/KETT/01/01: Kettle Papers, Draft for 'Recollections of a Younger World', Interview with Murdoch Taylor, Mar. 1983, p. 52.
59. Jackson, *Solo Trumpet*, pp. 58–9, 64 and 128.
60. Samuel, 'British Marxist Historians', pp. 42–55.
61. On the use of such rhetoric by the ILP, see: Knox, 'The Red Clydesiders and the Scottish Political Tradition'.
62. Knox (ed.), *Scottish Labour Leaders*, pp. 81–6; LHASC CP/IND/MISC/10/1: Crawfurd Papers, TS Unpublished Autobiography, pp. 12 and 24–5.
63. LHASC CP/IND/MISC/10/1: Crawfurd Papers, Autobiography, pp. 44, 49–51, 86–101 and 222–41.
64. LHASC CP/IND/MISC/10/1: Crawfurd Papers, Autobiography, pp. 53–4, 60 and 96.
65. An estimated 1,000 Party members were arrested during and immediately after the general strike, a period during which membership of the CPGB peaked at approximately 12,000. See: Ewing and Gearty, *The Struggle for Civil Liberties*, pp. 155–213.
66. LHASC CP/IND/MISC/10/1: Crawfurd Papers, Autobiography, p. 289.
67. Bell, *Pioneering Days*, pp. 79–80, 92 and 98–9. Kirkwood was, like Wheatley, later elected as a Labour MP.
68. On Newbold and the 1922 contest, see: Howell, *MacDonald's Party*, p. 395; Duncan, 'Motherwell for Moscow', pp. 47–69.
69. Bell, *Pioneering Days*, pp. 263–4.
70. MacDougall (ed.), *Militant Miners*, pp. 142–3, 288 and 301.
71. Gordon, 'The Scottish Trade Union Movement, Class and Gender'; Knox, *Industrial Nation*, p. 143; Morgan, Cohen and Flinn, *Communists and British Society*, pp. 143–83.
72. LHASC CP/IND/MISC/10/1: Crawfurd Papers, Autobiography, p. 233.
73. Docherty, *A Miner's Lass*, p. 138. On Selkirk, see: Selkirk, *Life of a Worker*; Docherty, *Auld Bob Selkirk*.
74. LHASC CP/IND/MISC/10/1: Crawfurd Papers, Autobiography, pp. 243–4 and 284–6.

75. Female membership of the CPGB fluctuated between 10 and 20 per cent during the 1920s: Hunt and Worley, 'Rethinking British Communist Party Women', pp. 3–8.
76. Bell, *Communist Party Training*, p. 86; Bell, *Pioneering Days*, p. 88.
77. Bell, *Communist Party Training*, pp. 86–7.
78. Rafeek, *Communist Women in Scotland*, p. 54; Hunt and Worley, 'Rethinking British Communist Party Women', p. 27. See also: Bruley, *Leninism, Stalinism and the Women's Movement in Britain*.
79. On the ILP, see: Hughes, *Gender and Political Identities in Scotland*, pp. 38–59.
80. *Aberdeen Citizen*, 10 Aug. 1928.
81. Stewart, *Breaking the Fetters*, pp. 174–6.
82. On the extent to which the radical political tradition was expressed in overwhelmingly masculine terms, see: MacDonald, 'Their Laurels Wither'd and their Name Forgot'.
83. Walker, *Juteopolis*, pp. 199–228.
84. Brooksbank, *No Sae Lang Syne*, pp. 36–9; Knox, *Lives of Scottish Women*, pp. 212–15.
85. *Dundee Free Press*, 25 Oct. and 1 Nov. 1929.
86. For the former, see: Pelling, *The British Communist Party*; Kristjansdottir, 'Communists and the National Question in Scotland and Iceland'. For the latter, see: Howkins, 'Class Against Class'; Redfern, *Class or Nation*.
87. AUL MS 2664/2/10: *Programme of the Pageant of Scottish History* (Aberdeen, 1938), pp. 5–12.
88. Pentland, 'Betrayed by Infamous Spies?', pp. 162–8.
89. Hobsbawm, *Primitive Rebels*, p. 127.
90. Knox (ed.), *Scottish Labour Leaders*, pp. 26–34; Knox, *Industrial Nation*, pp. 180 and 187.
91. On Ruskin College, see: Simon, *Education and the Labour Movement*, pp. 311–26; Tsuzuki, 'Anglo-Marxism and Working-Class Education', pp. 187–91; Rée, *Proletarian Philosophers*, pp. 15–22.
92. For a summary of the WEA, see: Simon, *Education and the Labour Movement*, pp. 303–11.
93. The early years of the movement for independent working-class education are outlined in: Millar, *The Labour College Movement*, pp. 1–15.
94. See: Price, 'Contextualising British Syndicalism'.
95. See: Duncan, 'Independent Working-Class Education and the Formation of the Labour College Movement in Glasgow'.
96. Millar, *The Labour College Movement*, pp. 1–33.
97. *Scottish Labour College: To the Toilers of Scotland* (Glasgow, 1920).
98. *Organised Labour's Educational Needs: Being a statement submitted by the Scottish Labour College (Edinburgh District) to the Executive of the Edinburgh Trades and Labour Council* (Edinburgh, 1922).
99. NLS Acc. 11177/19: Edinburgh TLC Minutes, 8 Aug. 1922.

100. Scottish Labour College: Dundee and District Committee, *Circular to Trade Union Branches* (Dundee, 1922).

101. NLS Acc. 4251(1)(ii) John Maclean Papers: Scottish Labour College: Glasgow District Committee, *First Annual Report and Financial Statement, 21 Sept. 1922 to 30 Apr. 1923*.

102. The district colleges were located in Aberdeen, Ayrshire, Dumbarton, Dundee, Edinburgh, Fife, Glasgow, Greenock, Helensburgh, Lanarkshire, Oban, Paisley, Perth and Stirlingshire. See: NLS Acc. 5120/75/1: Scottish Labour College, National Committee Minutes, 1923–25.

103. John Maclean, *A Plea for a Labour College in Scotland* (Glasgow, 1916); *The Scotsman*, 14 Feb. 1916.

104. Economics here encompasses courses in economics, finance and the history of capitalism; history includes industrial history, labour history and the history of trade unionism. See: NLS Acc. 5120/88/1: NCLC Division 10 (Scotland), leaflets and syllabuses.

105. NLS Acc. 5120/88/1: *Syllabus for Evening Classes under the auspices of SLC Aberdeen District: Winter Session, 1923–24*; *Education for Emancipation: The NCLC History, Report and Directory* (Edinburgh, 1924), p. 13.

106. NLS Acc. 5120/6/8: J. P. M. Millar, *Edinburgh and Workers' Education* (TS, n.d.); Acc. 5120/77/2: SLC Edinburgh District Committee Minutes, 15 Feb., 16 Apr., 14 May, 16 Jul. and 2 Sept. 1920; Acc. 5120/78/1 SLC Edinburgh District Committee Minutes, 10 Dec. 1927.

107. NLS Acc. 5120/77/6: NCLC Edinburgh DC Minutes, 16 Nov. 1923 and 7 Mar. 1924; 7: Register of Delegates Edinburgh and District Scottish Labour College, 1 Mar. 1925.

108. NLS Acc. 5120/77/3: SLC Edinburgh District Committee Minutes 23 Apr. 1921; Acc. 5120/77/6: SLC Edinburgh District Committee Minutes, 16 Nov. 1923 and 7 Mar. 1924.

109. On the process of 'bolshevisation', see: Klugmann, *History of the CPGB: Volume 1*, pp. 196–213.

110. Macintyre, *A Proletarian Science*, pp. 77–87; Linehan, *Communism in Britain*, pp. 166–70.

111. CPGB, *The Plebs League and the NCLC* (London, 1927).

112. NLS Acc. 5120/79/1: Edinburgh Labour College Executive Committee Minutes, 22 Aug. 1931; Acc. 5120/75/2: SLC National Committee Minutes, 5 Feb. 1927.

113. Macintyre, *A Proletarian Science*, pp. 85–7; Rose, *Intellectual Life*, p. 299.

114. Tsuzuki, 'Anglo-Marxism', pp. 194–5; Rose, *Intellectual Life*, p. 279.

115. NLS Acc. 5120/75/2: SLC National Committee Minutes, 3 Dec. 1927, 4 Feb., 14 Apr., 4 Aug. and 1 Sept. 1928.

116. NLS Acc. 5120/79/2: SLC West of Scotland Executive Committee Minutes, 6 and 12 Oct., 30 Nov. 1928.

117. NLS Acc. 5120/75/2: SLC National Committee Minutes, 6 Jul. 1929.

118. NLS Acc. 5120/88/1: NCLC Division 10 (Scotland): leaflets and syllabuses.

119. NLS Acc. 5120/75/2: SLC National Committee Minutes, 2 Mar., 4 May and 1 Jun. 1929.
120. NLS Acc. 7656/14/1: Arthur Woodburn Papers, Syllabuses of the Edinburgh Labour College; Acc. 5120/88/1: NCLC Division 10 (Scotland): leaflets and syllabuses.
121. *Plebs*, Apr. 1927, p. 123.
122. NLS Acc. 4977/8: Edinburgh Fabian Society Minutes, 5 Jan. 1929.
123. NLS Acc. 5120/78/1: SLC Edinburgh District Committee Minutes, 10 Dec. 1927. For the decision on Deas see: NLS Acc. 5120/79/1: NCLC Edinburgh and South East Area District Executive Committee Minutes, 22 Aug. 1931.
124. NLS Acc. 5120/75/2: SLC National Committee minutes, 13 Sept. 1930.
125. Tsuzuki, 'Anglo-Marxism', p. 197; A. Ellis, *A Secret History of the NCLC*, pp. 46–50.
126. *Aberdeen Evening Express*, 12 Oct. 1931.
127. NLS Acc. 5120/75/2: SLC National Committee Minutes, 5 Nov. 1932 and 11 Mar. 1933.
128. NLS Acc. 5120/75/2: SLC National Committee Minutes, 21 May 1927; Acc. 5120/78/3: SLC Edinburgh District Committee Minutes, 14 Feb. 1931.
129. NLS Acc. 5120/79/1: SLC Edinburgh District Committee Minutes, 1928–40; Acc. 7656/14/1: Arthur Woodburn Papers, Syllabuses of the Edinburgh Labour College.
130. For contemporary observations see: Muir, *Scottish Journey*; Orwell, *The Road to Wigan Pier*. For the historical debate see: Stevenson and Cook, *The Slump*, pp. 74–93; Thorpe (ed.), *The Failure of Political Extremism in Inter-war Britain*; McKibbin, 'The "Social Psychology" of Unemployment in Inter-war Britain' and *Classes and Cultures*, pp. 151–63.
131. F. Douglas, 'The NCLC's New Start', *Communist Review*, vol. 8(4) (Apr. 1935), p. 66.
132. Graham, *Willie Graham*, pp. 93 and 103; NLS Acc. 7656/1/1: Arthur Woodburn Papers, W. Graham to A. Woodburn, 7 Feb. 1920; Brown, 'The Labour Party and Political Change in Scotland', pp. 103–4.
133. NLS Acc. 7656/1/2: Arthur Woodburn Papers, T. Drummond Shiels to A. Woodburn, 28 Feb. 1929 and 19 Sept. 1932.
134. Beers, *Your Britain*.
135. *Edinburgh Labour Standard*, 2 Mar. 1929.
136. *Dundee Free Press*, 8 Nov. 1929.
137. *The Labour Organiser*, vol. 98 (Aug. 1929), p. 161.

PART II

Locations of Radicalism

3

Public Politics and Demonstrations of the Unemployed

In 1952, Harry Pollitt, then in his second spell as general secretary of the Communist Party, wrote to Bob Stewart, offering his best wishes on the occasion of Stewart's seventy-fifth birthday.[1] Born in Dundee, Stewart was a founding member of the CPGB, and Pollitt was, accordingly, generous in his praise, querying whether he and his fellow Communists would 'ever fully realise the debt we owe to you and men like you'. While such platitudes were perhaps to be expected, Pollitt proceeded to eulogise Stewart's career in terms that highlighted the alteration which he felt had taken place within British political culture in the intervening decades. Celebrating with evident nostalgia Stewart's combative and theatrical approach to political campaigning, a style honed on the platform of the street corner and public square, he lamented his inability to convey the force of Stewart's oratory to a younger generation of Communist activists. He concluded that they would have had to

> see you in action, with that effortless flow of language, addressing huge crowds in the open air . . . They would need to watch your making a pawky hit that convulsed the crowd, turning aside from the main theme of your speech to deal with a particular point or rout an interrupter, and then taking up the thread of your case . . . No wonder the crowds used to roll up in Dundee by the thousands.[2]

Three years later, Fred Douglas, a prominent Communist activist in inter-war Edinburgh, composed a series of articles for the *Edinburgh Evening Dispatch* that likewise stressed the changed nature of public politics. Unlike Pollitt and Stewart, Douglas was, by the 1950s, a repentant ex-Communist; nevertheless, he reflected wistfully on his youthful efforts to organise the unemployed. Depicting the early 1920s as a golden age of popular political engagement, when 'any street-corner was liable to turn into a public forum', Douglas recalled addressing a vast crowd at Edinburgh's Mound, alleging that 'without mechanical aid my voice reached ten thousand people ... when the entire crowd reached the point of being visibly and also audibly stirred I had the sense of perfect performance'. He recognised, however, that the political culture that had sustained such traditions of popular protest had since dissipated, surmising that 'the time seems to have passed ... for the flourishing of a breed of agitators'; maybe, he concluded, 'the present is not so conducive to vigorous orators'.[3]

In their content and shared elegiac tone, Pollitt's letter and Douglas's reminiscences illustrate the degree to which inter-war Communist identity was shaped as much by practice as it was by theory, and existed within the contours of a popular tradition that rewarded the public assertion of political loyalties. Rooted in local custom, this confrontational tradition was sustained by involvement in mass rallies, demonstrations and street-corner meetings. This represented, in many respects, a continuation of the political culture of late nineteenth- and early twentieth-century Britain, in which a premium had been placed on the physical occupation of contested public spaces.[4] It was precisely within this milieu that the founding cohort of British Communism gained their first experiences of political activism, in the ranks of the pre-war ILP and the myriad smaller socialist and Marxist societies.[5]

During the 1920s, however, the public traditions of popular politics became increasingly problematic. The unprecedented expansion of the electorate acted alongside industrial unrest and the feared impact of the war to discredit the masculine culture of rowdyism that had long surrounded popular politics.[6] British politics was refashioned, as local traditions of popular protest gave way to national political concerns and modes of political campaigning.[7] Crucially, in British politics class identity was highly localised, indelibly linking the class rhetoric deployed so forcefully by Communists to direct, local forms of political engagement.[8] For Communists politics was a physical pursuit: writing in 1925, the Communist journalist William Paul decried those who defined politics in narrow parliamentary terms, arguing that political action 'was something much more important'.[9] Shapurji Saklatvala spoke in similar terms during his tenure as the Communist MP for Battersea North, arguing that his presence in the Commons was of value only as an opportunity to draw attention to the 'real fight', which was, of course, 'outside'.[10] Yet while it enabled the CPGB to secure support in specific regions, such public and highly visible methods of campaigning were difficult to deploy in the national political arena. As the inter-war period progressed, it was increasingly apparent that political debate no longer took place in the public squares evoked so vividly by Pollitt and Douglas; the public traditions of popular politics had been discredited, and reliance upon traditional forms of protest resulted in exclusion from national politics. In contrast to the Communist commitment to public politics, the Labour Party dissociated itself from local traditions of protest, preferring instead to stress the party's fitness for local and national office. Decisively, this perspective informed local Labour politics, as activists came to share the electoral focus of their leadership.

From the outset, then, British Communism's conception of class politics was entwined with traditional forms of local protest: the party was not, as has been suggested, forced from the factories to the streets by mass unemployment and the victimisation that followed the 1926 general strike: it had been there since its inception.[11] The true impact of the failure of the general strike was to encourage local Labour activists to forgo the politics of the street in favour of the legitimacy bestowed by success at the polls; their Communist counterparts found themselves isolated in their continued attachment to popular protest. Subsequent chapters explore this shift through studies of the commemoration of May Day and Armistice Day, and the conduct of local election campaigns. This chapter, however, approaches this question from the perspective of demonstrations of the unemployed in urban Scotland, and the response these protests elicited, paying particular attention to the role played in these protests by the Communist Party and its ancillary organisation, the National Unemployed Workers' Movement (NUWM). The chapter focuses first on the unrest witnessed during 1921 and 1931, exploring what such instances can reveal of changing perceptions of the relationship between popular protest, public space and political legitimacy. The shifting administrative response to the protests is then outlined, and the increasing restrictions placed on the use of public space detailed. Lastly, the reaction of the Labour movement to such protests is considered, and its wider implications assessed.

DEMONSTRATIONS OF THE UNEMPLOYED, 1921 AND 1931

In September 1921, as the unemployment insurance of 12,000 local residents neared exhaustion, Dundee parish council declared that it was unable to extend the provision of outdoor relief to the able-bodied unemployed; the ruling signalled the start of three days of extensive unrest. On the afternoon of 6 September 1921, a crowd numbering several thousand gathered outside the parish council offices: a deputation of the unemployed was at first refused entry, but secured admission after the office windows were broken. A further meeting of the parish council was convened the following day; the councillors postponed any judgement on the extension of relief until a joint meeting with the town council and education authority scheduled for 8 September 1921 had been held, a decision received 'with dissatisfaction' by the crowd which had again gathered outside. That evening a procession of the unemployed, headed by a red banner and singing 'The Red Flag', marched to the residence of the Lord Provost, who had the misfortune to arrive home in a taxi as the demonstrators gathered outside his house: stones were thrown, the windows of the taxi smashed, and the Provost's daughter injured. Despite this hostile reception, however, the Provost agreed to receive a deputation of the unemployed; when the delegates returned having failed to secure the extension of relief, the violence recommenced. The crowd was dispersed by a police baton charge; its members returned to the city centre, where systematic looting and further clashes with the police took place; there were twenty-three arrests.[12]

Less violent but comparable scenes were witnessed in Edinburgh, where, on 9 September 1921, 1,500 demonstrators marched to the local parish council offices, with a deputation sent to demand immediate relief for the unemployed.[13] Five days later a deputation was received by the town council; the councillors were informed bluntly that, unless concessions were granted, 'the day might come when the unemployed would not be organised as they are now, but simply a disgruntled mob, with which they might not be able to cope'.[14] On 20 September 1921 representatives of the unemployed attended a meeting of Edinburgh trades council, where they threatened to encourage the unemployed to undercut trade union rates of pay should the support of the Labour movement not prove forthcoming.[15] In Glasgow, left-wing activists led daily demonstrations of the unemployed, which included targeted excursions into affluent areas of the city, where marches through the streets were timed to coincide with church services.[16]

The disturbances reached Aberdeen on 19 September 1921. A crowd of 2,000 protesters gathered at the Castlegate in the city centre, cheering as a deputation, which included representatives from the Labour movement and ex-servicemen's organisations, was admitted by the town council. That evening an estimated 1,000 demonstrators reconvened at the Castlegate; from there they marched to the Wallace statue, a traditional site for radical oratory situated close to the offices of the parish council.[17] Here the crowd was addressed by the Labour councillor Adam Stewart, a member of the trades council's executive committee. Upon finding that there were no parish officials present, and amid shouts of 'What about Dundee?', the protesters marched to the home of the Dean of Guild of the town council. After attempts were made to enter the grounds of the house, the demonstration was broken up by police intervention.[18] The next day the demonstrators reassembled at midday to await a decision regarding the extension of relief; in spite of the disturbances of the previous evening, the parish council again agreed to receive a deputation.[19]

The autumn of 1931 saw remarkably similar protests take place. The collapse of the second Labour government, and the subsequent imposition by the National Government of a 10 per cent cut in unemployment relief, in conjunction with the household means test, resulted in demonstrations across the UK. In Dundee, where unemployment had risen to 40 per cent of the insured workforce, the result was an outbreak of mass public unrest.[20] On 8 September 1931, a demonstration was organised by the NUWM; replete with flags and banners, and singing revolutionary songs, several thousand demonstrators 'formed a procession, and marched through the principal streets in the city', a spectacle repeated eight days later. On 21 September 1931, 2,000 demonstrators assembled in the city centre; headed by two pipers, and with banners and flags once again at the forefront, the crowd marched through the streets of the city headed by Bob Stewart, the Communist candidate for Dundee at the forthcoming general election. Called upon by the Secretary of State for Scotland to account for the unrest, the chief constable of Dundee complained that the demonstrators had swiftly 'lost all semblance of order, [and] great difficulty was experienced in keeping the crowd under control'. There were six arrests, including that of Stewart, after which the demonstration 'broke up in disorder'. The NUWM continued to lead demonstrations twice daily until 24 September 1931, when a crowd, again headed by Stewart, and, according to the police, armed with sticks, 'marched off in a disorderly manner': they were, it was alleged, 'shouting, bawling, and conducting themselves like madmen and all were in a high state of excitement'. After clashes with the police the demonstration ended in violence and looting; there were fifty-four arrests in the days that followed. For his part in the unrest, Stewart was sentenced to thirty days in prison.[21]

The unrest in Dundee coincided with similar disturbances in Glasgow. On the evening of 23 September 1931, a crowd estimated to number 50,000, and described as resembling 'a solid mass of humanity', assembled in Glasgow Green. From there the protestors marched through the city centre, with the express intention of gathering outside the business premises of Bailie Fletcher, a leading Moderate councillor in Glasgow who was alleged to have made disparaging comments about the unemployed. Carrying flags and banners, as well as an effigy of Fletcher, the procession passed the council chambers, prompting, according to reports, an outbreak of 'cheering, hissing, and booing'. After repeated choruses of 'The Red Flag' and 'The Internationale', the demonstrators assembled in St Enoch Square, where the effigy of Fletcher was set alight to yells of 'delight'.[22] The demonstration was said to be the largest since the Armistice celebrations of 1918; when an attempt was made to repeat the endeavour a week later the result was chaos. The police intervened to prevent any march through the city, and clashed with the thousands of protesters who had gathered near Glasgow Green. Amid 'wild scenes' two police officers were injured, an estimated one hundred shop windows were smashed, and twelve protesters were arrested, including John McGovern, the ILP MP for Glasgow Shettleston, and Harry McShane, the organiser of the NUWM in Glasgow.[23] The account relayed to the chief constable of Glasgow by an officer present evoked the atmosphere. The 'whole scene', it was stated,

> was one of the utmost confusion and disorder, with a complete want of control ... the noise and bad language was appalling ... the crash of glass could be clearly heard above the general din. Stones and missiles of every description were being hurled at the foot contingent of police ... Weapons of various descriptions were being openly brandished ...[24]

Further serious disturbances took place the following night, as the police clashed with demonstrators in the working-class environs of the Trongate, the Gallowgate, and Bridgeton; there were fifty-six arrests, including five for looting.[25] Rallies of the unemployed continued to be held in the city throughout October and November.[26]

On 18 October 1931, a demonstration at the Castlegate in Aberdeen, which numbered some 3,000, was addressed by Peter Kerrigan, the Communist Party's Scottish organiser. On 29 October, a NUWM demonstration in the city, complete with piper and red banner and led by the labour college lecturer James Younie, marched through the city centre.[27] That same month 1,000 protesters gathered in central Edinburgh to denounce the introduction of the means test. Conducted by Fred Douglas and accompanied by a drummer, 200 members of the crowd marched through the city centre; they held aloft placards, banners, and, provocatively, an effigy of William Graham, the Labour MP for Edinburgh Central, who had in fact opposed the cuts in relief and would shortly lose his seat in the National Government's landslide victory at the 1931 general election. When the procession returned to the Mound, the effigy of Graham was set alight, as the demonstrators sang 'The Red Flag'.[28]

Outwardly, the protests of 1921 and 1931 were of a similar order; in both cases, the participants exploited a symbolic visual and aural language of flags, banners and music to assert control over specific local public spaces. Glasgow Green, Edinburgh's Mound, Dundee's Albert Square and the Castlegate in Aberdeen – each held special meaning as time-honoured sites for radical and religious oratory. By tradition, open-air religious and political debates ran from midday until ten o'clock at night at Glasgow Green.[29] Equally, if, in the words of Fred Douglas, the Mound had functioned as Edinburgh's 'city forum', then Albert Square was, as the radical Christian prohibitionist Edwin Scrymgeour argued in 1930, 'Dundee's public cathedral'.[30] Aberdeen's Castlegate had, in the recollections of the Communist organiser Bob Cooney, been both a 'form of open university', and the 'forum' of the working class.[31] The occupation of such spaces carried a significance that went beyond questions of public order alone. While we may treat with scepticism official claims that, during the unrest of 1931, Bob Stewart had been heard to cry out 'Down with the police!', the assertion that he followed this by declaiming 'This is *our* town', even if apocryphal, is suggestive of the manner in which the struggle for the control of specific public locations could serve as a proxy for more fundamental political tensions.[32] Between 1921 and 1931, however, the perceived legitimacy of this struggle was transformed.

The attempts of unemployed demonstrators to lay claim to public spaces evoked the tactics of the Radicals and Chartists before them, and are best understood as a continuation of this tradition.[33] The burning of the effigies of Fletcher and Graham in 1931 may well have been distasteful; it was, however, by no means a novelty, or a tactic devised by extremists. In 1889, appalled at the perceived treachery of those who had abandoned the Liberal Party over the issue of Irish home rule, Radicals in Dundee had set alight a similar effigy of Joseph Chamberlain, the foremost Liberal Unionist, in Albert Square before a crowd later reported to have totalled 20,000.[34] In tandem with this link to nineteenth-century radicalism, in their attempts to pressure local officials the unemployed demonstrators exhibited a close affinity with what Eric Hobsbawm characterised as the 'city mob'. For Hobsbawm, prior to the era of the mass franchise, the tactics of the 'mob' offered a route, understood by both the public and the authorities, by which urban populations could obtain assistance during periods of economic crisis. In such a model, the mob pre-dated mass democracy and the emergence of a coherent party system, its methods losing relevance with the growth of the modern labour movement and a corresponding rise in political consciousness and electoral participation.[35] This was, no doubt, a narrative to which the CPGB would have subscribed: certainly, British Communists believed that their party represented an advance on earlier forms of socialist organisation. Yet in practice British Communism proved far from incompatible with such traditional, direct methods; indeed, through the organisation of public demonstrations and rallies, the CPGB found its *métier* in local traditions of popular protest. And if these methods declined in importance during the twentieth century, it does not necessarily follow that this was the consequence of the emergence of a politically engaged working class; rather, rapidly shifting notions of the acceptable

limits of public participation in the political process were key, and operated in tandem with the centralisation of welfare provision to limit the
scope for popular protest.

The importance of such broader developments could be discerned in the
divergent official responses generated by the demonstrations of 1921 and
1931. While the unrest of 1921 was widely condemned, in comparison with
the failure of the protests of 1931 to convince the National Government
to abolish the means test, they were nonetheless conspicuously successful. Outdoor relief was granted to the able-bodied unemployed, in clear
contravention of the poor law, and by November 1921 central government
had moved to indemnify local parish councils against any potential legal
action from ratepayers opposed to the extension of welfare provision.[36]
This contrast was primarily a result of the fact that in the immediate post-
war period, the administration of poor relief remained the responsibility
of locally elected parish councils.[37] In consequence, protesters were able
to extract concessions by using public rallies, demonstrations outside the
homes of local officials, and, of course, the latent threat of popular unrest,
to influence decisions regarding the granting of relief. In Edinburgh, for
instance, the local unemployed workers' committee embarked upon what
were termed 'irritation marches', parading slowly along the main shopping
streets of the city. When ordered to cease by the police, the marchers would
begin to run at pace, letting out wild cries, causing fearful shopkeepers to
lock their doors.[38] In a very real sense, relief simply had to be granted in
order to maintain public order.[39] Notably, in Glasgow, where the disturbances in 1921 were of a lesser order than were experienced elsewhere in
urban Scotland, this relative calm was a consequence of the fact that the
local authorities had already granted substantial concessions a year earlier.
In November 1920, a demonstration of the unemployed, organised by John
Maclean and Harry McShane under the auspices of the former's 'tramp
trust unlimited', had sent a deputation to the town council, securing the
use of the city halls for meetings of the unemployed, as well as free access
to local baths, and the provision of relief work for those out of work.[40]

The obvious effectiveness of such tactics, especially during the mining
lockout that followed the general strike, when a number of parish councils
and boards of guardians (the equivalent body in England) extended relief
to striking miners and their families, stimulated proposals for the reform of
local government. In 1929, these locally-elected bodies were abolished, and
replaced by local authority public assistance committees; while still composed of elected councillors, the membership of the new committees was
to be decided by councils, not the local electorate. Six years later, the new
assistance committees were themselves replaced by a unified system of relief

under the auspices of the Unemployment Assistance Board (UAB).[41] By the close of the inter-war period, unemployment relief had been removed from local political control, to be administered instead by a centralised bureaucracy largely insulated from popular traditions of direct action.[42]

The relocation of the issue of unemployment from the local to the national political sphere, where traditional forms of political campaigning enjoyed little leverage, laid bare the dilemma facing those on the political left. Although the reforms were introduced by the Conservative government, they were broadly welcomed by the parliamentary Labour party, at least in so far as they represented a step towards placing the funding of unemployment relief on a national footing, and removed the traditional stigma attached to those in receipt of poor relief. In contrast, the CPGB opposed the reforms, arguing that they were an attempt to allow officials to escape their responsibility to local communities. But in calling for the retention of the hated regime of the poor law and the parish, British Communists displayed their reliance on local political identities and traditions, and in the process confused many of their supporters.[43] Writing in *The Communist* in early 1928, the party intellectual Jack Murphy argued explicitly that the proposals to abolish parish councils and boards of guardians were a direct response to the election of working-class representatives to such bodies, and an attempt to shift responsibility for relief to town and county councils, where the interests of property still dominated. Murphy further suggested that the government had realised not only that local institutions were more likely to succumb to direct action, but also, as Communists had long contended, that identities of class were more powerful in local Labour politics. As he explained:

> local pressure has much to do with Labour Party politics ... the higher the Labour Party gets in [the] hierarchy of administrative machinery of the state the less does the Labour Party express the demands of the workers, and the more it succumbs to the politics of maintaining the existing order.[44]

The politics of unemployment became, then, part of the contest between the competing local and national understandings of politics promoted by Labour and the Communists. During the 1928 parish council elections in Dundee, the proposed reforms were attacked by Charles Niccolls, standing for the CPGB in the city's first ward. Niccolls contended that the changes were an insult to democracy, and a reaction to the growing influence exerted by working-class electors over parish councils. To avoid the prospect of what he termed 'workers' control', he alleged that the Conservative government had been faced with two choices: either to 'disfranchise the workers or close down the councils before the workers gained a majority';

it had, he concluded, 'chosen the latter course'.[45] In contrast, his Labour opponents criticised the reforms for not going far enough, suggesting that the 'cost of relieving the unemployed should be a national burden instead of a local one'.[46] The support within the CPGB for the retention of parish councils could exasperate those who wished to see British Communists adopt a more coherent Leninist theory of the state as an instrument of class administration in all its forms. An article in the Communist *Labour Monthly* in 1930 accused party members of making the 'supreme error' of believing that the 'local institutions of the state' could be used to challenge central government, and demanded that local government be confronted on the same class basis as national institutions.[47] In the actual practice of Communist politics, there was, all the same, a preference for the tangible, more responsive machinery of local government as opposed to that of the central state.

The changes in the administration of unemployment relief necessitated changes in the focus of Communist campaigning. Upon its formation in 1921, the NUWM had been christened the National Unemployed Workers' Committee Movement, denoting the organisation's origins in the disparate local committees of ex-servicemen and unemployed skilled workers which had proliferated during the post-war economic downturn; it was not until 1929 that the 'committee' was dropped. The change of title betokened a shift in tactics: with the exception of the national hunger marches of 1922 and 1929, the NUWCM had focused upon local campaigns, fighting evictions and individual cases at the parish council, activities conducted at the level of the street and neighbourhood.[48] In contrast, the NUWM launched four national hunger marches between 1930 and 1936 in an effort to influence national policy in relation to unemployment, and, from 1932, to try to force the abolition of the means test.[49] We should not, however, construe this shift, as James Vernon has done, as an attempt to force central government to recognise unemployment as a national problem.[50] That was, in effect, what had been achieved by the reforms implemented between 1929 and 1936, and the decision of central government in 1934 to designate the regions worst afflicted by unemployment 'special areas', eligible for additional funding. The introduction of the means test represented, if anything, precisely the imposition of a national policy in relation to unemployment, which local officials were required to implement whatever their personal sympathies. What the NUWM desired was the reintroduction of a degree of local discretion in the imposition of the regulations, which local activists could then exploit. The unemployed protests of the 1930s were an ultimately fruitless attempt to deploy in the sphere of national politics tactics which had previously succeeded at a local level: the marchers failed to secure the concessions from central government that had, in the past, been sought locally. And while it is right to stress that the political apathy of the unemployed was attributable in large part to the consequences of poverty and social isolation, the absence of large-scale political unrest during the era of mass unemployment after 1931 was also a consequence of the removal of responsibility for relief from local authorities, since it rendered the forms of protest traditionally open to the unemployed little more than ineffectual gestures.

Even in the case of the mass demonstrations which followed the introduction of the new UAB scales of relief in January 1935, which, contrary to government claims, proved to be in many instances lower than the previous local authority scales, it is unlikely that the protests were the decisive factor in the ensuing climb-down. Although the demonstrations are often cited by historians as evidence of the effectiveness of popular protests, of greater importance was the reaction in the House of Commons, where the National Government was excoriated not only by Labour and ILP MPs, but also by many on the government benches.[51] Conservative and Unionist, National Liberal, National Labour and Independent members all voiced their concerns that the new scales were lower than anticipated.[52] Robert Boothby, the outspoken Unionist MP for Aberdeen and Kincardine East, condemned the new scales as 'brutal', and alleged that although the Prime Minister Ramsay MacDonald was content to make 'political capital' out of his poverty-stricken childhood in the north-east of Scotland, he had 'never raised a finger' on behalf of the people of that region once in office. Boothby's Unionist colleague in Edinburgh South, Sir Samuel Chapman, stated that if 'even a portion' of the complaints regarding the new scales proved to be true, then his 'constituents, who were the best off in Scotland, would be the first to resent regulations which would mean hardship to those in less fortunate circumstances than themselves'.[53] The retreat of the National Government represented a victory not for popular pressure as exerted on the streets, but for parliamentary politics. It was telling that when criticising the new scales, the Liberal leader, Sir Herbert Samuel, was at pains to make clear that he did not do so under the influence of the vocal protests from the gallery that had disrupted the parliamentary debates. 'The House', he stated, 'could never allow itself to be influenced by such demonstrations.'[54]

RESPONSIBLE CITIZENS? THE PUBLIC CONDUCT OF POLITICS

The failure of the demonstrations of the early 1930s to secure successes similar to those of a decade earlier was, however, not just the result of the creation of a system of relief less responsive to local pressure: crucial too was a change in the perceived legitimacy of such protests. In the early 1920s, there remained a sense that, while they were regrettable, public demonstrations of discontent were representative of a strand of public opinion that had to be taken into consideration. Equally, the demonstrations of 1921 were not easily dismissed as the work of political extremists: rather, they were conducted on a basis that reflected the absence of fixed party boundaries on the political left. Thus in Dundee, although the local Labour movement condemned the rioting, the ILP took responsibility for leading the deputation to the parish council; in Aberdeen, it was representatives from the trades council who acted as delegates.[55] In Edinburgh, the 1921 deputation to the town council included Communists, members of the ILP and representatives from the trades council, as well as Reverend Marwick, a radical minister in the Church of Scotland, and William Morton, a septuagenarian veteran of the unemployed protests in London in 1886.[56]

By the 1930s, however, perceptions of such protests had altered dramatically. In part, this was a result of the hardening of the boundary between the Labour Party and the CPGB, and the growing control exercised by the latter over the activities of the unemployed movement.[57] As a result, the protests and marches organised under the auspices of the NUWM received little support from the official Labour movement, and were more readily identified with the Communists. Yet while British Communism certainly became more confrontational in its outlook after 1926, a consequence both of the shifting policy priorities of the Comintern and indigenous disillusionment with the Labour leadership in the wake of the general strike, the importance of such policy changes can be inflated. Although the protests of 1921 may be treated as being representative of an older tradition of spontaneous direct action, from which party allegiances were largely absent, it would be wrong to imagine that all those in attendance in the early 1930s were active members of the CPGB.[58] And anyway, although Communist and NUWM organisers hoped to harness and lead such mass demonstrations, they could not summon them at will, whatever their faith in their own leadership abilities. The fundamental difference between the treatment of the protests lay in the way in which they were perceived by the authorities, and portrayed by others. The nuances of the Comintern analysis were of less importance than the extent to which marches, rallies, and demonstrations, had, by the end of the 1920s, come to be viewed as outmoded and unnecessary in a mass democracy, identified with political extremism, and seen as a harbinger of violence. During the 1920s, public opinion was reimagined as a private and passive force, an agglomeration of individual opinions, rather than something to be displayed assertively in public.[59] This changed conception was echoed by a similar shift in the perceived qualities of the ideal citizen, as the experience of war and the introduction of female suffrage eroded the masculine, aggressive Edwardian ideal.[60] Citizenship was a role performed individually, perhaps even privately, not collectively in the urban public sphere; public participation in the political process came to be understood primarily in terms of the ballot. As such, local demonstrations no longer represented public opinion, but were an attempt to subvert the constitution.[61] Declamations of local class loyalties, and an attachment to the traditions of popular politics, ensured, in effect, that those who participated in such demonstrations had isolated themselves from national politics, and could be dismissed as Communists. Reflecting on the September 1931 protests in Glasgow, *The Scotsman* declared confidently that, while the behaviour of the 'mob' was 'unruly and threatening', it was clear that it was the Communists who 'were at the bottom of the demonstrations'.[62] The accuracy of such claims may have been questionable; they served, all the same, to marginalise the demonstrators, and tar them as Bolsheviks.

In 1921, parish and town councils remained willing to receive deputations of the unemployed, even when these interventions followed instances of unrest. Similarly, while Andrew Bonar Law, the then Conservative Prime Minister, refused to receive a delegation from the hunger march that arrived in London in November 1922, he did agree to meet with delegates from Glasgow trades council and the local unemployed workers' committee when he visited Glasgow a month later, maintaining that he did so in his capacity as the Member for Glasgow Central.[63] Yet although similar delegations were attempted in 1931, they were frequently turned away; even when they were admitted, this was usually contingent upon the submission of a written request, not as the result of public protests. It was on such procedural grounds that the public assistance committee in Edinburgh refused deputations composed of unemployed activists seeking increased rates of winter relief in 1931, 1932 and 1933.[64] In January 1932, Edinburgh town council acted in a similar fashion, dismissing a deputation from a demonstration protesting against the imposition of the means test, which represented almost one hundred local left-wing organisations.[65] In October 1932, the local branch of the NUWM organised two deputations, both headed by a flute band. The first was sent to a public meeting addressed by members of the public assistance committee; the second visited the home of Sir Thomas Whitson, the Lord Provost of Edinburgh. Both were snubbed.[66]

A similar tendency to treat demonstrations as the actions of a dangerous minority, who, although they were undoubtedly vocal, nonetheless aimed to circumvent the electoral process and promote an acrimonious, divisive politics of class, was visible in Glasgow. Here, anti-means-test demonstrations continued after 1931, led by the Communist-dominated workers' council of action. For all the theatre and noise that accompanied such marches and rallies, and the occasional clashes with the police that they provoked, they received no succour from the local authorities, who routinely refused to speak with representatives, including when (or especially when) they visited the home of the Lord Provost; unlike in 1920, there was little willingness on the part of the town council to offer concessions.[67] The use of analogous tactics in Greenock elicited a brusque warning from police that gathering outside the residences of elected officials would be treated as intimidation.[68]

The changed response was not limited to an increasing unwillingness to engage with demonstrations: local authorities also began to curtail the political use of public space. Within days of the 1931 disturbances, the magistrates in Dundee prohibited all public demonstrations and processions in the city. Although the restrictions on demonstrations were lifted, subject to certain conditions, the following month, the ban on processions remained in force.[69] By 1935 similar limitations were in place in Edinburgh and Glasgow, again in response to the demonstrations allegedly organised by the CPGB and the NUWM.[70] Indeed, after the disturbances of 1931 local police forces were required to report all political demonstrations to the Secretary of State for Scotland.[71] If the inter-war decades witnessed a move towards a more ordered approach to the political use of public space, then the response to the unemployed demonstrations suggests that there was also a concerted effort to depoliticise local public spaces, which increasingly became sites for the provincial echoes of national occasions such as Armistice Day.[72] Party politics was now reserved for the reasoned atmosphere of national politics, and required little direct public input. It was in this context that the *Edinburgh Evening News* welcomed the National Government's proposals to withdraw the administration of unemployment relief from local control, commenting that the creation of the new UAB would 'increase the purity of British politics' by removing unemployment from the 'maelstrom' of local politics.[73]

The attempt to impose order within urban areas which, by the 1930s, had become increasingly homogeneous working-class spaces was accompanied by a curbing of popular political traditions.[74] In this regard, the events of 1931 merely hastened a process already under way. During the 1928 parish council elections in Greenock, six members of the local Communist Party branch found themselves in court after allegedly leading a 'riotous mob' with the intention of 'intimidating' the current members of the council into increasing the relief available to the unemployed.[75] Similarly, in 1930 the police committee of Dundee town council voted to request powers from central government to ban chalking on public highways, the traditional method of advertising political meetings.[76] Ostensibly the request was motivated by concerns that slogans chalked on the road were a public safety issue: the messages were reportedly a distraction to road users. However, the councillors' focus soon departed from such altruistic concerns, and turned instead to the content of the slogans, alleged to be the work of local members of the NUWM. It was claimed that the slogans contained personal attacks on members of the local public assistance committee: the concerned councillors cited examples, including 'Public Assistance Committee Filthy Dope. Official to starve ex-servicemen into poorhouse' and 'Executioner and Informer: salary, £1000 per year'. The treasurer of the town council argued that the chalking of such vulgar attacks in public places 'altered the atmosphere of the town. They wanted an atmosphere of goodwill, and instead of that certain people were bringing in an atmosphere of scurrility.' Yet despite such accusations of novelty, the sloganeers had openly referred to local traditions of public protest: one message specifically appealed to the spirit that had animated the protests of the previous decade, proclaiming 'Lest ye forget, 1921 Riots and Starvation'.[77] The disturbances in Glasgow in late 1931 had been the latest instalment in a longer contest over the right to hold meetings in Jocelyn (or 'Jail') Square, adjacent to Glasgow Green. The Square had originally been exempted from the restrictive by-laws that applied to the Green. However, this exemption was removed in November 1926 and speakers were now required to apply for a permit. In the summer of 1931, prior to the collapse of the Labour government and the arrival of the means test, there were disturbances between police and representatives of the local free speech council, an incongruous alliance of Communists, ILP activists, anarchists and tramp preachers.[78]

This reordering of local public space was accompanied by a change in the tenor of official language, and, indeed, a certain rewriting of history. The ardent public display of political allegiance was excised from British political culture alongside the events of 1921; such tactics were now alleged to have been introduced into British politics by extremists. As *The Scotsman* warned in the aftermath of the initial protests against the means test, 'the organised character of the demonstrations shows that the disturbances are not merely sporadic but part of a general plan to mobilise the discontent of the unemployed'. It was, moreover, the Communist Party that was stirring the unrest. While, it was concluded, free speech and freedom of assembly were important, 'a breach of public order is a breach of the rules of the game and a threat to the stability not of the National Government but of government itself'.[79]

In September 1931, the Communist-led Edinburgh workers' defence committee contacted Sir Archibald Sinclair, the Secretary of State for Scotland, to complain of police brutality during the recent protests. The committee appealed for the release of those imprisoned during the unrest in Dundee, including Stewart, Mary Brooksbank, and James Hodgson, the secretary of the local Communist Party branch.[80] The reply, composed by Sinclair's Under-Secretary at the Scottish Office, stated that 'no complaint of any kind had been received from responsible citizens as to the conduct of the police'.[81] This was more than bureaucratic hauteur; it also indicated the degree to which the forceful public conduct of politics was, in an era of mass democracy, considered incompatible with the duties of citizenship; the limits of the constitution had been delineated a little more exactly. Despite the abundant evidence to the contrary provided by the events of just a decade before, at the 1931 trial of those involved in the disturbances in Dundee, the procurator fiscal informed the court that 'such demonstrations ... as had been held, were somewhat alien to this country [and] would be checked always by the strong arm of the law'.[82]

'THAT METHOD OF DEMONSTRATING': LABOUR AND POPULAR PROTEST IN THE 1930S

Crucially for both the fate of British Communism and the wider course of Scottish and British politics, such changes in attitude were echoed within the Labour movement. While the Labour leadership had long harboured doubts about the wisdom of crowds, prior to 1926 Labour and Communist activists had, locally at least, operated within a shared public political tradition; after the general strike, however, Labour activists became increasingly conscious that the means by which political messages were expressed could be as important as the message itself.[83] Previously, the question of unemployment had, through the joint advisory council established in 1923 by the TUC and the NUWCM, provided one of the few instances where the national institutions of the Labour movement were willing to co-operate with members of the Communist Party; in 1927 the TUC disbanded the council.[84] Although the decision was partly a consequence of the relationship between the NUWCM and the CPGB, locally it was the methods employed by Communist activists that proved critical in entrenching divisions, as the longstanding distaste of the Labour leadership for the politics of the street came to be more widely shared. Emblematic of such changing attitudes was the career of James McRae, a councillor in Aberdeen.

Elected in the working-class Greyfriars ward in 1921 as an ex-serviceman's candidate, McRae was closely aligned with the Labour group on the town council, and was a member of the local Labour ward committee.[85] In December 1923, McRae intervened during a council session to raise the issue of those receiving support from the parish council being forced to undertake relief work without being provided with suitable clothes, and not being paid trade union rates of pay. The vehemence with which he did so resulted in him being requested by the Lord Provost to try to 'maintain the dignity' of the council. He replied that he seen no evidence of this dignity, and told the Lord Provost that his name was 'a stench in the nostrils of the people of Aberdeen'.[86] Yet within just a few years McRae's attitude had changed. In 1927, he severed his ties with the Labour group, and secured re-election as an Independent candidate. This change was commended by the *Aberdeen Evening Express*, which praised the 'former "wild man" of the council' for settling down to 'real business as convener of the water committee'.[87] By 1932, he had renounced his former political approach entirely: at a ward meeting held during the municipal elections of that year he informed an unemployed member of the audience, who had asked whether he would participate in demonstrations against the means test, that 'if you think I am to head any procession in the streets with a big drum you are living in a fool's paradise'.[88]

McRae offers but one example; indeed, he was defeated at the 1932 municipal elections in a three-cornered contest caused by the disaffiliation of the ILP. Nonetheless, his relatively speedy transformation from 'wild man' to respected councillor points to a wider shift, which saw direct forms of political intervention replaced by a faith in the electoral process, and in the institutions of government. This indicated, in part at least, the experience of elected office, and participation in local administration, which softened the radical edges of many Labour candidates. As the *Glasgow Evening Times* reflected during the 1928 municipal elections, Labour candidates were offering less of the 'hot-headed enthusiasm' of old, a shift that was attributed to 'the sobering effect of office'.[89] This new perspective, and acceptance of the limits of politics, extended to attitudes towards agitation among the unemployed. In 1928, the NUWCM organised a march of unemployed miners from the coalfields of Scotland to Edinburgh, which culminated in the sending of deputations to the Secretary of State for Scotland, and to the offices of the boards of Health and Labour.[90] Although the marchers were accorded a sympathetic welcome, and the local Labour movement arranged open-air rallies to greet them, the political tactics they personified were the cause of some division. Writing in the *Edinburgh Labour Standard* on the day of the marchers' arrival, Arthur Woodburn, then the secretary of Edinburgh labour college, and the prospective Labour candidate for Edinburgh South, described the marchers as 'capitalism's deathless army'. While sympathetic to the plight of the unemployed, Woodburn was dismissive of the methods employed by the NUWCM, maintaining that marches and demonstrations could change nothing: the unemployed simply had no economic power with which to challenge the state, and until Labour gained power and implemented socialism, there could be no remedy for the problem of unemployment. This vision of socialism as rational, gradual and inevitable produced an understanding of politics that could verge on the passive: the march was, Woodburn argued, little more than a stunt, one that would 'only bring temporary relief, like brandy to the toothache'; there could, it appeared, be no shortcuts. Equally, however, there was a strong strand of moral disapproval in Woodburn's criticisms, a belief that the working class could never advance 'as the result of either emotional or violent speeches'. Fred Douglas, who as Scottish organiser for the NUWCM had co-ordinated the marchers' arrival, criticised Woodburn, alleging that he had 'expressed his real feelings for the unemployed mob or crowd, which are feelings of patronage and contempt'. Woodburn repudiated such accusations as being indicative of a 'romantic temperament', one which would always 'seek dramatic moments of hero-worship or traitor-finding'.[91]

The contrast offered by Woodburn between the rational and respectable methods of the Labour movement and the embarrassing histrionics of the Communists illustrated the conflicting tactics adopted by the two parties. By the time of the 1933 Scottish 'hunger march' to Edinburgh the division was even starker. While this estrangement has understandably been viewed in the context of Communist attacks on the Labour Party, of more importance was the changed political outlook of the latter. The reorientation of local understandings of Labour politics, away from a conception of the party as a broad-based regional protest movement, and towards efforts to promote Labour as an alternative national government, altered at a fundamental level the terrain within which the Communists and their allies operated. Labour had ceased to be a heterogeneous federal organisation, under whose banner sheltered a variety of political viewpoints and local traditions, but was now a centralised party that abjured the non-parliamentary methods proposed by the CPGB. Labour's focus was on securing control of the levers of government, and the 1920s saw the party undertake intensive efforts to extend Labour's appeal beyond the organised working class. Central to the failure of British Communism, and to the ostracising of the ILP, was the growing conviction among Labour activists that the traditional forms of popular protest were a discredited inheritance, unbecoming to a party of government.

Thus in August 1929, with Labour returned to power three months earlier, the Edinburgh Labour movement rejected a call from the NUWM to hold a joint demonstration with a view to sending a deputation to the town council, and voted instead to leave the issue of unemployment in the hands of the Labour councillors.[92] The following January a motion appeared before Edinburgh trades council declaring support for the ILP MPs who, led by James Maxton, had opposed the inclusion of a clause denying benefit to those 'not genuinely seeking work' in the Unemployment Insurance Bill introduced by the Labour government.[93] The motion was, however, defeated by an amendment that instead offered bland support to the Labour government 'in its work both at home and abroad'. In March 1930, the Edinburgh branch of the NUWM was informed tersely that the local Labour movement could offer no assistance to the proposed national 'hunger march', since there was no belief that 'such methods are productive of any good results to the unemployed as a whole'. Reverend Marwick, a veteran of the 1921 demonstrations and trades council delegate, could not even find a seconder for his motion calling on the Labour government to at least receive a deputation from the marchers upon their arrival in London.[94]

This transition was personified by Frank Smithies. Initially nominated as a delegate to the trades council by the SDF, Smithies had been a prominent participant in the 1921 protests, acting on the numerous deputations seeking relief, and criticising local trade unionists for their failure to support the unemployed demonstrators.[95] Indeed, months before the 1921 protests, Smithies had called on all unemployed trade unionists in Edinburgh to 'organise a procession and demonstration . . . as a united front against the inadequate provisions of the government and local authorities in dealing with the present situation'.[96] By 1933, Smithies was the trades council's political officer; his earlier association with Douglas and the local branch of the Communist Party notwithstanding, he opposed supporting that year's Scottish hunger march, advising the trades council to offer the marchers no assistance. But this was not a simple rejection of Communist ideology: the previous year he had organised an exhibition on Soviet education in Edinburgh.[97] Rather, Smithies concurred with the Labour leadership that the tactics pursued by the CPGB and the NUWM were now 'detrimental' to the interests of the Labour Party. He was supported in this assessment by the secretary of the trades council, who asserted that the 'crux of the situation' was whether the Labour movement was 'in favour of that method of demonstrating', an enquiry to which he answered firmly: 'they

UNEMPLOYED MARCH THROUGH EDINBURGH.

To celebrate International Unemployed Day, which was recognised by Communist organisations throughout the world yesterday, a number of Edinburgh's unemployed marched through the city. They are seen here passing up the High Street carrying aloft posters of Russian origin.

Mr Fred Douglas addressing a crowd at Fountainbridge, where one of many meetings was held.

Figure 3.1 The marking of International Unemployed Day by the Communist Party in Edinburgh. *Edinburgh Evening Dispatch*, 7 March 1930. © The Scotsman Publications Ltd. Image reproduced courtesy of the National Library of Scotland.

were not'.[98] Both Labour and the CPGB were opposed to the means test, but where local Communists sought to resuscitate the popular methods of 1921, Labour activists were committed to supporting the return of a Labour government.

Politics had become, then, not just a matter of policy, but a question of methods and means, of what conduct could be labelled constitutional, and, conversely, what could be deemed dangerous or extreme. The result was a narrowing of the meaning of politics, and the elevation of national, electoral, party perspectives. When asked by a member of the audience at an election meeting in Aberdeen in 1931 if he would 'organise and lead' the local unemployed, Wedgwood Benn replied calmly that the 'best thing anyone could do for the unemployed … was to organise the Labour Party'.[99] And if such sentiments were to be expected from as dedicated a parliamentarian as Benn, a similar reluctance to repeat the campaigns of 1921 was evident among local Labour Party members. A series of attempts by the NUWM in the city to draw the trades council into taking part in protests against the means test were rebuffed. The nadir was reached in early 1933 when the police were called to remove members of the Communist-aligned 'united front council', who had forced their way into a meeting of the trades council and placed their banner defiantly before the chairman.[100]

Such conflict reflected one facet of Labour's emergence as a national political party based upon individual membership rather than the affiliation of socialist societies. The Labour Party was no longer dedicated to the making of socialists through education and agitation: as Woodburn suggested, although 'the pioneering of those men and women who have done the work on stool and platform' could never be forgotten, Labour had now to 'seriously consider whether the tactics which succeeded for many years have not lost their strength', and whether the party should 'not now adapt methods suitable to the new circumstances'. He noted poignantly that 'some will not be able to adapt themselves, and we will see old comrades drifting away into little Plymouth brother sects'.[101] As a description of the CPGB and the ILP this was harsh, but neither was it inaccurate.

Labour's rejection of popular protest gave added credibility too to official accusations that such forms of political engagement were alien to British politics, and the last resort of political extremists. Denied the veneer of legitimacy offered by the participation of the local Labour movement, public protests were more easily portrayed as 'rough'. Wal Hannington, the national leader of the NUWM, visited Aberdeen in October 1934; a notorious local orator, Albert Gow, having addressed a crowd of approximately 2,000 at the Castlegate, marched with 200 supporters to the theatre where Hannington was speaking and attempted to force his way inside.

Refused entry, Gow returned to the Castlegate, where, after trying to once more address the crowd, he was arrested. The demonstration ended in violent clashes between the police and demonstrators, as bottles and stones were thrown, and the police responded with a baton charge.[102] The roots of Gow's disagreement with Hannington and NUWM are obscure, although he had certainly been a member of the CPGB in Edinburgh in his youth. However, having spent time in prison for assault, theft and housebreaking, Gow was far from the ideal of party propaganda, and local Communists were keen to distinguish their own brand of protest, supposedly marked by discipline and bravery in the face of police provocation, from such behaviour.[103] Yet during Gow's trial it was made clear by both the presiding Sheriff and the procurator fiscal that not only were riots and disorder unacceptable, but also even peaceful demonstrations had no place in British politics. Concluding the prosecution's case, the fiscal stated that if 'political convictions came into conflict then the way to settle them was not by committing breaches of the peace, assaults and disturbances of the general peace', but via elections.[104] Issuing a custodial sentence of six months, the Sheriff wondered why, if Gow had not intended disorder, had he 'taken with him a large crowd . . . heralded by a piper'.[105] The support of the crowd was not, as it had been during the nineteenth century, an indication of popular backing, but prima facie evidence of political extremism, and even criminal intent.[106]

Communist attempts to resurrect the tactics of 1921 were as ill-fated in Dundee as they were in Edinburgh, Glasgow and Aberdeen. In the months following the protests of September 1931, the local Labour movement had echoed Communist condemnation of both the means test and the restrictions imposed upon local meetings and processions. The initially heightened political atmosphere encouraged the trades council to revert to earlier forms of protest and rhetoric, with what was termed a 'monster meeting' calling for the ban on public processions to be overturned advertised in October 1931.[107] There was, however, to be no repeat of the joint protests of 1921.

In March 1932, the Labour Party held a rally at the Caird Hall to denounce the means test; the Communists, revelling in the confrontational melodrama of 'class against class', sought to turn the traditions of popular politics against the Labour Party. Local Communists hijacked the procession to the hall that preceded the meeting, loudly singing 'The Red Flag'. The local Labour press expressed its displeasure in revealing terms, complaining that such behaviour had ruined 'an opportunity for impressing the public'. Inside the hall individual Communists positioned themselves strategically within an audience of 3,000; when the platform party attempted to begin the meeting, they were drowned out by repeated choruses of 'The Red Flag' and 'The Internationale'.[108] The rally was abandoned as fights broke out among members of the audience. While this disruption must clearly be placed within the context of the 'class against class' era, there was more to the Communist intervention than mere thuggery, and there are two aspects of the meeting that illustrate the continued attachment of the CPGB to a form of politics with which the Labour Party no longer wished to be associated. Firstly, acting out a custom that had its roots in the hustings of the late eighteenth and early nineteenth centuries, the Communists attempted to seize control of the platform, and implored the audience to pass a resolution condemning the Labour Party. Secondly, breaking with the tradition whereby the maintenance of order at political meetings was considered to be the responsibility of the party holding the meeting, and, indeed, the ability to keep order at a meeting was considered a matter of honour, members of the Labour Party instead invited the police to clear the hall.[109] The police, in a significant echo of the language now employed by government officials, appealed to the Communist interrupters 'to "be citizens", and to set aside party politics for the moment'.[110]

In the aftermath of the meeting the gulf between the two parties' understandings of political conduct was obvious. The *Dundee Free Press* attacked the Communists in language reminiscent of that which, a decade before, had been directed against Labour. In the aftermath of the 1921 riots the Liberal *Dundee Advertiser* had accused the Labour Party of being responsible for 'an unceasing bubble of vituperation and menace' as a result of its 'incessant clamour of agitation', concluding that the 'whole tone of the agitation, the Labour Party's method of "calling attention", has been wrong'.[111] A decade later the Labour *Free Press* questioned why 'rowdy elements' had been allowed to participate in the procession and meeting. Similar sentiments were voiced in letters to the paper. James Hazel of the Dundee Fabian Society called for the rules regarding the exclusion of individual Communists from the Labour movement to be more rigorously policed. Another correspondent wondered whether it was 'too much to hope that the Dundee branch of the Communist Party will learn some day that hooliganism has no place in politics but inevitably leads to trouble'.[112]

It was indeed too much to hope. The following month, after their deputation had been refused admission, three members of the NUWM were arrested after forcing their way into a meeting of Dundee town council, where they threw the councillors' papers to the floor and spilled ink across their desks. Leading the protests was Mary Brooksbank, who was heard to shout 'We are going to be heard'; she was instead detained and subjected to medical observation.[113] It must be understood that such tactics were nothing new, but were a mere facsimile of the those of the Edwardian era, when the entry of Edwin Scrymgeour and his Scottish Prohibition Party into local politics had transformed council meetings into a spectator sport, filled with lurid accusations, petty recriminations, and fistfights conducted in the council chambers. Bob Stewart, when elected as a Prohibition Party town councillor in 1908, had received the financial support of the local Labour movement: there was to be no echo of this cross-party co-operation on the political left during the 1930s.[114]

By December 1932, the separation between Communist and Labour tactics was absolute. At a Communist rally in Dundee held to protest against the means test the audience was addressed by Pollitt and Gallacher. In his address Gallacher complained that the TUC leadership had drawn 'a sanitary cordon around the trade union movement', refusing to become involved in the popular struggle against the means test. In language that betrayed where British Communists believed politics took place, he demanded to know why the Dundee Labour movement was not 'out in the streets'. Gallacher's belief in the continued vitality of the politics of the street had been outlined five months earlier. Writing in the *Labour Monthly*, he had called for the campaign for the abolition of the means test to be conducted via 'chalking . . . street meetings, marches from one street to another . . . back court meetings, slogan shouting . . . all the methods of rousing the workers'.[115] The following evening a Labour Party recruitment meeting in the city was addressed by Arthur Greenwood, who had served as Minister of Health in the second Labour government. In the audience were local Communists, who disrupted the meeting by attacking Labour's performance in office. Greenwood first defended Labour's record; he then launched a furious attack on the 'gibbering people who sit in the gallery and gibe at public men', stating that they 'should not be allowed in a hall of respectable people'. He concluded by declaring that 'you people . . . will never rule Dundee'. Greenwood received strong support in the *Free Press*, which derided those who had taken part in the disruption as being 'representative of two types of mentality': the first were described as 'complete morons'; the second were disparaged as 'a peculiar brand [who] for want of a better name must be known as the "Hilltown Marxists"'. The editorial was even more strident, declaring that the 'anti-social instincts of the rabble present a problem in every form of civilisation. In Russia the answer is Siberia'; the hope was expressed that 'when socialism comes to this country a more humane way will be found to deal with those who refuse to accept the elementary principles of citizenship'. Far from considering Communism an alien doctrine, the *Free Press* was keen to salvage the ideology of Marx and Lenin from the ignominy of association with the methods of the local Communists, deploring the fact that 'the names of such geniuses ... should be connected, however remotely, with creatures of such puny intellect'.[116]

CONCLUSION

If claims that, during the inter-war era, British politics became a mediated spectacle are overstated, an analysis of the unemployed protests in Scotland suggests nonetheless that a fundamental alteration in political conduct did take place.[117] Traditional explanations for the inability of the CPGB to secure mass support have focused upon perceptions of Bolshevism as an alien ideology, and, by extension, on the negative impact of the policy shifts imposed by the Comintern. Yet methods too were crucial in defining the division between Labour and Communism; although Labour activists continued to believe that they shared the broad aim of socialism with their Communist counterparts, however misguided the latter, at issue were the tactics used by the CPGB. Labour's socialism was a national project to be achieved via electoral means; local public protests and demonstrations were obsolete and a source of embarrassment. As Arthur Woodburn argued in 1930, Labour could 'still spread its net much wider'; however, this 'encircling movement' was being 'hindered by the rough-and-tumble methods being proposed by extremists': the Labour Party needed to talk firmly with these 'fellow-workers'.[118] Communist activists failed not because they were identified with the ideology of Marx or Lenin, but because they were felt to represent the politics of the 'mob' and the 'rabble', those groups beyond the limits of the reformed political nation created by the new franchise, who threatened Labour's image as a party of government.

This should not, however, be construed as equivalent to the facile contrast between democracy and dictatorship offered by the Labour leadership; neither should we be distracted by the supposed distinction proposed by the Communists between their own revolutionary policy and the bourgeois reformism of Labour. Whatever the undoubted policy clashes that existed between the Labour Party and the CPGB, it was Communism's continued use of traditional forms of public protest, and the feared impact of such methods on Labour's electoral appeal, which provided the crucial dividing line. Communist methods were not imported into British politics under the influence of a foreign ideology; instead, they were useless within a national politics in which local protests were no longer relevant or justifiable. Communist activists appeared unaware that the locus of political debate had shifted in the years following their party's foundation; street rallies and demonstrations bore neither the political threat nor the moral validity they had in an earlier era; form, as much as content, proved to be the undoing of their ambitions. The inability of the CPGB to adjust its political practice to the changed nature of popular politics in twentieth-century Britain revealed a dependence upon a form of campaigning supplanted during the 1920s. Despite its revolutionary rhetoric, the party looked to the past rather than the future, seeking to mobilise local forms of political engagement and class identity inapplicable in the context of mass democracy. It is, then, the failure of Communism to play a significant role in British politics which speaks to the changing nature of public politics in the inter-war decades. British Communists defined themselves, and were defined by others, by their methods and behaviour; more importantly, as the following chapters illustrate, others increasingly delineated acceptable political conduct with reference to – and in opposition to – the CPGB.

NOTES

1. Elements of this research appeared previously in: Petrie, 'Public Politics and Traditions of Popular Protest'.
2. LHASC CP/IND/MISC/9/9 Stewart Papers: H. Pollitt to R. Stewart, 15 Feb. 1952.
3. *Edinburgh Evening Dispatch*, 8 and 9 Aug. 1955.
4. See: Lawrence, *Speaking for the People*, pp. 163–93, and *Electing Our Masters*, pp. 71–83.
5. See the accounts in: Bell, *Pioneering Days*, pp. 67–9; Gallacher, *Last Memoirs*, pp. 29–31; LHASC CP/IND/MISC/10/1: Crawfurd Autobiography, pp. 86–101.
6. Lawrence, 'Forging a Peaceable Kingdom'.
7. Beers, *Your Britain*, pp. 11–26.
8. Joyce, *Visions of the People*, pp. 137–41 and 329–30; Fentress and Wickham, *Social Memory*, pp. 114–26.
9. Paul, *The Path to Power*, p. 29.
10. S. Saklatvala, 'The House of Commons', *Communist Review*, vol. 6(12) (Apr. 1926), p. 563.
11. LaPorte and Worley, 'Towards a Comparative History of Communism', p. 240.
12. *Dundee Advertiser*, 7 and 8 Sept. 1921; *The Scotsman*, 7 and 8 Sept. 1921.
13. *Edinburgh Evening Dispatch*, 10 Sept. 1921.
14. *The Scotsman*, 15 Sept. 1921.
15. *Edinburgh Evening Dispatch*, 21 Sept. 1921; *The Scotsman*, 21 Sept. 1921.
16. *The Scotsman*, 19 and 21 Sept. 1921.
17. On the Wallace statue's use during the First World War, see: Paton, *Proletarian Pilgrimage*, pp. 306–10.
18. *Aberdeen Daily Journal*, 20 Sept. 1921; *Aberdeen Free Press*, 20 Sept. 1921.

19. *Aberdeen Free Press*, 21 Sept. 1921.
20. Jackson (ed.), *The Third Statistical Account of Scotland: The City of Dundee*, p. 461.
21. *Dundee Courier and Advertiser*, 22 and 25 Sept. 1931; NRS HH55/661: Dundee Unemployed Demonstrations 1931, Report of Chief Constable (Dundee) to Under Secretary of State for Scotland, 29 Sept. 1931.
22. *The Scotsman*, 24 Sept. 1931.
23. *The Scotsman*, 2 Oct. 1931. For McShane's account of the demonstration, and the decision of the police to charge the protesters, see: McShane, *No Mean Fighter*, pp. 174–9.
24. NRS HH55/664: Glasgow Disturbances, Notes of information furnished by Chief Constable (Glasgow) on telephone (n.d. but Oct. 1931).
25. *The Scotsman*, 3 Oct. 1931.
26. *The Scotsman*, 7, 9 and 26 Oct. 1931.
27. *Aberdeen Evening Express*, 19 and 30 Oct. 1931; *Aberdeen Press and Journal*, 30 Oct. 1931.
28. NRS HH55/673: Edinburgh Unemployed Demonstrations, 1931–32, Report of Chief Constable (Edinburgh) to Under Secretary of State for Scotland, 17 Oct. 1931.
29. McShane, *No Mean Fighter*, p. 12.
30. *Edinburgh Evening Dispatch*, 8 Aug. 1955; *Dundee Free Press*, 26 Sept. 1930.
31. IWM Acc. 804: Interview with R. Cooney, Reel 1; MML: Cooney, 'Proud Journey', pp. 22–3.
32. *Dundee Courier and Advertiser*, 25 Sept. 1931.
33. On this tradition, see: Vernon, *Politics and the People*, pp. 208–30; Taylor, 'Commons-Stealers'; Roberts, 'Spatial Governance'.
34. *Dundee Courier and Argus*, 15 Feb. 1889. On the place of effigy-burning in radical politics, see: Joyce, *Visions of the People*, pp. 232–5.
35. Hobsbawm, *Primitive Rebels*, pp. 111–17.
36. Levitt, *Poverty and Welfare in Scotland*, pp. 107–25.
37. Croucher, *We Refuse to Starve in Silence*, pp. 18–19.
38. *Edinburgh Evening Dispatch*, 12 Aug. 1955.
39. A point made convincingly in: Levitt, *Poverty and Welfare in Scotland*, p. 121.
40. Milton (ed.), *John Maclean*, pp. 204–6; McShane, *No Mean Fighter*, p. 121.
41. See: Croucher, *We Refuse to Starve in Silence*, pp. 78–80 and 167–71; Flanagan, *Parish-Fed Bastards*, pp. 165–7.
42. Garside, *British Unemployment, 1919–1939*, pp. 71–4. This centralisation was a trend discernible across Western Europe: Croucher, 'History of Unemployed Movements', p. 9.
43. Croucher, *We Refuse to Starve in Silence*, pp. 80–4.
44. J. T. Murphy. 'Relations of the Parties in the Forthcoming Elections', *The Communist*, vol. 3(2) (Feb. 1928), p. 67. A similar stance was adopted by the CPGB in the pamphlet *Communism and Industrial Peace*, pp. 13–14. On

Murphy, who left the CPGB under a cloud, see: Darlington, *The Trajectory of J. T. Murphy*.

45. DPL Dundee Trades Council Collection: Acc. 2419, *Mr Charles Niccolls: Communist Candidate Parish Council Election, Ward One* (Dundee, 1928), p. 4. Niccolls represented the Boilermakers on the local TLC, and his membership of the CPGB had resulted in his removal from the TLC Executive Committee in 1926.

46. DPL Dundee Trades Council Collection: Acc. 2419, *Labour Party Parish Council Election Address Ward One 1928: G. S. Ireland, R. M. Smith, H. Hird* (Dundee, 1928), p. 2.

47. B. McIntosh, 'A Revolutionary Municipal Policy', *Labour Monthly*, vol. 12(9) (Sept. 1930), p. 560.

48. McShane, *No Mean Fighter*, pp. 131–2.

49. For a sympathetic account of the hunger marches, see: Kingsford, *The Hunger Marchers in Britain*.

50. Vernon, *Hunger*, pp. 246–9.

51. For the view that the retreat of the National Government in 1935 represented a success for demonstrations of the unemployed, see: Perry, *Bread and Work*, pp. 44–5; Reiss, 'Marching on the Capital', p. 167; Ward, 'The Means Test and the Unemployed', pp. 120–1.

52. *The Times*, 29 and 30 Jan. 1935.

53. *The Manchester Guardian*, 29 Jan. 1935.

54. *The Times*, 30 Jan. 1935.

55. *Dundee Advertiser*, 7 Sept. 1921; *Aberdeen Daily Journal*, 20 Sept. 1921; *Aberdeen Free Press*, 20 Sept. 1921.

56. *Edinburgh Evening Dispatch*, 21 Sept. 1921; *Edinburgh Evening Dispatch*, 11 Aug. 1955.

57. Campbell and McIlroy, 'The NUWM Revisited'.

58. Flanagan, *Parish-Fed Bastards*, p. 121.

59. Lawrence, 'The Transformation of British Public Politics', pp. 188 and 212–13.

60. Beaven and Griffiths, 'Creating the Exemplary Citizen', pp. 213–15. See also: Clark, 'Gender, Class, and the Nation', pp. 251–3.

61. These concerns were present as early as 1921 in the debate surrounding 'Poplarism' and the political influence of the unemployed at a local level in London: Thackeray, 'Building a Peaceable Party', pp. 663–6.

62. *The Scotsman*, 24 Sept. 1931.

63. McShane, *No Mean Fighter*, pp. 147–8; *The Scotsman*, 21 and 23 Dec. 1922.

64. NRS HH55/673: Edinburgh Unemployed Demonstrations, 1931–32, Report of Chief Constable (Edinburgh) to Under Secretary of State for Scotland, 18 Dec. 1931; NRS HH55/674: Edinburgh Unemployed Demonstrations 1932, 19 Nov. 1932; NRS HH55/675: Edinburgh Unemployed Demonstrations, 1932–34, 29 Sept. 1933.

65. NLS Acc. 11177/24: Edinburgh TLC Minutes, 2 Feb. 1932.
66. NRS HH55/674: Edinburgh Unemployed Demonstrations 1932, 17 and 29 Oct. 1932.
67. See the reports of deputations being refused in: NRS HH55/682: Glasgow Unemployed Demonstrations, 12, 19 and 20 Jan. 1932; HH55/683: 5 Apr. 1932; HH55/684: 16 Sept., 28 Oct., 25 Nov. and 22 Dec. 1932, 2 and 16 Mar. 1933; HH55/685: 30 Mar. 1933, 22 Jan. and 3 Feb. 1934.
68. NRS HH55/670: Greenock Unemployed Demonstrations, William Mitchell (Detective Inspector) to Chief Constable (Greenock), 20 Dec. 1932.
69. *Dundee Courier and Advertiser*, 26 Sept. 1931 and 9 Oct. 1931.
70. NRS HH55/676: Edinburgh Unemployed Demonstrations, 1934–36, Report of Chief Constable (Edinburgh) to Under Secretary of State for Scotland, 2 May 1935.
71. This was required by Scottish Office Circulars 2589 and 2662. See: NRS HH55/704: Demonstrations in Aberdeen, 1937, Letter from Under Secretary of State for Scotland to Chief Constable (Aberdeen), 7 Oct. 1937.
72. On the inter-war era, see: McCarthy, 'The League of Nations Union', p. 116. On Armistice Day, see: Gregory, *The Silence of Memory*, pp. 133–42.
73. *Edinburgh Evening News*, 10 Nov. 1933.
74. Worley, *Labour Inside the Gate*, p. 172; Savage and Miles, *The Remaking of the British Working Class*, p. 73.
75. *The Scotsman*, 28 Sept., 24 Nov. and 7 Dec. 1928.
76. Chalking on pavements had already been prohibited in late 1925: *Dundee Evening Telegraph and Post*, 30 Dec. 1925.
77. *Dundee Free Press*, 12 Dec. 1930. Capitalisation in original.
78. McGovern, *Neither Fear nor Favour*, pp. 67–80; McShane, *No Mean Fighter*, pp. 172–4; Caldwell, 'The Battle for Glasgow Green'.
79. *The Scotsman*, 3 Oct. 1931.
80. NRS HH55/661: Dundee Unemployed Demonstrations 1931, Letter from Secretary of the Edinburgh Workers' Defence Committee to Secretary of State for Scotland, 29 Sept. 1931. On Brooksbank see her memoir, *No Sae Lang Syne* and Knox, *Lives of Scottish Women*, pp. 203–19.
81. NRS HH55/661: Dundee Unemployed Demonstrations 1931, Letter from Under Secretary of State for Scotland to Secretary of the Edinburgh Workers' Defence Committee, 1 Oct. 1931.
82. *Dundee Evening Telegraph and Post*, 30 Dec. 1931.
83. On the attitude of the Labour leadership to the political dangers of the 'mob', see: Lawrence, *Electing Our Masters*, pp. 120–3.
84. Croucher, *We Refuse to Starve in Silence*, pp. 81–4.
85. AUL MS 2270/3/1/12: Aberdeen TLC Minutes, 7 May 1924; MS 2270/3/1/13: Aberdeen TLC Minutes, 9 Sept. 1925.
86. *Aberdeen Evening Express*, 3 Dec. 1923.
87. *Aberdeen Evening Express*, 31 Oct. 1927.
88. *Aberdeen Evening Express*, 28 Oct. 1932.

89. *Glasgow Evening Times*, 6 Nov. 1928.
90. *Edinburgh Evening Dispatch*, 21 Sept. 1928.
91. *Edinburgh Labour Standard*, 22 Sept., 6 and 13 Oct. 1928.
92. NLS Acc. 11177/23: Edinburgh TLC Minutes, 23 Aug. 1929.
93. On the Bill, see: Howell, *MacDonald's Party*, pp. 289–92.
94. NLS Acc. 11177/23: Edinburgh TLC Minutes, 1 Jan., 14 and 16 Mar. 1930.
95. NLS Acc. 11177/19: Edinburgh TLC Minutes, 20 Sept. 1921; *Edinburgh Evening Dispatch*, 11 Aug. 1955.
96. NLS Acc. 11177/19: Edinburgh TLC Minutes, 17 May 1921.
97. NLS Acc. 11177/24: Edinburgh TLC Minutes, 12 Apr. 1932.
98. *Edinburgh Evening Dispatch*, 10 May 1933.
99. *Aberdeen Evening Express*, 6 Oct. 1931.
100. AUL MS 2270/3/1/14: Aberdeen TLC Minutes, 12 Oct. and 21 Dec. 1932, 22 Mar. and 5 Apr. 1933.
101. *Edinburgh Labour Standard*, 15 Nov. 1930.
102. *Aberdeen Press and Journal*, 8 Oct. 1934.
103. NRS HH16/515–17 and HH18/167–8: Albert Percival Gow Papers. By the late 1940s Gow had been detained at Broadmoor, suffering apparently from 'paranoid dissociation'.
104. *Aberdeen Evening Express*, 30 Oct. 1934.
105. *Aberdeen Press and Journal*, 2 Nov. 1934.
106. On the crowd in the nineteenth century, see: Joyce, *Visions of the People*, pp. 48–9.
107. *Dundee Free Press*, 9 Oct. 1931.
108. *Dundee Free Press*, 1 Apr. 1932.
109. NRS HH55/662: Dundee Unemployed Demonstrations 1932–33, Report of Chief Constable (Dundee) to Under Secretary of State for Scotland, 28 Mar. 1932.
110. *Dundee Evening Telegraph and Post*, 28 Mar. 1932.
111. *Dundee Advertiser*, 13 Sept. 1921.
112. *Dundee Free Press*, 1 Apr. 1932.
113. *Dundee Courier and Advertiser*, 8 Apr. 1932; *Dundee Free Press*, 8 and 15 Apr. 1932.
114. Walker, 'The Scottish Prohibition Party'; *Juteopolis*, pp. 333–93.
115. *Dundee Free Press*, 23 Dec. 1932; W. Gallacher, 'Advancing the Fight of the Unemployed', *Labour Monthly* 14(7) (Jul. 1932), pp. 425–6.
116. *Dundee Free Press*, 23 Dec. 1932. Hilltown was a working-class district of Dundee directly north-east of the city centre and Albert Square.
117. Beers, *Your Britain*, p. 5.
118. *Edinburgh Labour Standard*, 4 Oct. 1930.

4

May Day, Armistice Day and the Politics of Public Space

In his 1933 novel *Cloud Howe*, James Leslie Mitchell, writing as Lewis Grassic Gibbon, recounted the events of Armistice Day in 1922 in the fictional town of Segget. The setting for the service of remembrance was the town square; here local residents had gathered, and, as the assembled choir began to sing, a crowd comprising twenty spinners from the local mill came, in Mitchell's words, 'marching down through the close . . . their mufflers on, not in decent collars, their washy faces crinkled with grins'. At the forefront, and wielding a red flag, was Jock Cronin, organiser of the local Labour Party; he instructed the demonstrators to form a circle in the town square, where they proceeded to give a rendition of 'The Red Flag', drowning out the choir. The police considered intervening, but were shamed into refraining when they saw the medals on the spinners' chests, indicating their war service. Scaling the local war memorial, Cronin addressed those present, declaring,

> Comrades – not only mill folk . . . WE went to the war, we know what it was, we went to lice and dirt and damnation: and what have we got at the end of it all? Starvation wages, no homes for heroes, the capitalists fast on our necks as before . . . that's our reward . . . that's the thing we must mind today . . . It's the living that's our concern . . . Come over and join us, the Labour Party.[1]

With its hedonistic and despised spinners, whose presence was resented by inhabitants of longer standing, Mitchell's Segget owed much to Dundee. But beyond such surface similarities, his depiction of Armistice Day as an occasion for the contestation of the legacy of the First World War, and for the right to occupy local public space, was also founded in reality. The 1921 Armistice Day service in Dundee had been disrupted when members of the local unemployed workers' committee, ex-servicemen prominent in their ranks, clashed with those observing the two-minute silence. Anticipating Mitchell's rendering, the *Dundee Advertiser* reported that, as the silence approached, 'a procession of unmistakable composition' made its way towards the city centre; in the lead were the male members of the demonstration, who drew behind them a lorry bearing women and children surrounded by 'banners, red flags, and red rosettes'. At the sound of the gun that marked the start of the silence, 'the hooligans raised cheers and commenced bawling in varying degrees of untunefulness the "red flag"'. The *Advertiser* had few doubts as to who was to blame, decrying the local 'Communist crew', who, with 'their blood-red banners and singing their unmusical dirge', had done 'their best to rob the digni-fied ceremonial of all its solemnity and simple grandeur'. Those who had gathered to observe the silence persevered in the face of such provocation, a reaction considered a 'striking tribute to the law-abiding qualities of the vast throng of Dundee manhood ... the very contrasts of the scene emphasised the impressiveness of the silence so religiously observed ... all honour to them for doing it'. As soon as the silence had ended, however, the demonstrators were confronted by a group of enraged ex-servicemen, who, it was reported with some relish, seized the protestors' flags and banners, and used them as 'weapons to belabour any of the processionists within reach'. As in Mitchell's fictional depiction, a local minister pleaded forlornly with the demonstrators to cease their protest in a futile attempt to avert a violent confrontation.[2]

Arriving so soon after the unemployed disturbances of September 1921, the disruption of the remembrance service was widely condemned. It was, above all, the highly visible and audible tactics of the demonstra-tors that were deemed most reprehensible; ideology, in contrast, received little mention, the extremism of the protesters treated, perhaps, as implicit within their conduct. The *Advertiser* felt that the protest had been 'on a par with an outrage at an open grave', and had exposed to the 'public the real human quality of the tail of riff raff and unemployables which daily parades the city under The Red Flag'. The demonstrators' claim to rep-resent the unemployed was disputed: the true unemployed – and not just the idle – would 'angrily reject the implication that they are represented by the shouting band', which, it was repeated, 'daily parades the streets with the red flag'. The flag itself caused especial offence: it was a 'symbol of social hatred and ravin ... an offence to good citizenship and a provoca-tion to dispeace [*sic*]'. Similar sentiments were expressed in the letters from members of the public selected for publication by the *Advertiser*; these too condemned the noise and spectacle of such processions, and their intoler-able monopoly of local public space. Thus the 'red flag pestilence' had become 'more unruly and noisy'; the 'discordant, raucous, "red flag" din' savoured of 'Sinn Fein, Bolshevism, and Communism'; 'all these troubles' were 'hatched' at Albert Square by a 'herd of "redflaggers"'; the 'hooligans' had 'made Albert Square their headquarters'. The protagonists were felt to have forfeited the right to share in the civic spaces of the city: why, it was demanded, should 'the beautiful Albert Square be handed over daily to a band of foul-mouthed orators, who would not be permitted to use the same language in any other street'. 'The Red Flag' was condemned as 'an emblem of blood, tyranny and oppression', and Labour was advised to 'see and get another'.[3]

As was the case with protests of the unemployed, such advice was taken seriously by the Labour Party as it strove to project an image appropriate to national politics. By the early 1930s, Labour had not only started to abandon popular demonstrations and deputations: party figures were also increasingly ill at ease amid the pageantry and symbolism central to local identities of class. In *Cloud Howe*, Mitchell allowed the career of Cronin to illustrate this shift. Having led the local protests in 1922, Cronin had, by the end of the decade, accepted a paid position as a trade union official in Glasgow, from where he now, in Mitchell's acerbic words,

> went lecturing here and went blethering there, in a fine new suit and a bowler hat, and spats . . . and brave yellow boots [He had] a fine house on the Glasgow hills; and wherever he went Jock Cronin would preach alliance between all employers and employed and say to folk that came to hear that they shouldn't strike, but depend on their leaders – like himself.[4]

For Mitchell, sympathetic to Communism if not a party member, the lesson was clear: class identity was linked to local radicalism, and the acceptance of national office necessitated the betrayal of both.[5]

Labour's rejection of public political traditions ensured not just that these were identified largely with the CPGB, but also that such customs were no longer viewed as a threat to political stability. Stripped of the broader support they had received in the immediate post-war era, and as local public space ceased to be an acceptable forum for the display of competing political identities, by the 1930s rallies, processions and the material trappings of the working-class movement came to be mocked rather than feared. The role of place remains a neglected factor in the political history of modern Britain; yet where and how parties conducted their political campaigns was of fundamental importance in conferring legitimacy on movements and causes. As Simon Gunn has argued, public space must be understood as an 'active ingredient in the historical process', and not simply as the 'bare stage on which the historical drama was enacted'.[6] In Dundee, carrying a red flag, or indeed singing 'The Red Flag', at Albert Square inspired support and provoked condemnation of a different magnitude from if the same act were performed in a working-class area such as

Hilltown: these were contested public political spaces. Yet between 1920 and 1939 the political meaning attached to such spaces altered; they were drawn into the sphere of national politics, and deprived of their ability to grant meaning to sections of the local community.

This waning in the public display of local class identity is considered first through an examination of the changing composition, location and reception of May Day celebrations in the urban centres of Scotland. Despite the near-universal adoption of May Day by the international labour movement after 1890, it has, with the exception of an essay by Eric Hobsbawm, received little attention from historians. As Hobsbawm noted, this was an occasion when those normally 'invisible . . . captured the official space of . . . society'.[7] More than this, May Day provides a remarkable annual visual appraisal not merely of relations on the political left, but also of changing attitudes towards public politics more generally. The rejection of processions, and the adoption of indoor rallies as opposed to outdoor demonstrations, laid bare the wider failure of local class identities and the political forms through which they had been expressed, as political meetings became occasions for the dissemination of national programmes. By way of contrast, the local enactment of Armistice Day, and the use of the occasion to assert a shared national identity that, while superficially apolitical, had profoundly political connotations, is assessed.

'WORKERS, THINK FOR YOURSELVES': MAY DAY, 1920–1926

Inaugurated in 1890 by the second Socialist International as part of the campaign for the eight-hour day, the labour and socialist celebration of May Day subsequently, and almost accidentally, became an annual occasion.[8] Although by 1914 the standard May Day imagery of youthful optimism, flowers and the red flag had become well-established, the occasion was nonetheless revitalised in 1920 by the widespread disillusionment occasioned by the First World War, and the threat posed by outside intervention to Bolshevik Russia. In consequence, the demonstrations held across Britain on Saturday 1 May 1920 were widely recognised to be the largest since 1890. An estimated 8 million people participated in what was described as a 'festival' of labour, many of whom had refused to work a standard half-day shift, opting to celebrate on the first of May and not the more commonplace first Sunday of the month.[9]

In Aberdeen, as elsewhere, the celebrations in 1920 were 'on a bigger scale than ever before'.[10] A procession of 1,000 marched from the Castlegate in the city centre to the beachfront, where they were met by a crowd estimated at ten times that number. The demonstration was addressed by councillor Fraser Macintosh and John Paton of the Aberdeen ILP; in his speech, Paton stressed the 'essential unity of working-class aims'. The procession had included contingents from the ILP, the local Socialist Sunday School movement, the SLP, and the local Labour housing association, whose placard declared 'socialism' to be 'the hope of the workers'. At the rear appeared the embryonic Aberdeen Communist group, with a banner urging the workers to 'follow Bolshevik Russia'.[11] Also prominent were the Aberdeen Boilermakers, who had resolved that, work day or not, the day had now come 'when all trade unionists should recognise [May Day] by making it an annual holiday'. This resolution had been partially successful, with two shipyards closing for the day, and one-sixth of the workforce at the largest, that of Hall Russell, taking the day as an unofficial holiday.[12]

Beyond its sheer scale, the procession in Aberdeen was notable for the widespread use of vivid banners and tableaux, which, steeped in a suspicion of central government, expressed the dignity, solidarity and, most stridently, the political independence of labour. The local branch of the National Union of ex-Servicemen challenged notions of the First World War as a moment of national unity with a 'grimly humorous' display, the centre-piece of which was a large white cross upon which was emblazoned: 'Land fit for heroes: promise made by the government to the men while serving: died 11th November 1918'. Beneath this were two smaller white crosses, which together marked the hoped-for political demise of 'Lloyd George' and 'Winston Churchill's way of government'.[13] Offsetting such belligerent political statements were optimistic and youthful depictions of the future, such as the four young girls seated in a rowboat and dressed in the national costume of Britain, the Netherlands, Russia and Spain, who represented collectively the unity of the international working class.[14] The most striking imagery, however, was provided by the Aberdeen branch of the Painters' Society, whose tableau comprised 'a white-robed girl seated on a pedestal', who, blindfolded and carrying the sword of truth and the scales of justice, appeared alongside a male counterpart, who, with torch in hand, was illuminating the path forward; together they symbolised the justice of the cause of labour. In front was a large white cross, denoting 'the death of servile labour and the birth of new labour'. The central meaning of the imagery was expressed in the slogan on the side of the lorry, which declared that 'independence and justice' would 'fetters break'. The underlying message of the occasion was, however, perhaps encapsulated best in the slogan painted on the side of yet another tableau, which stated simply: 'Workers, think for yourselves'.[15]

This display of trade and class identity, and the defiant occupation of local public space, was evident that year too in Edinburgh, where the

May Day Procession in Aberdeen.

Figure 4.1 Local class identity on display in Aberdeen on May Day 1920. *Aberdeen Evening Express*, 3 May 1920. © Aberdeen Journals. Image reproduced courtesy of the National Library of Scotland.

procession marched provocatively in military formation from the city centre to Leith Links, accompanied by several brass bands. Present in the parade were the Leith shipwrights, who displayed a series of miniature sailing ships, complete with masts and rigging.[16] Similarly, in Dundee, a crowd of over 1,000 assembled in Albert Square, where they passed a resolution in support of Soviet Russia and those striving for Irish independence.[17] In Glasgow, the main rally was estimated to have attracted 50,000 participants, with almost 300 organisations represented in the pageant.[18] And though not always celebrated on the scale of the demonstrations of 1920, and from 1921 onwards as a rule on the less contentious first Sunday in May, until 1926 May Day remained an occasion when local trade unionists and members of the various socialist societies could voice in public a shared political identity framed in terms of class. In this vein, the May Day demonstration at Dundee's Albert Square in 1921 was addressed jointly by Labour and Communist speakers, with banners 'conspicuously displayed', and proceedings punctuated by songs performed by a youthful choir.[19] The 1921 procession in Glasgow was even larger than in the previous year, attracting an alleged 150,000 participants from a variety of socialist and labour organisations, and stretching to two miles in length. Events concluded at Glasgow Green, where those gathered could hear addresses from twenty-four platforms.[20]

In Aberdeen, the procession in 1921 again numbered 1,000, with the marchers accompanied by two brass bands. Present, and proudly displaying banners, were numerous trade union branches, the ILP, the Communist Party and the proletarian school.[21] The demonstration attracted a crowd of 5,000, with the trades council, the ILP and the CPGB each granted a platform. Following a performance by the socialist Sunday school choir, a joint resolution condemning capitalism and offering fraternal greetings to Soviet Russia was approved, echoing that passed in Glasgow.[22] The role of May Day in providing an occasion for the display of a common class identity by the local political left was mirrored in Edinburgh, where, in 1921, 'with the usual pageantry', a procession numbering approximately 2,000, and which represented some seventy working-class organisations, marched to the East Meadows in the south of the city centre. The most impressive feature of the procession was the number of trade unions who had 'their "colours" out', and the 'socialist bannerettes' carried by children in fancy dress.[23] At the Meadows eight separate platforms passed a joint resolution condemning capitalism and declaring support for the Bolshevik regime in Russia, a format repeated a year later.[24]

Yet notwithstanding these ritual declarations of international solidarity, May Day was a platform for the expression of an avowedly local political identity, one shaped by notions of trade and class, which could clash with the national electoral imperative to distinguish Labour from Communism. It was the unity of the local labour movement that was on physical display, a loyalty that was relatively ambivalent about institutional boundaries: conspicuous among the banners exhibited in Edinburgh in 1922 was the call to 'watch your trade union leaders'.[25] Such faith in the primacy of the local political and industrial experience was apparent in the identity of those invited to address May Day demonstrations, which in the early 1920s remained an honour bestowed chiefly upon those who had served the local Labour movement with distinction rather than national Labour Party figures. In 1923, for example, Robert Foulis, refused the Labour nomination in Leith the previous year by the party's Scottish executive in view of his Communist links, addressed the May Day demonstration in Edinburgh in his capacity as a labour college tutor.[26]

Conflict between this exhibition of local political identity and the concerns of the national party sharpened with the election of the first Labour government. Locally, Labour activists continued to appear alongside their Communist counterparts: the 1924 May Day celebrations in Dundee combined dancing to the accompaniment of music provided by the trades council's brass band with the crowning of a May Queen, as well as a rather confrontational display of drilling by members of the local branch of the YCL.[27] Addressing that year's rally in Glasgow, James Maxton dismissed Tory calls for a period of more tranquil politics: he would, he assured those present, assume such a state only when he was dead; politics, he maintained, was 'a very definite and bitter class war, which could not be fought with kid gloves'.[28] Maxton's rhetorical resolve was echoed from the same platform by Alec Geddes, a Communist fresh from standing as an unsanctioned Labour candidate in Greenock the previous year; Geddes informed the Glasgow audience that, when it came to fighting the 'boss class', they had to show a 'united front'.[29] The most memorable image in the 1924 Aberdeen procession was 'a horse-drawn lorry carrying a company of juveniles dressed in the national costumes of the various countries in which Communism has a hold'. Here a 'boy in the front represented Russia, and displayed a banner bearing the words, "Russia leads the way"'. The demonstration was addressed by the veteran socialist James Leatham. Sharing a platform with William Joss of the CPGB, he berated the failure of the Labour government to pursue a more vigorous socialist policy while in office, declaring that he had not been active in the socialist movement for four decades to see a Labour government deliver merely 'a halfpenny off the ale'. If the concerns of Labour continued to trump those of socialism, he concluded, he would be forced to join the CPGB.[30] A similar note of provincial anger with the national leadership was struck in Edinburgh, when at a May Day meeting George Buchanan, ILP MP for Glasgow Gorbals, complained that, with the influx of professional politicians into the party, Labour activists needed to take care to ensure that 'their movement's ideals and outlook . . . remain the same'.[31]

Until 1926, local May Day processions and demonstrations continued to be characterised by slogans and imagery which bore a militant political message, whether explicitly, or, as in the case of the near-ubiquitous colour red, implicitly, and which was at odds with the measured approach preferred by the Labour leadership. In 1925 in Glasgow, amid a procession that took a full fifteen minutes to pass a single point, 'scarcely a button-hole was empty of its rosette', while in 'scarlet-festooned drays and charabancs [socialist] Sunday school scholars sat and sang unfamiliar hymns . . . of incendiary hues'. The colour scheme was sustained throughout: spectators could gaze at the 'vermilion' uniforms of the bands, the red 'banners and bannerettes', and 'all the other paraphernalia of the pageant'.[32] Those who lined the streets in Edinburgh that year were met by the sight of a procession led by a man dressed as John Ball, who marched beneath a banner upon which were inscribed Ball's famous words from the peasants' revolt of 1381: 'When Adam delved and Eve span, who was then the gentleman?' After Ball appeared numerous red banners, men sporting red rosettes, women in red hats, and a dog decorated with red bows. Next arrived a group of children dressed in tattered rags, their outstretched hands clasping begging bowls as they paraded beneath the words 'as it is'; in their wake, under a banner which declared 'as it should be', came children dancing round a maypole, while joyfully singing 'The Red Flag'.[33] The 'red' element within the labour movement was reported to be similarly 'conspicuous' in Aberdeen, where the local Communists took their place in the procession bearing a 'huge scarlet flag with a picture of Lenin emblazoned upon it'.[34] The following year the female members of the Aberdeen parade 'displayed prominently the badge of their political and industrial favour in the shape of large red and orange artificial roses'.[35]

Communism, despite its international pretensions, was in Scotland a political stance which found a receptive audience at the level of the neighbourhood, where it could build upon a strong pre-existing class identity. May Day, as observed in the early 1920s, offered, through the display of banners, flags and working models, evidence of a powerful blend of class, trade and locality shared across the political left, which Communists could hope to exploit. At the 1926 Glasgow parade, the Communists could take their place within a parade that was the largest in the city's history, alongside the socialist Sunday schools, the myriad sections of the labour movement, thirty-seven branches of the ILP and twenty-five brass, pipe and flute bands.[36] On the eve of the general strike, members of Edinburgh trades council appeared on a May Day platform beneath a large picture of Karl Marx, flanked on one side by Keir Hardie, and on the other by Lenin.[37] Afterwards it was noted with approval that there appeared to be increased interest in May Day, and the trades council recommended that 'all working class bodies . . . take their share in bringing its message and spirit before the workers'.[38] Local public space, not yet absorbed into the political nation, remained something open to competing sections of society; this, however, was to change radically after 1926.

A CONTINENTAL CULT? REACTIONS TO MAY DAY, 1920–1930

The public celebration of May Day in the early 1920s induced a reaction from concerned local elites, expressed via the editorials and reports of the Liberal and Unionist press, which condemned the method and the message of the occasion. Initially, the labour and socialist commemoration of May Day was decried as an unwanted import from the continent, unsuited to British politics. As the *Aberdeen Evening Express* remarked, the British preferred to demonstrate, on the 'rare occasions' when they chose to do so, 'in a strictly constitutional manner, free from that spirit of narrow-minded and peevish acerbity' witnessed elsewhere in Europe.[39] This perspective was shared by the *Aberdeen Free Press*, which declared that, while the demonstrations of 1920 had undoubtedly been successful in numerical terms, and represented a 'very good first attempt' at instituting a new tradition, the 'cult' of May Day remained a 'continental one'. It concluded that if 'May Day was to be established in this country, it would do . . . better than to be used for class and . . . propagandist ends'.[40]

It was the form of politics embodied by the processions and demonstrations of May Day that was subject to the greatest criticism, and which concerned commentators were especially keen to denounce as alien to British politics.[41] After 1926, such public displays of class allegiance fell into disuse, as, with the adoption of *Labour and the Nation* in 1928 and the election of the second Labour government in 1929, Labour politics assumed a national rather than a class hue. As with the traditions of popular protest, May Day demonstrations became the refuge of those whose politics depended most clearly upon a combination of a strong local class identity and a confrontational campaigning style, namely the CPGB and, in Glasgow, the ILP.

Prior to the decisive victory of the government during the general strike, however, the rhetoric and imagery prevalent in the processions and demonstrations of May Day could be interpreted as evidence of the seemingly inexorable growth in the power of the organised working class.[42] Furthermore, the prevalence of post-war industrial unrest, and the apparent emergence of a class-based politics under conditions of near universal suffrage, made the ultimate victory of socialism appear inevitable.[43] The sheer breadth of local participation on May Day seemed to indicate a disturbing unity among the working class, and perhaps even evidence of

foreign influence, increasing further the concerns of a local press unsympathetic to the Labour Party. The *Aberdeen Evening Express* observed
anxiously that, notwithstanding their 'noise and the whole-hog character
of their view', the Communists had not dominated the procession in 1921:
'all shades of Labour opinion, from the mildest and most moderate of
constitutionalists to the fire-eating "Bolshie"', had been present. Indeed,
a 'noticeable feature' of the procession had been 'the youthfulness of the
red-ribboned Communist and Socialists, of both sexes', marching 'behind
a red banner'.[44] The *Glasgow Herald* took issue with the endless choruses
of 'The Red Flag', finding it 'disquieting' that such a 'lugubrious' and
'inferior' German dirge was being performed by children.[45] A new political
generation, it appeared, were ascendant after 1918.

The perceived threat posed by the expression of class identity on May
Day encouraged local authorities to seek to curb what were, in truth,
relatively innocuous public political traditions. In 1923 Edinburgh town
council refused the organisers of the May Day procession permission to take
street collections; the decision was subsequently extended to reject similar
applications from the local unemployed workers' committee and even the
railwaymen's widows and orphans fund. Unable to provide evidence of any
specific complaint, the Lord Provost nonetheless declared that 'citizens were
tired of collections and [that] he was acting in the best interests of citizens'.
The oppositional nature of relations between the local Labour movement
and the town council was illustrated by the decision of the trades council to
ignore the ruling and proceed with the planned collection anyway.[46]

In this context, the celebrations in Aberdeen in 1924 gave rise to the
complaint that May Day was no longer 'a real festival for nations', but
had become 'a day of political propaganda for sections'. The *Evening
Express* invited readers to contrast the May Day celebrations of the 1920s
with those before 1914, which were remembered rather imaginatively as
an occasion for the expression of the 'jollity of spirit of old and young,
rich and poor'. Since 1920, it was alleged, 'politics has taken the place of
sociability; class warfare has supplanted the mutual goodwill [and] grum-
bles and threats are there instead of merriment and hope'. Elsewhere it was
contended that May Day had become little more than an opportunity for
'hundreds of vociferous individuals [to] employ their throats, tongues, and
arms to spread abroad the tale of capitalist iniquity'.[47] By 1927, councillors
in Aberdeen had extinguished a forty-year tradition by refusing applications to sell political literature during the summer months at the customary
political meeting place of the beachfront links.[48]

If the May Day processions and demonstrations of the early 1920s
reflected a political tradition which was shaped by the physical contest for

public space, and which rewarded the emphatic public assertion of political creeds, then their decline exposed the failure of this tradition. The defeat of the general strike revealed the threat posed by local proclamations of class identity to have been illusory, and ended the ability of May Day celebrations to unite the disparate elements of the local political left. Where processions and demonstrations had once been an omen of looming conflict, by the latter 1920s they were atavistic anomalies, objects of derision rather than alarm.

At the May Day demonstration in 1927 in Aberdeen, Dan Gillies, a Communist councillor from Greenock, addressed a crowd that numbered just 200; however, rather than seeing his rhetoric as an incitement to class war, the local press preferred to ridicule Gillies' speech and appearance. Mocking his accent, the *Evening Express* remarked that Gillies was a 'typical example of the "I'm agin the government" tub-orator type . . . Comrade Gillies is probably "agin" the British language as well.' He was, apparently, 'full of the mannerisms of the tub-orator. There is the hoarse voice, the long hair, the frequent repetition of blood-curdling invective . . . devoid of any point or meaning.' The demonstration ended, it was noted contemptuously, with a 'rather feeble rendering of that very dismal ditty, the red flag'.[49] This confident dismissal of May Day as the preserve of an insignificant coterie of extremists was echoed in Edinburgh, where in 1930 the *Evening Dispatch* observed playfully that 'the merry month of May is now-a-days noted by two factors – the tramwaymen wear white tops on their hats, and the Communists get excited over the anniversary of the Russian revolution'. Readers may, the *Dispatch* charitably realised, have been surprised to learn there was an active Communist Party branch in Edinburgh; they were informed sardonically that 'to-day it is going to be exceptionally active', with a 'procession of Communists with banners bearing Communist slogans' planned, and a demonstration, where the audience would be subjected to 'a feast of oratory'.[50]

DISILLUSIONMENT AND HOPELESSNESS: MAY DAY AFTER 1926

The serenity with which conservative opinion now confronted the celebration of May Day was a result of the degree to which the Labour Party had distanced itself from the public display of class identity. For Labour, the refutation of Conservative accusations of sectionalism required the demonstration of a commitment to governing in the national interest; May Day processions, with their red flags, red banners and choruses of 'The Red Flag', proclaimed a discredited local identity of class. The response of Labour to the defeat of the miners and the imposition of the Trades

Disputes Act was to accuse the Conservative government of pursuing the politics of class, not to promote an equal and opposing class identity. As such, leading Labour politicians, seeking inclusion within the constitution, proved increasingly uncomfortable with such expressions of working-class exceptionalism. Conversely, the Communist Party and the ILP believed that a rising tide of militancy could be discerned in the aftermath of the general strike, which could be expected to continue after the 'betrayal' of the striking miners by the Labour leadership. The CPGB, now positioned as 'the sole independent political force in opposition to the bourgeoisie', attacked Labour as simply another of the 'component elements of the single capitalist bloc'.[51]

These opposing responses were on display at the May Day rallies of 1928. The Aberdeen May Day committee, which in previous years had purported to co-ordinate the procession on behalf of all working-class bodies in the city, was sundered by a series of disagreements over the resolution to be passed at the demonstration. The committee, influenced by local Communists, had drafted a resolution repudiating the policy of industrial peace pursued by the Labour leadership and the TUC since January 1928 via the Mond–Turner talks, asserting that there was 'no peace possible with capitalism'.[52] The trades council rejected this criticism of the national leadership, and proposed an alternative statement that called only for the election of a Labour government.[53] The committee ruled that this had been submitted after the agreed deadline; the trades council withdrew in protest.[54] With the exception of the Aberdeen Boilermakers and the Painters' Society, the latter still represented on the trades council by the Communist William Morrison, the Aberdeen Labour movement played no official part in the May Day commemorations that year. The traditional procession comprised only the Painters, the ILP and the Communists, who appeared with banners depicting Marx, Lenin and the hammer and sickle. The refusal of the trades council to abide by the majority decision of the committee was criticised from the platform at the May Day demonstration, and was juxtaposed with the alleged efforts of the Communists to secure one hundred per cent trade union membership in the city's industries.[55] In contrast, the decision of the Labour movement to decline to participate in proceedings was welcomed by the local press, with it being suggested that the dispute simply emphasised the extent to which 'the sensible working men of Aberdeen' had become 'averse to such public exhibitions in the company of Communists'. The labour correspondent at the *Evening Express* concurred, arguing that, since the occasion had come to be dominated by the partisans of the ILP and the Communist Party, it was no longer representative of the real Aberdonian working class, who were 'not particularly fond of spectacular displays of that type'; Labour was counselled to abandon the celebration of May Day completely, since it was at odds with the moderate and reserved culture now held to prevail in British politics.[56]

Similar divisions arose in Edinburgh, where, although the Labour movement held its normal parade and demonstration, the Communist contingent was prevented from taking part in the official procession. This exclusion was enforced by the police at the request of Frank Smithies, the trades council's political officer. The segregation was repeated at the demonstration in Edinburgh's Meadows, where those assembled listened to speeches delivered from separate party platforms; there were few banners present.[57] It was asserted that the dispute was a result of the Communist decision, soon rescinded, to challenge the Labour Party at the Linlithgowshire by-election earlier in the year. However, the trades council's annual report suggested other motivations too: here it was argued that, unlike the CPGB, Labour was no longer confined to 'merely making propaganda speeches explaining the reasons for unemployment', but had 'as practical people . . . set ourselves the task of [making] proposals to the powers that be'.[58] May Day, in this sense, offered another site where the debate over the future direction of the Labour Party could be conducted. On one side were those such as Smithies, who, having renounced their earlier attachment to the traditions of popular protest, saw the occasion as an opportunity to communicate Labour's national policy to the public. On the other was William Marwick, Smithies' partner during the unemployed protests of 1921, who continued to believe in a shared local political identity. In June 1928, a resolution condemning the decision to request police assistance as a violation of 'all socialist principles' was defeated at a meeting of the trades council, but still drew the votes of one third of the delegates present. An amendment, proposed by Marwick, declaring Smithies' actions to have been 'both wrong and stupid', was defeated by just fifty-seven votes to fifty-two.[59]

If the priority of the Labour Party was now engagement rather than denunciation, and government not opposition, the potential dangers posed by involvement in overt displays of class identity were outlined with clarity by the local press. Before 1926 May Day had been presented as a generic working-class display: by the end of the decade the event was identified with an isolated Communist Party, and any perceived lack of enthusiasm on Labour's part was reported in favourable terms. In 1928 the *Aberdeen Evening Express* argued that, since the traditions of May Day had been adopted so visibly by the CPGB, if members of the local Labour movement wished to 'be free from misunderstanding as to their attitude to the Communists . . . they should hold no communication with them . . .

Figure 4.2 The Communist procession in Edinburgh, May Day 1928. *Edinburgh Evening Dispatch*, 7 May 1928. © The Scotsman Publications Ltd. Image reproduced courtesy of the National Library of Scotland.

and if they cannot help walking in the same street with the extreme men, it should not be in a procession'.[60] In Glasgow, the strength of the ILP ensured that the experience was different. Here May Day celebrations continued, at least in the years immediately after the general strike, to be conducted on a scale similar to that of those which had taken place earlier in the decade, drawing strength from the opposition to the 1927 Trades Disputes Act, which had imposed legal restrictions on the trade unions. Even so, the prominence of the Communists at the 1928 demonstration at Glasgow Green was noted.[61] And while there was, the *Evening Times* granted, a certain 'nobleness' in the 'fanaticism about people who take part in a procession intended to demonstrate to the world the strength of one's conviction', most of the public were, thankfully, 'not so gloriously fanatical about any of [their] faiths to forget [their] decorum'. It appeared, the report concluded, as if the devout socialists had 'inherited the procession'.[62] The following year the *Dundee Courier and Advertiser* lamented that, in contrast to the May Days of decades before, which had apparently been 'a joyous occasion, celebrated by the proletariat with song and dance', since

1918 the occasion had been used 'for the recitation of . . . grievances, and that particular section which looks to Moscow for its inspiration has dedicated May Day as . . . the day of class war'. Nevertheless, where May Day had previously united the working class, it was now almost exclusively the preserve of the CPGB: the *Courier* noted 'that in proportion as the devotees of Moscow have captured the occasion, the interest in it of other sections of the wage earning classes has cooled off'.[63]

Assertions that May Day processions had changed in composition, and were now the domain of those to the left of the Labour Party, were, in one sense, didactic, an attempt to influence behaviour; they were, however, also founded in truth. In 1929, the Aberdeen May Day committee was dissolved entirely owing to a lack of support from the Labour movement, with the Communist-aligned Painters' Society, which in the past had dedicated no little time and expense to preparing and maintaining its May Day banner, expressing disappointment that other trade unions 'had failed to respond to appeals as in previous years'.[64] The trades council abandoned the traditional procession, holding only a demonstration at which the resolution passed was the official one issued by the Labour national executive.[65] A year later, with a Labour government in office, the trades council decided against holding even a demonstration; it was now only the ILP among the ranks of the Labour movement that maintained what were described revealingly as the 'old traditions'.[66] There was a similar lack of interest in 1931, while the following year the growing dominance of national political concerns was plain. Whereas May Day platforms in the early 1920s had been dominated by local speakers, in 1932 plans for a Labour demonstration in Aberdeen were cancelled when a national speaker could not be secured.[67] A demonstration was held in Aberdeen in 1933, but only after a speaker from the national Labour Party had been secured. The Painters' Society, sensing an opportunity to rekindle the public traditions of May Day, indicated its intention to prepare a new banner for any procession to be held. Owing to a lack of interest from other organisations, however, the proposed procession was cancelled, and the Painters' new banner remained unused. The Society's trades council delegate reported that 'one or two members' had wanted to launch an 'unofficial march'; such plans, however, came to nothing.[68]

Likewise, in Edinburgh a decision was taken in 1930 to replace the usual procession and demonstration with a 'sports meeting' and indoor rally.[69] In 1932 the rally was again held indoors, and attracted a disappointing audience.[70] The process witnessed in Aberdeen, whereby May Day celebrations ceased to be the remit of an autonomous local committee that represented a variety of organisations, was also replicated: between 1931 and 1933 the

Edinburgh May Day committee was absorbed into a subcommittee of the trades council.[71] By 1933 the Labour movement in Edinburgh was content to set aside the public traditions of May Day in their entirety, electing to mark the occasion with an indoor rally, 'and thereat deliver Labour's May-Day message'.[72] May Day was a now an occasion for the expression of party rather than class loyalty; further, Labour politics was no longer conducted on the streets or in public squares, but indoors.

In Glasgow, too, Labour's involvement in public displays of political identity on May Day declined. The 1929 demonstration, held just weeks before the general election of that year, was reputedly a 'tame affair', considered by local observers to be 'symbolic' of the party's aspiration to assume an appearance of 'respectability'.[73] A year later, only organisations affiliated to the trades council were permitted to take part.[74] At the official Labour demonstration, from which the Communists were, of course, excluded, the musical accompaniment was provided by the brass band of the Corporation Gas Department, not, as it had been for the previous twelve years, the Clyde Workers' Band. Such symbolic changes mattered: the Workers' Band arrived at the Labour demonstration uninvited, played 'The Internationale' in protest, and promptly left to join the Communist counter-demonstration.[75] By 1931, as the second Labour government moved towards its ignominious conclusion, there were two distinct May Day committees in existence in Glasgow, one directed by the trades council and divisional Labour parties, and another self-consciously 'socialist committee' for May Day, dominated by the ILP.[76] This division of effort resulted in a markedly smaller turnout, with just five platforms at Glasgow Green, and only fifty organisations represented.[77] As the *Evening Times* remarked, such instances of 'political exhibition' had fallen from favour with the mainstream of the Labour movement, which now regarded the 'orthodox procession and meeting in Glasgow Green as too hackneyed for enjoyment'. It was, then, only the radical left which still clung to the traditional May Day rally.[78] The division between the 'official' Labour demonstration and the efforts of the ILP and Communists was replicated the following year, denoting the growing disillusionment of the left after 1931, and foreshadowing the disaffiliation of the ILP at a national level in July 1932.[79] Perhaps surprisingly, the electoral tumult of 1931 found little public expression in May Day demonstrations; indeed, participation continued to decline in Glasgow, and in 1933 the focus of the official Labour celebrations had shifted to the formal evening concert, to be held at St Andrews Hall.[80]

The progressive reluctance of Labour figures to engage with the public traditions of May Day was a consequence of the dominance of national electoral concerns in Labour politics, and especially the change in perspective created by the return of the second Labour government, a shift experienced locally as well as at Westminster. The outcome of the general strike had, in the words of the Labour *Aberdeen Citizen*, been 'worse than nothing', leading to 'disillusionment and hopelessness' at a local level.[81] The victory of the government in 1926 represented a triumph for a national, electoral understanding of politics at the expense of a class-based industrial interpretation, and across Britain Labour went to great lengths to affirm its commitment to exerting power solely through the attainment of elected office. Curiously, perhaps, for those who declined to follow the path taken by the ILP, the collapse of the Labour government in 1931 reaffirmed this basic faith in democracy, and the primacy of politics over economics. Speaking at the official Labour May Day rally in Glasgow in 1933, Rosslyn Mitchell, the Labour MP for Paisley between 1924 and 1929, made clear the extent to which the party was convinced that, in a mass democracy, there was no barrier to what could be achieved. Further, the British experience of slow, incremental advance towards democracy was infinitely preferable when compared to the upheavals evident elsewhere in Europe. While the rest of the world was 'rocking and reeling', Mitchell urged those present 'to stand fast to those principles of government which had made us if not the greatest at least the freest people that history had ever known'. Mitchell concluded by demanding to know what it was that, if the British people had by 'laborious processes' been 'able to snatch from the hands of those who held them in thrall the priceless possessions of physical, religious, and political liberty', was to prevent them from using the same methods to 'win liberty from such a trifling and unimportant thing as economic slavery'.[82]

Even those unsympathetic to Labour recognised the shift that was taking place. Following the marking of May Day in 1929, the *Dundee Courier and Advertiser* accepted that, in the case of Ramsay MacDonald and his colleagues, the protestations of moderation and commitment to the constitution were 'as near as may be true'. Nonetheless, for the *Courier*, behind such figures remained the looming spectre of 'class hate'. These sentiments were clearly identified with the local and public traditions of popular politics: it was claimed that the politics of class continued to rise 'like a reek from the multitude of street meetings'. This distinction between indoor and outdoor meetings was crucial, and provided a means of distinguishing between political approaches. When the 1929 May Day demonstrations in Dundee's Albert Square were spoiled by rain, the official Labour platform party made for the shelter of the Labour Hall beneath their umbrellas. As they did so they were sardonically 'cheered . . . on their way' by the rival Communist demonstration, which, significantly, remained outside.[83] For Communists, politics remained a public pursuit, one best undertaken outdoors. The contrast between indoor and outdoor meetings was also employed by the *Aberdeen Evening Express*, which noted that the programme embodied in *Labour and the Nation* had 'shattered . . . the class-war theory', which, while it remained a 'hot subject for street-corner propaganda', was 'useless' in an election campaign. With affected concern, it was indicated that longstanding members of the local socialist movement, such as the ILP councillor Fraser Macintosh, had been forced to accept that Labour's election manifesto was no longer drafted for their benefit: the old campaigners would have to 'forget their Castlegate gospel' until the election had passed. 'How galling it must be', the *Evening Express* observed wryly, 'for men who have been waving the red flag from their youth to have to tell the electors . . . that their views are subject to modification from headquarters when occasion demands.'[84]

Unsurprisingly, the Communists condemned Labour's abandonment of public politics, and willingly assumed responsibility for maintaining May Day as an occasion for the assertion of an independent class identity. Writing in the *Labour Monthly* in 1932, the Communist intellectual Emile Burns criticised the 'tendency to avoid the class form of the May Day demonstration', and denounced the Labour leadership for having 'whittled away' the 'militant spirit' of the occasion. He argued that, since 1927, Labour had attempted to 'represent May Day as some form of gala festival, stripped of any class significance'. The Labour Party's insistence on separate platforms for Labour and Communist speakers was 'the most open and definite betrayal of the whole position of May Day'. For Burns, the primary objective of the 1932 demonstrations should be to 'revive the spirit of 1890 and 1920'.[85] This was a call to which local Communist activists responded. In Dundee, where, as a result of the unemployed protests the previous September, the local magistrates had prohibited all public processions, the CPGB organised a May Day rally with the express intention of challenging the ban. The demonstration, which attracted an estimated 3,000 participants, ended in twenty-one arrests, as the demonstrators, who had assembled carrying flags, banners and sticks, engaged in running battles with the police that lasted for half an hour. Those arrested were conveyed to the police station to the sound of a 'Communist chorus'; among their number was a youth dressed in what was described as the 'uniform' of the YCL: 'blue dungarees, khaki shirtwaists, and the hammer and sickle badge'. But the efforts to rekindle the militant spirit of 1920 failed to rouse the interest of the Labour movement, which maintained a studious distance from the procession.[86] Although lacking the bellicosity on display in Dundee, May

Day in Edinburgh that year provided further evidence that the customs so prominent in the period before 1926, especially the use of banners, music and processions to proclaim a public political identity, were now being maintained only by the CPGB. Amid what were described as 'quiet May Day celebrations' at the Meadows, the Communist procession arrived, 'carrying about a score of banners', and commenced a series of musical and theatrical performances.[87]

By the 1930s, the traditions once characteristic of May Day had lost their force, despite the stimulus that public politics received from the growth of anti-fascist sentiment.[88] There was a fundamental difference between the May Day demonstrations of the early 1920s and those of the mid-to-late 1930s, with their condemnations of fascism and declarations of support for Republican Spain. The latter were less a proclamation, through pageantry, procession and song, of the dignity and independence of labour than they were a call for the national institutions of government and the Labour movement to take action. The primacy of the national over the local was no longer contested; the 'workers' were not implored to think for themselves. Local Labour activists did not, as they had in 1920, assert their self-sufficiency, or their contempt for the prevailing political settlement, but rather requested that their leaders provide appropriate guidance for the movement as a whole.

The triumph of national party loyalty over local class sentiment could be witnessed in Edinburgh. In 1934 plans were made for a 'united working-class demonstration' that would bring together the trades council, the Communists and the ILP. The CPGB had, in response to the rise of fascism, traded the sectarian purity of the 'class against class' era for the pursuit of a united front on the political left that would, in subsequent years, grow into calls for an even broader popular front. Nationally, however, Labour rejected these overtures consistently, seeing relations with the Communist Party as toxic to any hopes of securing a return to national office.[89] The local plans for a display of unity were thrown into disarray when Arthur Woodburn, by now Scottish secretary of the Labour Party, intervened to point out that anyone opposed to the constitution of the party was ineligible to appear on a Labour platform. The original roster of speakers was duly replaced by the four official Labour candidates selected for the forthcoming general election.[90] Discontent was expressed over Woodburn's intervention, as well as the restrictive nature of the Labour constitution: there were complaints that the plans for a united demonstration had been 'frustrated by the intervention of a higher authority'.[91] Yet there were many local activists who were fully supportive of the ruling. The decision to allow the CPGB to affiliate to what was now the Labour May Day committee had resulted in the boycotting of May Day by the divisional Labour party in Leith, which had been reconstituted in 1931 after similar issues; the local mining unions also shunned proceedings as a result of Communist participation. Even among those who agreed to work with the CPGB, loyalty to the national Labour Party clearly trumped the cross-party local unity typical of the May Day celebrations of a decade earlier. Although the trades council was unimpressed by Woodburn's interference, when he refused to disclose who had alerted him to the possible infringement of the constitution, the matter was promptly dropped.[92]

In Aberdeen, similar efforts to use anti-fascism to resurrect the traditions of the early 1920s also foundered upon the dominance of national politics. Attempts to hold a joint demonstration in 1934 were derided by the *Evening Express* as a 'fiasco', as the various competing elements within the May Day committee failed to agree on a resolution. The endeavour was not repeated the following year.[93] When, in 1936, Edinburgh trades council felt that a 'spectacular show' should be organised in an attempt to rekindle popular interest in May Day, it decided not to organise the traditional procession and outdoor demonstration, but to concentrate on securing a 'national speaker' to address an indoor meeting, where they would be joined by an orchestra and choir.[94]

THE NATION AS A VAST CATHEDRAL: ARMISTICE DAY, 1919–1939

The decline in the display of local class identity on May Day took place in inverse proportion to the entrenchment of Armistice Day, an occasion for the expression of sentiments that indicated membership of a national community. The post-war coalition government, searching for a suitable format with which to commemorate the first anniversary of the Armistice, appointed Lord Curzon to co-ordinate the arrangements in London; the King issued the appeal for the two-minute silence a mere four days before 11 November 1919.[95] The ceremony, initially intended as a unique occasion, became an annual tradition; Sir Edward Lutyens' temporary Cenotaph of 1919 was replaced by a permanent construction, unveiled in 1920 by George V. That year the Tomb of the Unknown Warrior was installed in Westminster Abbey; the shrine received more than half a million visitors in the first week.[96]

The silent national reverence of Armistice Day provided a stark contrast to the clamorous local class identity on display on May Day, drawing together individual sentiments unmediated by class or sectional loyalty, and offering an alternative vision of the ideal nation, one unsullied by social and economic division. There are few clearer manifestations of what

Benedict Anderson described as the 'imagined community' of the nation, with his two prerequisites for national consciousness, 'calendrical coincidence' and 'simultaneous consumption', pristinely embodied in the shared and synchronised national silence.[97] During the industrial and social upheaval of the early 1920s Armistice Day could thus embody a desired national consensus. In November 1920, the *Dundee Advertiser* contrasted the 'national unity and readiness for sacrifice' believed to have typified domestic responses to the outbreak of war in 1914 with the post-war culture of 'self-interest' and 'class interest'. Hope was expressed that the Tomb of the Unknown Warrior would become a lasting monument, and grow into 'even more of a solemn shrine than [it is] to-day'. The warrior was a symbol of national identity, representing 'all who made the sacrifice, and the tokens of national honour bestowed upon his dust are given to all of them'.[98] The change in form this use of public space represented was recognised explicitly: unlike traditional public rallies, Armistice Day was an act of emotional rather than physical belonging, performed by the individual not the crowd. The nation was required to play 'a thinking part', not to demonstrate or rally, nor even celebrate military triumph; the nation must, it was concluded, 'give our minds to those we owe so much'. The *Glasgow Herald* placed similar emphasis on the way in which the occasion offered an opportunity for class conciliation and national unity, noting in 1921 that the crowd that gathered in the city to mark the silence was 'only equalled in its class comprehensiveness by the great glorious dead'.[99] A year later, when Armistice Day coincided with the 1922 general election campaign, the *Herald* observed that such political battles, with their attendant 'strife of tongues', did not always display the nation at its best. The act of remembrance, however, stood in contrast to such narrow, sectional concerns, and gained 'added solemnity' by the comparison.[100]

In 1925 the 'spirit of national unity and high purpose' and 'pacifism' evident on Armistice Day was again contrasted with the 'war of classes' witnessed at other times of the year in Dundee.[101] That year in Aberdeen Armistice Day was characterised as an occasion when 'the whole Nation joined ... in paying honour to the heroes who laid down their lives in the Great War'; the Cenotaph, the Tomb of the Unknown Warrior, and, indeed, the silence itself, were all 'symbols of national piety'.[102] Such depictions of national unity were granted an additional potency after moments of extreme political conflict. In the wake of the general strike, and with the subsequent lockout of the miners only now coming to an end, Armistice Day in Aberdeen was lauded as a 'homage by all classes' to the memory of those who died serving the nation.[103] In Glasgow, the analogy was made even more explicit. The 'annual companionship' of the silence was, the

Evening Times emphasised in 1926, a moment when 'all classes sink their differences': 'for two minutes today', the report continued, 'we paused in our common task in a communion of peace and silence, while the bitterest industrial war in our history was still being waged'. Surely, it was concluded, the greatest way of recognising the sacrifice of those who 'fell in a war to end war' was to pursue 'industrial peace'.[104] As British politics adjusted to the spread of democracy, the commemoration of the war assisted the construction of a national polity by fashioning a sense of belonging around notions of duty, loyalty and sacrifice.[105] As Jay Winter has noted, commemoration was 'an act of citizenship' that asserted membership of the national community, and, by implication, excluded those who did not participate.[106] By 1931, clear comparisons were being drawn between the election of the National Government, and the 'national unity' on display on Armistice Day.[107]

Nevertheless, the manner in which individual memories and acts of remembrance were unified under the rubric of the nation was perhaps the most lasting effect of the occasion. As the franchise expanded, the political nation was understood to be composed of individuals, not competing sections: public expressions of class identity were both unnecessary and illegitimate; the electoral link between the individual and national politics should be direct, not refracted through the intervening lens of class or locality. The event was accordingly purged of discordant elements; the local organisations of ex-servicemen, a key component of the unemployed workers' committees formed in 1920–1, who, as in Aberdeen in May 1920 or Dundee in November 1921, could challenge the dominant portrayal of the war as a sacrifice duly honoured, faded from public view. It has been suggested that the consensus surrounding the meaning of the conflict had begun to fragment by the end of the 1920s.[108] Yet, while this may be true in cultural terms, it seems doubtful that this chronology was replicated at the level of popular politics. In the immediate post-war years there was a readiness to challenge the legacy of the war, and the Labour movement remained willing to question an inclusive national interpretation.[109] In Edinburgh in 1925 the trades council refused an invitation from the city's Remembrance Day committee to send representatives to a service at the Usher Hall, to be addressed by Earls Haig and Jellicoe, and 'where master and men would be asked to sit side by side'.[110] By the 1930s this political contest had been decisively settled in favour of a singular narrative of national loss. Indeed, the sheer scale of the casualties caused by the conflict made remembrance a truly national event. Moreover, given the losses sustained by working-class communities, attacks by the political left on the legacy of the war could easily be construed as an insult to the families of the dead.[111]

Armistice Day performed the opposite function to May Day, asserting the primacy of the nation above class, and offering an alternative function for public space as a sight of national unity rather than political conflict. When Dundee's new city square was completed in 1933, it was felt to be 'most fitting' that the first public meeting to be held there was 'Dundee's homage to her citizens who fell in the war'.[112] Further, the two-minute silence was an innovation which had the most impact in those urban centres where the popular traditions of public politics held greatest sway: in the words of the King 'all work, all sound, and all locomotion should cease', an instruction aimed primarily at those living in towns and cities.[113] Equally, the holding of ceremonies of remembrance and the widespread erection of war memorials proclaimed, in physical form, membership of the British nation, replicating the ceremony at Whitehall in a multitude of local arenas. Jenny MacLeod has explored the meanings attached to the Scottish National War Memorial erected at Edinburgh Castle in 1927, stressing that it commemorated a Presbyterian and martial tradition within an imperial context, and allowed for the expression of a specifically Scottish identity in a manner not reflected elsewhere in the UK.[114] Although this was undeniably the case, and the National War Memorial in Edinburgh symbolically incorporated the numerous local memorials in Scotland, there is no doubt that it was, in turn, subsidiary to the Cenotaph in London. This process of memorialisation drew opposition from the Labour movement, which, in 1924, protested against the construction of a war memorial in Edinburgh on the grounds that the money would be better spent providing housing for those who had served in the war.[115] Yet it proved almost impossible for those on the political left to counter the inclusive message of Armistice Day. This is not to suggest that the act of commemoration was the cynical 'invention' of a national tradition: the occasion clearly performed an important function as an outlet for mass grief on a hitherto unimaginable scale.[116] However, such nationwide acts of remembrance could not be 'politically neutral', since they excluded from the nation those who contested the prevailing interpretation.[117]

The silence itself allowed, within reason, for a variety of interpretations: each individual present could, internally and according to their belief, choose either to regret the war as a tragic waste of life or celebrate a military victory. However, the observation of the silence itself became close to compulsory, containing dissent and debate within the confines of a single moment of national commemoration.[118] It was in their undermining of this spectacle of unity that the protesters in Dundee in 1921 with whom this chapter began were considered to have behaved so disgracefully: by pitting different factions of ex-servicemen against one another, they had shown that the legacy of the war remained open to public challenge. What is more, during the inter-war decades, Armistice Day became an occasion for recognition of the stoic sacrifice of wives, mothers and sisters: by the 1930s it was this wider national and domestic loss that was granted primacy.[119] Here too the conception of the public political sphere as a contested masculine realm predicated upon physical strength was deprived of legitimacy.[120]

The ability of the memory of the war to limit the appeal of a politics based upon class identity was revealed in the extent to which remembrance services did not just become an opportunity for the proffering of national sentiment in local public space, but were increasingly conducted nationally. While local memorials and services played a key part in the early commemoration of the war, by the late 1920s the national service at the Cenotaph in London predominated. When the BBC began to broadcast the service from the Cenotaph, local ceremonies were scheduled to avoid clashing with proceedings in London.[121] The mere observation of the silence no longer sufficed: the very national silence itself, relayed from London, was now required. In fact, despite the BBC only beginning to officially broadcast the service from the Cenotaph in 1928, as early as 1923 'hundreds' of radio listeners in Aberdeen were reported to have participated in the London service of remembrance: 'at 10.55am they heard "London calling," the "Last Post" sounded by bugles, followed by 11 o'clock striking. Then the two minutes' silence and "Reveille".' The effect was 'deeply impressive'.[122]

The nationalisation of Armistice Day was assisted by the fact that in Britain the government assumed responsibility for the commemoration of the war. The contrast with Germany, where defeat in 1918 had led to the collapse of the Imperial regime, is instructive. With the legacy of the war tainted by defeat and accusations of betrayal, the maintenance of military cemeteries fell to the private 'Black Cross' organisation until 1925; the memorial at Tannenberg did not appear until 1927, again financed by private donations. Here the war remained an issue that could be contested politically, not contained and legitimised by the nation.[123] Contrariwise, in Britain the occasion drew participants into a grieving community that could encompass all shades of political opinion, so long as the basic validity of the nation and the constitution were accepted. In 1927, the Labour *Aberdeen Citizen* complained that 'it should be remembered that one's duty is not performed by observing the two-minute's silence. It must be done by struggle and effort and a determination to leave this world much better than one found it.'[124] But such complaints were ineffectual: it was reported by the local press, under a headline declaring the 'Hush that deepens year by year', that the 'Two Minutes' Silence [had] transformed the whole country into one vast cathedral, and chief among the services of Remembrance was the ceremony at the Cenotaph in Whitehall'.[125] In Dundee, the 1930 Armistice Day service was reportedly the largest yet witnessed.[126]

Against this growing immutability, the Communist Party in Edinburgh attempted to replicate the protests witnessed in Dundee in 1921. However, the growing distance between the local traditions of public politics and the concerns of national politics, and the speed with which the former became discredited, were evident in the changed reactions inspired by these efforts at disruption. In November 1932, in a cul-de-sac near Edinburgh's Tollcross, less than a mile from where the official Armistice Day service was taking place in Parliament Square, Fred Douglas erected a small platform, with the intention of leading a 'No Silence' demonstration. Ordered to move by the police, who accused him of obstructing a public thoroughfare, Douglas sullenly dragged his platform ten yards along the pavement, and began once again to address the crowd who had gathered as rumours of a disturbance spread. As the silence approached he was arrested amid scuffles with police officers; he was convicted of breach of the peace at Edinburgh Police Court a week later.[127]

REMEMBRANCE DAY SCENES IN EDINBURGH

Figure 4.3 The ordered use of public space: the official Armistice Day service in Edinburgh in 1932. *Edinburgh Evening Dispatch*, 11 November 1932. © The Scotsman Publications Ltd. Image reproduced courtesy of the National Library of Scotland.

Figure 4.4 The Communist counter-demonstration in Glen Street. *Edinburgh Evening Dispatch*, 11 November 1932. © The Scotsman Publications Ltd. Image reproduced courtesy of the National Library of Scotland.

The disruption of the silence echoed that witnessed in Dundee a decade earlier; however, the responses of the public and the press were informative. The protests of 1921 had taken place in a local public sphere where the legacy of the war could still be physically contested; as a result, the demonstrators had become engaged in violent clashes with unsympathetic ex-servicemen. In 1932 the crowd of spectators who assembled did so largely out of curiosity. Similarly, the violent reaction of the ex-servicemen to the breaking of the silence in 1921 had been reported in approving terms: the physical control of public space, through force if necessary, remained valid, contingent, of course, upon the particular political creed being espoused. A decade later, although still condemned, similar incidents could be viewed with a degree of detachment. Such conduct was no longer a threat to political stability, nor even an affront to the same degree as before; there was little fear that the tactics of the Communists would find sympathy among the wider public. As *The Scotsman* reported, at eleven o'clock an impressive hush spread over the area, in which about a dozen, from the vicinity where the Communist demonstration was being held, were heard in an effort to lead a political song. No one except those immediately concerned joined in, and the volume of sound only seemed to emphasise the surrounding silence.

The absence of the confrontational, masculine politics of the immediate post-war years was accentuated by the 'large number of young mothers with children in their arms, most of them accompanied by their husbands, who were amongst the crowds'. Here the feminisation of both the act of remembrance and public politics indicated that Communist attempts to make politics a question of conflict and not unity, and about class and not the nation, had failed. Men were present as husbands and fathers, not as soldiers or political activists, the family serving as metaphor for the nation.[128]

Two years later Edinburgh's Communists repeated their attempt to dispute the legacy of the war. On Armistice Day 1934, an anti-war demonstration was held at the Mound; when the two-minute silence began a cry of 'red front' was heard, and the demonstrators began to sing 'The Internationale'. The demonstration was left unmolested by those observing the silence; when the two minutes had passed a spectator, rather than attacking the demonstrators, informed those who had taken part in the breaking of the silence that they 'ought [to] be ashamed', since 'this kind of action does nothing but alienate those citizens who are interested in the unemployed'.[129]

CONCLUSION

In the first half of the 1920s, politics remained something that was performed in public. The processions and demonstrations of May Day provided an occasion on which a local class identity opposed to the existing political and economic settlement could be exhibited. What was crucial was that this identity be placed on display in the recognised political spaces of each city: the Castlegate and Links in Aberdeen; Albert Square in Dundee; the Mound, Meadows and Leith Links in Edinburgh; in Glasgow, the Green and George Square. In this respect the politics of class were bound to the politics of place: rather than being contained just within a specific ideology, militancy was expressed in how and where politics was conducted. Until 1926 this was a political tradition that united the bulk of the Labour movement, the ILP and the CPGB, in tandem with the remnants of the pre-1914 socialist societies, in a shared understanding of politics rooted in the locality, and in a sense of politics as a public act.

During the inter-war period this conception of politics was steadily eroded as a result of two factors. First, the extension of the franchise undermined a class-based politics, and gave credence to those who constructed British politics around an exclusive belief in constitutional means. Second, the failure of the general strike fatally wounded the confidence of the Labour movement in the efficacy of industrial action, and brought to a close the syndicalist tradition of direct action on the British left. Politics was no longer something performed in the local public sphere; the physical, visual and audible occupation of public space through demonstrations and processions, and banners, flags and song, was irrelevant in national politics; crucial now was the print and broadcast media. As one delegate to Glasgow trades council's May Day committee put it in 1932, they should aim to use the occasion to create a 'holiday feeling', one more suitable for families, and there should be 'no more "tub-thumping" at [Glasgow] Green'.[130]

British politics ceased to take place across a patchwork of local political arenas, and came instead to be performed within the forum of a singular national politics, one without a specific physical location. If the decline of May Day as an occasion for the promotion of craft pride and political independence revealed the fading of public political traditions from one angle, then the extent to which Armistice Day achieved a near-universal level of observance indicates the growing power exerted by national occasions and sentiments. This was a change in the use of public space of critical importance. Labour's increasing national focus and disillusionment with the local traditions of public politics was signified by the abandonment of the processions and pageantry of the early 1920s in favour of indoor rallies and demonstrations at which the national policy of the party could be explained. The traditions of May Day became, then, the preserve of an impotent Communist Party and an isolated and disaffiliated ILP. It was striking when, in 1935, Patrick Dollan, alongside Arthur Woodburn the leading Labour figure in Scotland after 1932, announced, in his capacity as treasurer of Glasgow Corporation, that the use of bands in public processions would be made conditional on the issuing of a licence by local magistrates. In the face of protests from his former colleagues in the ILP, who were adamant that the 'democratic rights of the working classes to demonstrate on the streets should be protected', Dollan argued that 'all parties, great or small, irrespective of their colour or religion, must maintain the good name of the city, and . . . no section should be allowed licence to provocation or disorder'.[131] There was, for Labour, now a loyalty which outranked that of class.

A final example from Edinburgh will suffice to demonstrate the change. The 1938 May Day celebrations were considered to be the largest in the city for many years, with the civil war in Spain providing the key motivation for a number of those present. Yet those who gathered in Edinburgh's Saughton Park on the first of May that year, or who took their seats among the audience at the Tivoli Cinema later that evening to witness the Unity Theatre Players' production of the American labour drama *Waiting for Lefty*, did so not in order to declaim the essential independence of the labouring classes, or to protest their unwavering opposition to what their syndicalist forebears would have termed contemptuously 'the wages system'. Rather, they were demanding, however stridently, that the National Government amend its foreign policy to better respond to the threat posed by fascism.[132] As the trades council subsequently reflected, there may have been a 'greater mustering of the workers than before', but few of the trade unionists present appeared to 'realise that it is much more important' that they 'take their place in the procession as active demonstrators instead of standing on the side-walk as spectators'.[133] But despite such evidence of disquiet, the central attraction of the preparations for May Day in 1939 nevertheless proved to be the hiring once more of the Tivoli Cinema, and the screening of *The Black Legion*, a Humphrey Bogart vehicle in which an American factory worker falls under the malign influence of a band of white supremacists after being passed over for promotion in favour of a Polish workmate. After some discussion, it was agreed to allow the main feature to be prefaced with a selection of musical shorts.[134] The transition from demonstrators to spectators continued.

NOTES

1. Grassic Gibbon, *Cloud Howe*, p. 102. Capitalisation in original.
2. *Dundee Advertiser*, 12 Nov. 1921; *Aberdeen Evening Express*, 11 and 12 Nov. 1921.
3. *Dundee Advertiser*, 12 and 14 Nov. 1921.
4. Grassic Gibbon, *Cloud Howe*, p. 182.
5. On the personal politics of Mitchell, see: Malcolm, *A Blasphemer and Reformer*, esp. pp. 1–25.
6. Gunn, 'The Spatial Turn', pp. 3–4. See also: Epstein, *In Practice*, pp. 106–25; Warf and Arias (eds), *The Spatial Turn*.
7. Hobsbawm, 'Birth of a Holiday', p. 164.
8. Hobsbawm, 'Birth of a Holiday', pp. 166–8.
9. *The Times*, 3 May 1920.
10. *The Scotsman*, 3 May 1920.
11. *Aberdeen Daily Journal*, 3 May 1920; *Aberdeen Evening Express*, 3 May 1920; *Aberdeen Free Press*, 3 May 1920.
12. *The Scotsman*, 3 May 1920; *Aberdeen Free Press*, 3 May 1920; AUL MS 2269/10: United Society of Boilermakers and Iron and Steel Shipbuilders

(No. 2 Branch) Minutes, 20 Jan. 1920; *Aberdeen Daily Journal*, 3 May 1920.

13. *Aberdeen Free Press*, 3 May 1920.
14. *Aberdeen Daily Journal*, 3 May 1920.
15. AUL MS 2657/6: Scottish Painters' Society (SPS) Minutes, 13 Jan. and 12 Mar. 1920; *Aberdeen Evening Express*, 3 May 1920; *Aberdeen Free Press*, 3 May 1920.
16. *The Scotsman*, 3 May 1920.
17. *Dundee Advertiser*, 3 May 1920.
18. *Glasgow Evening Times*, 1 May 1920.
19. *Dundee Advertiser*, 2 May 1921.
20. *Glasgow Evening Times*, 2 May 1921; *Glasgow Herald*, 2 May 1921.
21. *Aberdeen Daily Journal*, 2 May 1921.
22. *Aberdeen Evening Express*, 2 May 1921; *Aberdeen Free Press*, 2 May 1921.
23. *The Scotsman*, 2 May 1921.
24. *Edinburgh Evening Dispatch*, 2 May 1921 and 1 May 1922.
25. *Edinburgh Evening Dispatch*, 1 May 1922.
26. NLS Acc. 5120/77/5: NCLC Edinburgh District Committee Minutes, 14 Apr. 1923.
27. *Dundee Advertiser*, 5 May 1924.
28. *Glasgow Evening Times*, 5 May 1924.
29. *Glasgow Herald*, 5 May 1924.
30. *Aberdeen Press and Journal*, 5 May 1924.
31. *The Scotsman*, 5 May 1924.
32. *Glasgow Herald*, 4 May 1925.
33. *Edinburgh Evening Dispatch*, 4 May 1925; *The Scotsman*, 4 May 1925.
34. *Aberdeen Press and Journal*, 4 May 1925.
35. *Aberdeen Evening Express*, 3 May 1926; *Aberdeen Press and Journal*, 3 May 1926.
36. *Glasgow Evening Times*, 3 May 1926; *Glasgow Herald*, 3 May 1926.
37. *Edinburgh Evening Dispatch*, 3 May 1926.
38. Edinburgh TLC, *Annual Report for the Year Ending 31st March 1927*, p. 17.
39. *Aberdeen Evening Express*, 3 May 1920.
40. *Aberdeen Free Press*, 3 May 1920.
41. See variously: *Dundee Advertiser*, 3 May 1920; *Glasgow Herald*, 3 May 1920; *Aberdeen Press and Journal*, 2 May 1923; *The Scotsman*, 2 May 1923.
42. On middle-class disillusionment in the post-war years, and accompanying fears of the working-class, see the insightful discussion in: Green, *Ideologies of Conservatism*, pp. 114–34; McKibbin, *Parties and People*, pp. 35–49.
43. The number of days lost to industrial disputes totalled 35 million in 1919, 26 million in 1920 and 85 million in 1921. The figure did not fall below 10 million until 1924. In both 1927 and 1928 the comparable figure was little more than one million days; between 1933 and 1942 the average annual number of days lost to industrial action was less than two and a half million.

See: Stevenson, *British Society, 1914–45*, p. 197; Clegg, *A History of British Trade Unions since 1889: Vol. III*, p. 421. On Conservative fears that mass democracy would lead automatically to socialism, see: Jarvis, 'The Shaping of Conservative Electoral Hegemony'.

44. *Aberdeen Evening Express*, 2 May 1921; *Aberdeen Daily Journal*, 2 May 1921.
45. *Glasgow Herald*, 2 May 1921.
46. NLS Acc. 11177/20: Edinburgh TLC Minutes, 22 and 25 Apr., 1 May 1923.
47. *Aberdeen Evening Express*, 5 May 1924; *Aberdeen Press and Journal*, 2 May 1924.
48. *Aberdeen Citizen*, 19 Sept. 1927.
49. *Aberdeen Evening Express*, 2 May 1927.
50. *Edinburgh Evening Dispatch*, 1 May 1930.
51. R. P. Dutt, 'Notes of the Month: The General Election and the Working Class', *Labour Monthly*, vol. 10(11) (Nov. 1928), p. 646.
52. *Aberdeen Citizen*, 11 May 1928.
53. AUL MS 2270/3/1/13: Aberdeen TLC Minutes, 11 and 25 Apr., 2 May 1928.
54. *Aberdeen Evening Express*, 3 May 1928.
55. *Aberdeen Citizen*, 11 May 1928.
56. *Aberdeen Evening Express*, 26 Apr. 1928.
57. *Edinburgh Evening Dispatch*, 7 May 1928.
58. Edinburgh TLC, *Annual Report for the Year Ending 31st March 1929*, pp. 13–14.
59. NLS Acc. 11177/22: Edinburgh TLC Minutes, 12 Jun. 1928; *Edinburgh Labour Standard*, 14 Jun. 1928.
60. *Aberdeen Evening Express*, 3 May 1928.
61. *Glasgow Herald*, 2 May 1927 and 7 May 1928
62. *Glasgow Evening Times*, 7 May 1928.
63. *Dundee Courier and Advertiser*, 1 May 1929.
64. AUL MS 2657/9: SPS Minutes, 1 Apr. 1929. For the banner preparations, see: AUL MS 2657/7–8: SPS Minutes, 25 Apr. 1921 and 21 Apr. 1924.
65. AUL MS 2270/3/1/14: Aberdeen TLC Minutes, 6 Feb. and 1 May 1929; *Aberdeen Evening Express*, 2 May 1929.
66. AUL MS 2270/3/1/14: Aberdeen TLC Minutes, 9 Apr. 1930; *Aberdeen Evening Express*, 1 May 1930.
67. AUL MS 2270/3/1/14: Aberdeen TLC Minutes, 30 Mar. and 27 Apr. 1932.
68. AUL MS 2270/3/1/14: Aberdeen TLC Minutes, 25 Jan. and 26 Apr. 1933; AUL MS 2657/11: SPS Minutes, 5 Apr. and 8 May 1933.
69. Edinburgh TLC, *Annual Report for the Year Ending 31st March 1931*, p. 6.
70. Edinburgh TLC, *Annual Report for the Year Ending 31st March 1933*, p. 6.
71. Edinburgh TLC, *Annual Report for the Year Ending 31st March 1932*, p. 6; *Annual Report for the Year Ending 31st March 1933*, p. 6; NLS Acc. 11177/24: Edinburgh TLC Minutes, 19 and 23 Jun. 1931.
72. NLS Acc. 11177/24: Edinburgh TLC Minutes, 12 and 14 Mar. 1933.

73. *Glasgow Evening Times*, 6 May 1929.
74. *Glasgow Herald*, 5 May 1930; ML: Glasgow TLC Minutes, 18 and 19 Mar. 1930.
75. The incident was recounted, strangely, in the *Dundee Courier and Advertiser*, 5 May 1930.
76. ML: Glasgow TLC Minutes, 17 Feb. 1931.
77. *Glasgow Herald*, 4 May 1931.
78. *Glasgow Evening Times*, 1 May 1931.
79. ML: Glasgow TLC Minutes, 1 Mar. 1932.
80. *Glasgow Herald*, 2 May 1932; ML: Glasgow TLC Minutes, 2 May 1933.
81. *Aberdeen Citizen*, 16 Sept. 1927.
82. *Glasgow Herald*, 7 May 1933.
83. *Dundee Courier and Advertiser*, 6 May 1929.
84. *Aberdeen Evening Express*, 3 May 1929.
85. E. Burns, 'Class Against Class on May Day', *Labour Monthly*, vol. 14(4) (Apr. 1932), pp. 241–2.
86. *Aberdeen Press and Journal*, 2 May 1932; *Dundee Free Press*, 6 May 1932; *The Scotsman*, 2 May 1932; NRS HH55/662: Dundee Unemployed Demonstrations 1932–33: Chief Constable of Dundee to Under Secretary of State for Scotland, 1 May 1932; *Dundee Courier and Advertiser*, 2 May 1932.
87. *The Scotsman*, 2 May 1932; *Edinburgh Evening Dispatch*, 2 May 1932.
88. See for example the glowing report of May Day in 1937 in: Edinburgh TLC, *Annual Report for the Year Ending 31st March 1938*, p. 12.
89. For a summary of this standpoint see: Statement of the Labour Party NEC, *Labour and the Popular Front* (London, 1937).
90. NLS Acc. 11177/24: Edinburgh TLC Minutes, 10 Apr. and 1 May 1934.
91. Edinburgh TLC, *Annual Report for the Year Ending 31st March 1935*, p. 8.
92. NLS Acc. 11177/24: Edinburgh TLC Minutes, 27 Apr., 1, 18 and 22 May, 5 Jun. 1934.
93. *Aberdeen Evening Express*, 6 and 10 May 1934, 2 May 1935.
94. NLS Acc. 11177/24: Edinburgh TLC Minutes, 10 and 21 Jan. 1936.
95. Homberger, 'Story of the Cenotaph', p. 1429; Mosse, *Fallen Soldiers*, p. 95. For the King's appeal, see: *The Times*, 7 Nov. 1919.
96. Gregory, *The Silence of Memory*, pp. 8–31.
97. Anderson, *Imagined Communities*, pp. 28–40. Anderson uses the example of the daily national newspaper as an illustration.
98. *Dundee Advertiser*, 11 Nov. 1920. The importance of the Tomb of the Unknown Warrior as a national symbol is a point raised by Anderson. See: *Imagined Communities*, p. 17.
99. *Dundee Advertiser*, 11 Nov. 1920; *Glasgow Herald*, 12 Nov. 1921.
100. *Glasgow Herald*, 13 Nov. 1922.
101. *Dundee Advertiser*, 11 Nov. 1925.
102. *Aberdeen Evening Express*, 11 Nov. 1925; *Aberdeen Press and Journal*, 11 Nov. 1925.

103. *Aberdeen Evening Express*, 11 Nov. 1926.
104. *Glasgow Evening Times*, 11 Nov. 1926.
105. King, *Memorials of the Great War in Britain*, pp. 195–200.
106. Winter, *Sites of Memory, Sites of Mourning*, p. 80.
107. *Glasgow Evening Times*, 11 Nov. 1931.
108. MacLeod, 'By Scottish hands, with Scottish money, on Scottish soil', p. 74.
109. For example, there were similar disturbances to those in Dundee in Liverpool in November 1921: *The Scotsman*, 12 Nov. 1921.
110. NLS Acc. 11177/21: Edinburgh TLC Minutes, 20 Oct. 1925.
111. I am indebted to Dr William Knox for highlighting this aspect.
112. *Dundee Courier and Advertiser*, 13 Nov. 1933.
113. Gregory, *Silence of Memory*, p. 13; *The Times*, 7 Nov. 1919.
114. See: MacLeod, 'By Scottish hands, with Scottish money, on Scottish soil'; 'Memorials and Location'; 'Britishness and Commemoration'.
115. NLS Acc. 11177/20: Edinburgh TLC Minutes, 19 Feb. 1924.
116. A point well made by MacLeod: see 'Memorials and Location', p. 75.
117. See: Goebel, 'Remembered and Re-mobilized', p. 488.
118. See the perceptive discussion in: King, *Memorials of the Great War*, pp. 216–45.
119. Gregory, *Silence of Memory*, esp. pp. 33–40, 51–92 and 225–7.
120. Clark, 'Gender, Class, and the Nation', pp. 251–2.
121. Gregory, *Silence of Memory*, pp. 84 and 133–42; King, *Memorials of the Great War*, pp. 22–4.
122. *Aberdeen Evening Express*, 12 Nov. 1923.
123. Mosse, *Fallen Soldiers*, pp. 80–93 and 159–81.
124. *Aberdeen Citizen*, 11 Nov. 1927.
125. *Aberdeen Evening Express*, 11 Nov. 1927. Capitalisation in original.
126. *Dundee Courier and Advertiser*, 12 Nov. 1930.
127. *Edinburgh Evening News*, 11 Nov. 1932; *The Scotsman*, 12, 14 and 18 Nov. 1932.
128. *The Scotsman*, 12 Nov. 1932. On the feminisation of English national identity during the inter-war decades, see: Light, *Forever England*.
129. *Edinburgh Evening Dispatch*, 11 Nov. 1934.
130. ML: Glasgow TLC Minutes, 8 Mar. 1932.
131. *Dundee Evening Telegraph and Post*, 16 Nov. 1935.
132. *Edinburgh Evening Dispatch*, 2 May 1938; NRS HH55/679: Edinburgh Demonstrations 1937–39, Chief Constable of Edinburgh to Under Secretary of State for Scotland, 4 May 1938.
133. Edinburgh TLC, *Annual Report for the Year Ending 31st March 1939*, pp. 8–10.
134. NLS Acc. 11177/25: Edinburgh TLC Minutes, 3 and 31 Mar. 1939.

5

Popular Politics and Electioneering between the Wars

In October 1922, as the annual local elections and a general election approached, the *Dundee Courier* commented drolly that 'a great deal of free entertainment will be offered to the electorate during the next few weeks'. Election meetings were, its readers were told, 'primarily places of entertainment', and 'the public halls of the country would be crowded every night', as 'perspiring and ambitious men, eager for public office harangue and extort in the honoured manner of the orator'. This would be followed by the 'fine art' of heckling, as members of the audience took the opportunity to inspect, interrogate, and perhaps even ridicule, their prospective representatives.[1] The *Courier's* remarks were suggestive of the extent to which, in the immediate aftermath of the First World War, elections continued to be held within a political culture that prized a certain physical proximity between candidates and the public. Closed meetings, with entry restricted to the party faithful, were an act of political cowardice; open public meetings remained central to the conduct of election campaigns. Indeed, prior to the extension of the franchise, such meetings had offered those excluded from the ranks of the electorate an opportunity to participate in the political process. That this interaction with the public could be an ordeal for candidates was well understood; nonetheless, the election meeting, as the successor to the open hustings of the nineteenth century, was a forum in which candidates were expected to assert their 'manly' character, to be 'bonny fechters', or good sports, able to face down hecklers and earn the respect of the audience.[2] Only the timid approached public meetings with trepidation: for those in possession of the requisite blend of self-confidence, physical fearlessness and wit, an election campaign was an occasion for the display of their charisma, and capacity for leadership.

Soon, however, the assumptions that sustained this acceptance of popular intrusions during election campaigns began to be questioned. Official tolerance of rowdyism and disruption at political meetings, as well as rallies and demonstrations, rested upon an implicit but crucial distinction between a

The Heckler—Dread of Timid Candidates.

Figure 5.1 The heckler at work. *Aberdeen Evening Express*, 11 November 1922. Note the difference in clothing and demeanour between the heckler and the candidate, and the fact that in 1922 it remained only the 'timid' politician who feared audience interjections. © Aberdeen Journals. Image reproduced courtesy of the National Library of Scotland.

political class drawn almost wholly from the middle and upper ranks of society, and a popular audience composed overwhelmingly of members of the working class. Equally, the pre-war willingness to humour heckling and interruptions during election meetings was encouraged by the comforting – if not always accurate – belief that the most raucous elements of the popular crowd were either too young or too poor to vote. And although it has been contended that such popular electoral participation declined during the nineteenth century as a consequence of the progressive extension of the franchise, Jon Lawrence and James Thompson have demonstrated persuasively that political disorder in fact increased amid the heady populism of late Victorian and Edwardian politics, as politicians struggled to come to terms with the problems of communicating with a newly enlarged electorate.[3] Rather, it was the post-war creation of a genuine mass democracy, coupled with the rise of Communism in Europe and Labour's breakthrough at the 1922 general election, that ensured that such behaviour was reinterpreted as a threat to the constitution. Popular disruption during election campaigns, and especially the deliberate wrecking of political meetings, appeared no longer as working-class high jinks, but as something altogether more sinister. In consequence, during the 1920s a new understanding of acceptable political conduct was established, one which privileged the figure of the rational, individual elector, and from which violence and disorder were excluded.[4]

Inter-war politics was, then, about more than party labels or particular policies: fitness to govern was denoted too by behaviour. And if the positioning of Labour as a party capable of representing the nation required that the boundaries of party membership be policed rigorously, and individual Communists expelled, it also demanded that Labour candidates distance themselves from the rambunctious populism which surrounded local election meetings in the early 1920s, but which, by the second half of the decade, had become synonymous with a confrontational, and unacceptable, politics of class. As a result, heckling and rowdyism disappeared from local Labour politics, as the party made a concerted effort to appeal to the mass of voters who did not attend political meetings, and who, it was believed, were repelled by traditional methods of campaigning. As *The Labour Organiser*, journal of the party's election agents, argued in 1929, activists should not be fooled by triumphant rallies, since these were almost always attended only by the converted: the true purpose of electioneering was to reach the 'great phlegmatic remainder of the electorate'.[5] By the close of the 1920s, the desire of the Labour Party to appear as a party of government, committed to the constitution rather than the representation of class interest, saw the party adopt centralised, national methods of campaigning, engaging with the emergent mass media. While, as Laura Beers has shown, this change reflected in part the practical difficulties posed by the creation of a mass electorate, the use of national print and broadcast media was also intended to reinforce Labour's nationwide electoral appeal, and the party's essential respectability.[6] In the years that followed the defeat of the first Labour government in 1924 and the fiasco of the 1926 general strike, participation in the popular disorder previously typical of British elections declined. This was a shift most marked at a local level, where a clear physical distance emerged between the politics of the Labour Party and those of the Communists, and, to a lesser extent, the ILP.

This chapter explores this shift through a consideration of municipal and parliamentary electioneering in urban Scotland, as revealed by a study of local newspapers. It suggests that this change in electoral culture was most apparent in Labour politics, as the party strove to counter accusations that, as exposed by the conduct of its supporters, it represented a masculine class politics that threatened the constitution, and excluded newly enfranchised female voters.[7] In turn, the popular traditions of electioneering came to be associated with a dangerous extremism, and, especially, with the Communist Party. Despite its numerical insignificance, the CPGB thus performed a central, if unintentional, role in inter-war politics as a political negative against which other identities could be defined. The attachment of British Communists to traditions of popular politics that were viewed as objectionable within mainstream politics does not only explain (in part at least) the failure of the CPGB to secure wider support: the association of street-corner meetings, heckling and electoral rowdyism with the threat of Bolshevism strengthened the desire of others, especially Labour, to abandon the politics of the street. The period between 1922 and 1926, when perceptions of popular electoral culture were revised drastically, and the informal electioneering alliance which had been established at a local level between Labour and Communist activists collapsed, is explored first; second, the years from 1926 until 1931 are assessed, and Labour's conscious adoption of more reputable methods of campaigning considered; lastly, the post-1931 era is surveyed, as electoral rowdyism became the preserve of those excluded from mainstream political debate, primarily the Communists and the ILP, but also Oswald Mosley's British Union of Fascists, and the militant Protestant movements which emerged in Glasgow and Edinburgh.

'THE AGE OF THE BOLSHEVIST': ELECTIONEERING TRANSFORMED, 1922–1926

The welcome extended to the resumption of electoral hostilities in Dundee, and the portrayal of political meetings as an opportunity for entertainment as much as edification, had its counterpart elsewhere in Scotland. In provincial newspapers, the heckler remained an essentially comical figure, a local 'character'. In Glasgow, the *Evening Times* commented that general election campaigns contributed

> a considerable quota to the fun of any constituency, if not to the gaiety of the nation. The element of mischief, often of devilry itself, is always more or less in evidence at political meetings. Tricks and dodges to prevent the opposition from getting a hearing are continually resorted to; occasionally a meeting is broken up in disorder, and without the 'enemy' having had the ghost of a chance to air his views.

The onus, the *Evening Times* maintained, was on candidates to demonstrate they could cope with such vagaries, and to fend off, with style if possible, any interventions. The 'supreme quality' in any candidate was 'readiness in retort', and the greatest importance was attached not to what a candidate said, but to the 'neat and sudden' way in which they said it.[8]

This understanding of electoral politics was apparent in the behaviour displayed by Unionist and Liberal candidates during the 1922 general election, who found their meetings subjected to repeated disruption at the hands of hecklers proclaiming their support for Labour candidates. Events in Dundee, where Winston Churchill saw his re-election campaign derailed by the concerted opposition of local Labour, Communist, Prohibition Party and Sinn Fein supporters, have entered Scottish political legend.[9] Yet even if shorn of the visceral personal hatred that Churchill attracted, elsewhere the campaign was similarly unruly. In Aberdeen North, the coalition Liberal William MacKenzie Cameron, challenging the Labour incumbent Frank Rose, saw his meetings targeted relentlessly. All the same, Cameron continued to uphold the 'manly' traditions of the platform, refusing to be cowed by hecklers, and instead confronting his tormentors. During one especially rowdy meeting, Cameron demanded a fair hearing, and appealed to the 'sporting instincts' of the audience; his chairman asserted that 'whatever the audience might think of Mr Cameron's political views . . . they must all recognise that he was a "bonny fechter"'.[10] This assessment was shared by the local press, with it being suggested that, despite his defeat, Cameron would 'long be remembered' for his 'splendid fight against the red flag'.[11]

Cameron's commitment to platform tradition was shared by Sir George McCrae, his coalition Liberal colleague in Edinburgh Central. McCrae had served as the Liberal member for Edinburgh East before 1914, was the founder of the 16th battalion of the Royal Scots, and had been awarded the Distinguished Service Order; nevertheless, this record attracted little respect. Labour and Communist supporters flooded McCrae's meetings, drowning out the platform speeches with choruses of 'The Red Flag' and chants of 'Long live the Bolsheviks' in what were described as not just instances of 'lively heckling', but a series of 'persistent and apparently organised interruptions'.[12] But when a police cordon proved necessary to clear a safe path for McCrae through a hostile crowd following his eve-of-poll rally, the primary concern of his chairman appeared to be protect McCrae's 'manly' reputation, as he went to great lengths to assure the assembled crowd that the police presence had not been requested by his candidate, who remained able to maintain order at his own meetings.[13]

As the conduct of Cameron and McCrae suggests, at the 1922 election candidates remained willing to engage with hecklers at open election meetings in the traditional manner: as the independent Liberal Arnold Fleming remarked during the contest in Glasgow's St Rollox constituency, candidates still required 'sufficient sporting instinct' to demonstrate they were 'game for the fight'.[14] Yet the extent of Labour's success at the polls that year – the number of Labour MPs in Scotland rose from six to twenty-nine – caused an abrupt change in perceptions, which reflected the changing nature of political representation. Election campaigns had previously affirmed rather than challenged the established order; when, however, this political division of labour was threatened by the combined uncertainty engendered by the advent of mass democracy, Labour's electoral advance, and the perceived threat posed by Communism, the traditional willingness to tolerate the boisterous excesses of election meetings soon evaporated.[15] The expansion of the franchise appeared to concerned commentators to render a class-based political settlement inevitable, one in which populist demagogues would pander to working-class grievances, and rouse popular discontent.[16] If such fears would prove in hindsight to be groundless, they were nevertheless widespread on the political right in the early 1920s, as the separation long upheld between government and the governed, between the platform and audience, seemingly gave way. Heckling, motions of no confidence, the seizing of the platform: all assumed a worrying new symbolism as electoral rowdyism became detached from the traditional parties of government, and appeared to have been commandeered by those committed to radical political change.

When the politically motivated heckling of 1922 was repeated at the December 1923 general election, it was no longer depicted by local newspapers as harmless entertainment or mere mischief; rowdyism and disruption was now the public manifestation of a dangerous class politics, redolent even of the violent extremes of Bolshevism. In Dundee, the *Courier* viewed the coming election with trepidation rather than the anticipation of previous years, bemoaning what was described as the 'decline of oratory'. There was little doubt that, in the *Courier's* opinion, this deterioration was the result not only of the elevation of the majority of the working class to the status of electors, but also of the return of significant numbers of Labour candidates to parliament the previous year. Political oratory, it was argued, had 'fallen upon its present decline because too many people practise it – or think they do. This is an age of the soap box, not of the august debating hall.' Since 1918, it was asserted, 'a man need not have the qualifications ... or even a command of the English language to open his mouth': what British politics had 'lost in oratory', it had 'also lost in dignity'.[17]

Similar complaints were aired in Glasgow, where it was suggested that the 'good-humoured' and 'genial' interventions characteristic of the traditional heckler had been replaced by obstruction of a more organised type. According to the *Glasgow Herald*, this was the responsibility of the Labour

Party, which had polluted public debate with the politics of class: the resort to 'bludgeon tactics' of shouting and abuse had 'been largely coincident with the growth of the Socialist-Labour Party [sic] . . . and it is invariably opponents of that party and its doctrine who are subjected to such treatment'.[18] There was certainly anecdotal evidence to support the *Herald*'s claims, with disruption of Liberal and Unionist meetings in Glasgow being widespread.[19] There were also a number of incidents that appeared to suggest that there had been a material change in the nature of rowdyism. In Glasgow Central, the Liberal candidate, Harold Tennant, until 1918 the MP for Berwickshire and a former Secretary of State for Scotland (and brother-in-law of the former Liberal Prime Minister Herbert Asquith), was humiliated when his meeting was broken up and his gold watch and chain stolen. In Tradeston, the Liberal candidate Douglas MacDonald left a rally to find that his car tyres had been slashed.[20] More controversially, in St Rollox it was alleged that the Unionist candidate, Violet Robertson, had been injured after being kicked by a Labour supporter.[21] The disorder extended westwards along the Clyde: in Greenock, Liberal meetings had to be abandoned, and at a Unionist meeting in Port Glasgow the platform was seized by Labour supporters amid flying chairs and choruses of 'The Red Flag'.[22]

There were similar examples across urban Scotland. Cameron repeated his candidacy in Aberdeen North in 1923, and continued to find himself faced with popular opposition. After the audience at one meeting at a local school grew too large for the venue, he was forced to speak in the playground, where he outlined his policy to a largely hostile audience estimated to number five hundred. When Cameron suggested that the election was a contest between free trade and protectionism, he was informed brusquely by one elector that the real contest was that between socialism and capitalism.[23] In Dundee, a Unionist meeting was marred by concerted opposition: the chairman was told bluntly to 'sit down' by the audience, and when the Unionist candidate Frederick Wallace tried to begin his address, he was at once informed that he was a liar.[24] Thomas Lamb, a town councillor who had replaced McCrae as the Liberal candidate in Edinburgh Central, was told by one audience member to just 'go away and read Marx'; a subsequent Liberal meeting was ruined when a number of those present began to sing 'The Red Flag', accompanied by a mouth organ. Such treatment was mirrored in Leith, where the platform at one Liberal rally in support of Captain Wedgwood Benn was commandeered by members of the local branch of the International Socialist Labour Party, while at a Unionist meeting in Edinburgh East a young Labour supporter simply walked on to the stage and assumed control of proceedings.[25]

The disruption of Unionist and Liberal meetings by hecklers who declared their support for the Labour Party, socialism, and even, at times, Soviet Russia, appeared to offer conclusive evidence of the rise of political extremism. For the *Glasgow Evening Times*, the disorder in 1923 demonstrated that Labour's appeal had a 'deplorable tendency to rouse class hatreds'.[26] As that year's campaign drew to a close, the Liberal *Edinburgh Evening Dispatch* identified a 'rapid deterioration in British electioneering [since] the wild wing' of the Labour Party has 'adopted organised hooliganism as one of its campaign weapons', and declared testily that Britain was not 'Communist Russia'.[27] At the same time, the *Aberdeen Press and Journal* warned that socialism was no longer the preserve of the 'pale and neurotic "intellectual"', but also now of the 'hooligan and the rough'; the 'fine art' of heckling had been supplanted by what was termed 'buffoonery' and, tellingly, 'impertinence'.[28]

Crucially, as rowdyism came to be identified with a dangerous appeal to class identity, Liberal and Unionist candidates began to abandon the role of the 'bonny fechter', and ceased to feel bound by the convention that election meetings should be open to the public. The *Dundee Advertiser*, broadly Liberal in sympathy, dismissed those who were critical of the growing preference for ticketed meetings, asserting that it had become the only means by which non-Labour speakers could gain an unmolested hearing.[29] The *Advertiser* called too for the enforcement of the 1908 Public Meetings Act, which had made the breaking up of meetings during parliamentary elections an offence under the 1883 Corrupt and Illegal Practices Act, a view echoed by the *Glasgow Herald*.[30] Before the 1920s, the 1908 Act had been largely unused, considered the humiliating last resort of candidates unable to muster sufficient supporters to defend their own meetings.[31] Yet the *Advertiser* argued that the introduction of class sentiment into British politics by the Labour Party had changed the basic rules of engagement: the party's rhetoric had liberated 'forces of social hate' that could not be controlled.[32] And even if the Labour leadership denounced the worst instances of disruption, it was clear that the old stoicism was now outmoded: a clear distinction was emerging between the collective public expression of political allegiance at election meetings and the casting of an individual vote: in a mass democracy, the latter was decisive. As the *Advertiser* stated, the electors would be able to deliver their rebuke to the socialist rowdies 'at the polling booth'.[33]

This faith in the wisdom of the electorate was, of course, by no means the only response to the disruption of the early 1920s. There were those on the political right who viewed with interest developments in Italy under Mussolini's Fascist regime.[34] In October 1922, in the immediate wake of the march on Rome, the *Aberdeen Evening Express* praised the Fascist movement as being made up of patriotic ex-servicemen who had been forced to intervene as Bolsheviks proclaimed the 'coming revolution . . . at every street corner, and in many places the red supplanted the national flag'.[35] Indeed, in Aberdeen the local press marked the anniversary of the Fascist seizure of power by praising Mussolini fulsomely.[36] For those who saw in the emergence of Labour the potential seed of a British revolution, Italy offered one example of how the forces of order could retaliate. As the *Aberdeen Press and Journal* phrased matters during the 1924 general election campaign, the 'Bolshevist tactics' of the local left could 'only continue for so long' before 'the long-suffering majority of the public, of all shades of opinion, will begin to bethink themselves of the success of the Fascists against similar hooliganism in Italy'.[37]

Some candidates were willing to take such sentiments beyond the realms of abstract sympathy, and hired stewards to maintain order at their rallies. Following the theft of his watch in 1923, Harold Tennant turned to the 'roll of voluntary workers', a right-wing organisation established to provide 'free' labour in Glasgow during the 1921 dock strikes, to ensure there was no repeat.[38] The following year, accusations were made that Robert Horne, the Unionist member for Glasgow Hillhead, had employed members of the British Fascisti as stewards at his meetings.[39] In Edinburgh Central, the Unionist candidate Allan Beaton, having endured continual disruption and abuse during the 1924 campaign, aborted his programme of open meetings, and, rather provocatively, recruited a number of well-built young men to act as stewards; these, outraged Labour supporters claimed, were members of the recently established Edinburgh branch of the Fascisti. Beaton rebutted these allegations, and claimed, perhaps a little absurdly, that the stewards were simply 'personal, individual friends' who wished to hear his speeches. Despite these protestations of innocence, it seems likely that the suspicions of the local left were correct: three days before Beaton unveiled his new recruits, a highly sympathetic report on the Fascisti had appeared in the *Evening Dispatch*, stressing their professional background, and desire to ensure that there was no repeat of the rowdyism of recent elections.[40] Beaton's efforts to counter disruption via the threat of force backfired: his actions simply encouraged Labour and Communist hecklers to redouble their efforts, and to make certain that they enjoyed a numerical advantage over their opponents. The night after the stewards made their first appearance, Beaton was forced to abandon a meeting after some three hundred Labour supporters forced their way into the venue; four days later the police were compelled to intervene after a hostile crowd gathered outside the hall where Beaton was speaking. Days before polling a Unionist rally degenerated into a free fight as members of the audience clashed with the stewards after waving red handkerchiefs at the candidate, refusing to stop unless the platform party removed their red, white and blue ribbons.[41]

Confrontational reactions such as Beaton's remained, all the same, relatively rare; by 1924, if not before, it was clear that there was greater political reward to be had by refraining from engaging with hecklers, and instead condemning the Labour Party for the offensive behaviour of its supporters. This approach was promoted in Aberdeen by the *Press and Journal*, which suggested that, owing to the antics of so-called socialists, elections had become wearisome affairs. Heckling, which 'under the fine old rules of free speech and fair dealing' had been a 'beautiful thing, like rapier play', was now the preserve of 'brazen . . . interrupters' who lacked 'the patience, the decency, or the intellect to fight fair': the sharp-witted and incisive heckler of the pre-war era had been 'engulfed [by] the Age of the Bolshevist'.[42] Such attacks provided a local adjunct to the controversy regarding the relationship between Labour and the Communists that defined the 1924 general election, suggesting that the denials of the Labour leadership of any links with the CPGB were exposed as dishonest by the conduct of Labour voters.[43] These criticisms were, moreover, lent credence by the highly vocal support Labour candidates received from local Communists, whether welcomed or not. The form of politics adopted by parties thus became one of the key dividing lines within inter-war politics, a means of assessing whether a party could be trusted to govern in a constitutional manner. The *Dundee Courier* mocked the efforts of the Labour leadership to highlight the ideological differences between their party and the CPGB. What truly mattered was how and where parties conducted their politics: for the 'man in the street', the *Courier* surmised, theoretical and doctrinal differences would appear 'rather fine-spun'. Whatever Labour's claims to be a 'non-class' party, their policy, 'as expounded', crucially, at the 'street corners', was 'as much an exclusive appeal to malcontents as that of the Communists'.[44]

Individual Labour candidates naturally attempted to distance themselves from any disruption, and to disavow any suggestion of an alliance with the CPGB.[45] Yet these efforts were consistently hampered by the predilection of those disrupting Unionist and Liberal meetings to align themselves with the Labour Party. At a Liberal rally in Dundee in 1924, the ejection of a heckler was followed by continuous chants of 'Good old Ramsay!' in support of the Labour leader James Ramsay MacDonald.[46] Likewise, at a Unionist meeting in Aberdeen, the traditional vote of confidence in the platform was sabotaged by three cheers for MacDonald, a tactic repeated throughout the campaign.[47] When the Aberdeen Unionists' eve-of-poll rally was wrecked by members of the audience singing 'The Red Flag', the *Press and Journal* concluded that the 'hooliganism' of 1923 had regrettably returned, and had even worsened: 'among the wilder supporters of socialism', it was suggested, there was now 'a decided leaning towards the favourite tactics of Bolshevist terrorism'. In the aftermath of the election, and with a Conservative government now returned to office, Labour was warned that a political party was 'to be judged, like individuals, by the association it keeps'.[48] The *Glasgow Evening Times* suggested in 1924 that while Labour nominees called on their followers to grant other candidates a 'fair hearing', the 'unmannerly behaviour' evident at Unionist and Liberal meetings was the inevitable result of 'long periods of bitter propaganda'. And although much of the disruption was ostensibly harmless, those who cheered 'revolution, Russian tyranny, sedition . . . even in fun, may come in time to lose a very necessary suspicion of these political expedients'.[49]

The shared repertoire of slogans and songs deployed by Labour and Communist supporters encouraged the Conservatives, and, in Scotland, the Unionists, to portray themselves as the party of patriotism, order and the constitution.[50] In addition, in depicting the rowdyism of Labour voters as evidence of Bolshevik leanings, the Conservatives hoped to appeal to female voters; by linking Labour to a masculine physical culture of public politics that was, correctly or not, thought to exclude women, the party's propaganda aimed to confine Labour's appeal to the organised male working class.[51] Alluding to the lurid tales of the forced collectivisation of family life emanating from Soviet Russia, the *Press and Journal* praised the Unionists as being the only party that stood for 'religion, morality, and decency'; Labour, with all its 'Bolshevist associations', represented a danger 'which women will be the first to feel and regret'.[52] It was in this changed context that candidates and their chairmen were willing to threaten persistent interrupters with prosecution under the 1908 legislation: the taint of illegality assisted the portrayal of Labour as a force beyond the constitutional pale.[53] Labour voices tried to contest Conservative claims to be the party of the constitution: a common response by hecklers to accusations of Bolshevism was to raise the issue of Ulster, and the Unionist challenge to parliamentary sovereignty before 1914.[54] Alternatively, memories of instances of Labour speakers being attacked by right-wing mobs during the First World War were exhumed. Writing in *Forward* during the 1923 general election, Patrick Dollan, chairman of the ILP in Scotland, noted the irony in the fact that 'the same people who are squealing for orderly assembly now are the same people who incited jingoes to break up our meetings during the war. We recollect how they shouted down free speech then and gloated when

A PUBLIC NUISANCE

Can it not be muzzled somehow?

Figure 5.2 The backlash against disruption. *Glasgow Evening Times*, 24 October 1924. © Glasgow Evening Times. Image reproduced courtesy of the National Library of Scotland.

our speakers were assaulted.'[55] Even so, the Conservative narrative of a Labour Party whose rhetoric, conduct and imagery exposed its commitment to an acrimonious class politics gained greater traction, and, in turn, persuaded all the major parties to abandon the traditions of public politics.

After 1924, a new conception of acceptable political behaviour began to emerge, as the rowdyism that had characterised late Victorian and Edwardian electoral culture was discredited. This shift went beyond condemning just the worst instances of disruption and violence: the very public conduct of politics itself began to bear the stigma of a class politics incompatible with national politics. Public opinion became something to be expressed at elections by an aggregate of enfranchised individuals. As the *Glasgow Evening Times* editorialised, candidates who measured their success by the size of the audiences they addressed, or the acclaim they received at rallies, were

> building on a shifting foundation. Crowded as most of these meetings are, they represent only a fraction of the voting power of the community. And of the meetings themselves, only a part is usually active. And not all of these are voters. And not all of these are serious. And that's a blessing.[56]

Labour's defeat at the 1924 general election allayed Conservative fears surrounding the expansion of the franchise, and transformed mass democracy from a threat to the constitution to its very guarantee. Conservatives and Unionists were now the defenders of the democratic 'public' in opposition to the narrow class sectionalism of Labour and the left.[57] The political consensus which arose, as Bill Schwarz has suggested, equated democracy almost exclusively with the act of voting, with Westminster functioning as the key repository of political legitimacy.[58] With there being now few who required representation at public meetings rather than through the ballot box, to attempt to circumvent the electoral process via public protest was unacceptable; as a result, traditions of heckling and disruption were pushed to the fringes of British political culture. A report of a meeting in the Glasgow Kelvingrove constituency addressed by the Unionist incumbent Walter Elliot provides a flavour of this outlook. Events were, it was claimed, 'rowdy beyond words . . . obscene language, such as is only used by drunks or abandoned persons, was loudly heard in the hall . . . these impossible interruptions supported vocally the Socialist Party'. Any alien visitor would, the account concluded, think they had 'wandered into a lunatic asylum'; they would 'find reason, courtesy and common sense set at naught, and in their stead mob emotion and vulgarity advanced and exalted'.[59] If the audience at election meetings had once been a synecdoche for the wider electorate, this was no longer the case: beyond the confines of the local classroom or town hall were millions of newly enfranchised voters, who, although believed to be unattached to a particular party, were nonetheless part of the political nation. In 1924 the *Aberdeen Press and Journal* dismissed political rallies as being of dubious worth in influencing 'public opinion', and cautioned against mistaking vocal 'enthusiasm' for electoral support.[60] A year later the *Dundee Advertiser* counselled that rowdyism could be defeated by the simple act of voting: 'shouting', it was suggested, 'counts for nothing at the polling station'; indeed, it was doubted if election meetings were of any political value whatsoever, since the 'great mass of the electors', and especially female voters, did not attend.[61]

Within this primarily electoral conception of politics resided a series of unspoken oppositions: between nation and class, democracy and dictatorship, the rule of law and revolution, which together mapped the borders of constitutional politics. Under the leadership of Stanley Baldwin, Conservatives portrayed their party as above sectional political conflict, able to represent the national interest in a way that Labour could not.[62] This commitment to constitutional politics was strengthened by Baldwin's willingness to accept the electorate's rejection of protectionism in 1923, which not only granted Labour the opportunity to govern as a minority, but also confined Labour politics within parliamentary limits.[63] Labour was forced to conduct its politics in accordance with these boundaries, and to risk exclusion from national politics if it engaged in class politics. The aggressive platform politics in which a generation of orators had been schooled was now a liability.

The transition from a political tradition that prioritised the physical immediacy of the election meeting to a national politics defined by the cumulative judgements of anonymous individual electors was hastened by technological advances. Clearly, it was futile to heckle a radio set: as the *Aberdeen Evening Express* noted drily during the 1924 campaign, 'many skilled socialist hecklers are said to have died of apoplexy while listening to Mr Baldwin on the wireless last night'.[64] But distance removed not only the opportunity for heckling: it also changed the style of political oratory itself. The platform speech delivered at the open election meeting, designed to rouse the passions of a partisan crowd, or win over a hostile audience, was, it soon became clear, less suitable for broadcast. Famously, when speeches by Baldwin and MacDonald were broadcast in 1924, the avuncular manner of the former was considered more effective. This judgement was certainly echoed locally; nonetheless, we should recognise that this assessment was neither impartial nor based solely on the addresses: rather, it formed part of a broader shift in opinion that saw the mass platform discredited, and Labour depicted as the party of the mob, unfit for

government office. Marvelling that 'thousands of people heard his message
. . . who would never have heard his voice in any other way', the *Evening
Express* praised Baldwin for his 'undisguised contempt for rhetoric', and
refusal 'to practise the wiles of the mob orator, on which his socialist
opponents . . . deliberately depend'.[65] The efforts of Ramsay MacDonald
were, in the opinion of the *Aberdeen Press and Journal*, unsuited to
the 'calm and rational atmosphere of the listener's own fireside'.[66] As
British politics was nationalised by the extension of the franchise and the
rise of a national print and broadcast media, it was also domesticated,
removed from the febrile atmosphere of the streets and public halls, and
reconstituted as a private interaction between national politicians and
enfranchised individuals.

Candidates were now increasingly unwilling to tolerate heckling, while
among audiences the belief that election meetings were an opportunity
for the public to communicate with their politicians, and not just for
candidates to disseminate party policy, declined. The Aberdeen municipal
elections of 1925 were devoid of any 'liveliness'; in Edinburgh, proceedings were considered to have been free from the 'unfortunate uproar' of
previous years.[67] When a candidate refused to allow questions at a meeting
held during the 1923 municipal elections in Dundee, more than half of the
audience left in disgust at such 'gross ignorance'.[68] Two years later George
Caldwell, a candidate in Dundee for the anti-Labour Municipal Electors'
Association, refused the traditional vote of confidence in the platform,
responding to muted complaints by declaring that the only vote of confidence that interested him was that held on polling day.[69] The Conservative
narrative which identified rowdyism with a challenge to the constitution
was strengthened by the events surrounding the general strike. Disruption
at election meetings was not treated in isolation, but was placed within
this wider context: in 1926 electors in Aberdeen were advised to remember
the strike, when 'the paramount needs of the public were flouted', and the
local Labour movement had 'maintained that the authority of the strik-
ers, and not the community, was supreme'.[70] This opposition between
class politics and the interests of the public and the community was key;
strident displays of political allegiance indicated an inability to represent
the interests of the nation as a whole. The correct form of political engagement was to cast an individual vote: as the *Evening Express* advised voters
in Aberdeen, 'silence is golden [and] silently the electors should now give
Socialism a back seat'.[71]

Significantly, this electoral emphasis was now shared by many in the
Labour Party, who considered any participation in popular disruption
a threat to their chances of electoral success. Such concerns were not

necessarily focused on the predominantly working-class constituencies and wards where disruption occurred; the fear was that alleged rowdyism in these areas would tarnish Labour's wider appeal.[72] At the 1926 municipal elections in Edinburgh, at a meeting in St Leonard's, scene of some of the wildest uproar of the early 1920s, councillor Hardie of the Labour Party successfully appealed to the 'honour' of his supporters, asking them 'to show Edinburgh that we in St Leonard's can conduct a meeting properly'. An election meeting in St Leonard's was, then, of relevance not merely to those in attendance, nor only to the electors of that ward; rather, it was an opportunity to display Labour's ability to govern the city, and, by extension, the nation.[73]

'A GENERAL ELECTION IS NOT A DEBATING SOCIETY': LABOUR POLITICS, 1926–1931

The abandonment of open ward meetings, and the wider decline in the traditional format of election meetings, with their generous allocation of time for audience questions, votes of confidence in the candidate and expectations of platform 'manliness', was under way by 1924. But it was after 1926 that this evolution gathered speed, and electoral rowdyism came to be associated decisively with political extremism. Driving this change was a shift in understandings of political representation, as the extension of the franchise dissolved the distinction between the public and the electorate, and equated political participation chiefly with the act of voting. Crucially, Labour, except for elements within the ILP, accepted that class strife had ended with the transition to mass democracy, and with it the need for confrontational forms of political campaigning.

Labour duly rejected the aggressive traditions of electioneering. In September 1926, *The Labour Organiser* announced that the era of mere 'propaganda fights' had passed: Labour now needed to promote a more expansive identity than that instilled by the institutions of the Labour movement. A prospective Labour candidate outlined his intended tactics: door-to-door canvassing would replace public rallies, and such meetings as were held would be addressed by speakers from the right wing of the party, since they were 'likely to gain more converts'. The unnamed candidate concluded by stating that they would, from the 'outset . . . make it perfectly clear that Communists were not to be retained in membership of the party, nor allowed to serve on any committee or be accepted as canvassers'.[74] Ramsay MacDonald spoke in similar terms in a Christmas message to the Aberdeen Labour movement in 1927. Summarising the progress he felt he and his colleagues had made during the preceding year in opposing the

Conservative government, MacDonald declared that Labour had 'done good work in the Commons and had fought every inch of the way, not by rowdyism as alleged in the Tory press, but by sound, reasoned argument'. Chiding those who advocated more forceful tactics, he advised activists that a rational approach was 'the only way for a party to make headway'; Labour 'had no time for rowdyism, and looked on it with disfavour'.[75]

Support for this new emollient and, in a certain sense, apolitical style of campaigning permeated elections in urban Scotland, with important consequences for those local Labour figures who remained committed to an aggressive platform persona. Robert Wilson, as we have seen, was cast aside unceremoniously after his defeat in the 1927 by-election in Leith. Wilson's removal was, of course, motivated partly by his controversial policy pronouncements; all the same, the by-election post-mortem prepared by the national executive emphasised Wilson's dogged reliance on street-corner meetings and public demonstrations, methods which, it was believed, had alienated female voters.[76]

The contrast between Labour's new approach to electioneering and that of the radical left was made ever more apparent as the Communists moved towards a policy of open condemnation of the Labour leadership during 1927 and 1928, and the ILP left, under the guidance of James Maxton, became increasingly disillusioned with the official stance of the Labour Party.[77] The boisterous traditions of disruption and heckling that had previously been the hallmarks of election meetings became the preserve of the radical left, allowing Labour to attribute rowdyism to Communists who appeared in public not, as they had earlier in the decade, as vocal left-wing allies, but now as bitter opponents. The true consequence of the adoption of 'class against class' was not that it isolated British Communists from potential supporters in the Labour movement; given the commitment of the Labour Party to enforcing the exclusion of individual Communists that would have happened in any case. Rather, Communist vitriol assisted the efforts of those endeavouring to present Labour as a responsible party of government, and as a credible alternative to the Conservative and Liberal parties: that is the narrow, but crucial, sense in which the CPGB mattered in inter-war politics. In the words of Herbert Morrison, Labour should 'thank Moscow' for ditching the policy of the united front, and 'for blowing to the winds at last the Tory fiction that Labour is a creature of Communism'.[78]

Notably, local newspapers, which had previously refused to differentiate between Labour and the CPGB, subsuming both beneath the umbrella epithet of 'socialist', began to associate political rowdyism and class politics specifically with the Communists. In January 1928, Robert Workman Smith, the Unionist member for Central Aberdeenshire, addressed a meeting at the city's music hall. According to the *Press and Journal*, the meeting was disrupted by 'extreme socialists'; while accepting that the Labour Party disowned those who participated in such behaviour, the report suggested that it was 'a fair deduction from the class and tactics of the offenders ... that they aspire to rule through socialism, as the Bolshevists came to control Russia through the weakness of the socialist Kerensky'.[79] The link between such disruption and extremism was assumed, and if Labour wished to be free from any association with Communism, it would have to distance itself from rowdyism; the Communist decision to oppose Labour candidates granted an opportunity to do so.

While the CPGB had considered challenging Labour at the Linlithgowshire by-election in April 1928, it was the contest in Aberdeen North four months later that represented the first parliamentary confrontation of the 'class against class' period. The selection of the former Liberal Wedgwood Benn as the Labour candidate exposed, as we have seen, the tension between national and local political identities: but the campaign also laid bare the sheer physical distance that had arisen between Labour and Communist politics in the wake of the general strike, and demonstrated that the disruption which had characterised previous elections was now exclusively in the service of the Communists. The Communist candidate, Aitken Ferguson, relied upon a welter of street-corner meetings, and the calculated disruption of his opponents' efforts. Even the *Aberdeen Evening Express*, which viewed the 'clamour and shouting' indulged in by the 'red rowdies' with distaste, was forced, however grudgingly, to recognise their work ethic, confessing that 'they have plenty of energy, those Communists, they started out ... this forenoon and will still be haranguing when most of the citizens are asleep'.[80] Nevertheless, the Communist emphasis on aggressive heckling and disruption was condemned as offensive to British political culture: who, the *Evening Express* demanded to know, 'would wish to ally themselves with or give a vote to the representative of such a band?'. Communist tactics were contrasted with the style of address adopted by Unionist speakers during the by-election, who, it was claimed, had abandoned the 'flights of oratory that were once so highly prized' in favour of 'a plain, unvarnished statement, lucidly and concisely put'.[81] Crucially, however, the hecklers' interventions were now directed at the Labour Party as well as the Unionists and Liberals.[82] Communist disruption at Labour meetings enabled the latter to assume a position in the mainstream of national politics. As the Labour correspondent of the *Evening Express* suggested during the campaign, 'the red propaganda has made clear ... that there is a big gulf between the frothy nebulosities of the Communists' and Labour's 'sound, practical programme of social reform'.[83]

Ferguson's performance was, relative to the wider Communist record between the wars, not disastrous; yet the enthusiasm on display at Communist rallies had convinced local activists that they were on the verge of a stunning victory. Bob Cooney, who abandoned the ILP to campaign for Ferguson, felt that, on the basis of the public response, 'we were winning hands down'. The eventual result thus came as a disappointment.[84] In contrast, the Labour Party understood that elections were no longer won or lost at the street corner, that public support was not measured by the size of the audience at party rallies. Benn declined to compete with the Communist campaign; even when Labour did hold public rallies, speakers refused to participate in the combative public debates favoured by their left-wing rivals. At a rally celebrating Benn's victory, Robert Morrison, a native of Aberdeen who now represented Tottenham North and served as Ramsay MacDonald's parliamentary private secretary, declared parliament to be 'the only means by which the people can be emancipated'. Communist demands that Ferguson be allowed to contest such an assertion were refused, and when it was suggested that Morrison return the following evening to participate in a full debate, he replied coolly that, as a member of parliament, 'he had to be careful to debate with a man of his own weight'.[85] In asserting that political discussion took place between elected public representatives, Morrison was following official party guidance, which had advised speakers to avoid acrimonious public arguments with left-wing critics. In 1927, *The Labour Organiser* had maintained that, despite their popularity during what were termed 'the early days of the socialist movement', such intra-left debates had become 'a favourite weapon of the extreme left wing', and were little more than 'cheap propaganda'. To attract what was described as the 'outside public', candidates were advised to debate only with 'prominent members of our Tory and Liberal opponents', and only with official sanction from the party leadership.[86]

By the time of the November 1928 municipal elections, heckling and disruption had almost vanished. Accounts of the polling in Glasgow stressed the apathy of voters.[87] In Aberdeen, the contest was reported to be 'placid' and even a 'little uninspiring'; the 'fierce controversies' of previous contests had, apparently, 'fallen out of favour'.[88] In Edinburgh too, it was felt that a 'a gradual change [had come] over the municipal elections'. Previously, great weight had been attached to open ward meetings, 'where all parties had a "look in" on the same platform and hecklers had lively but invariably good-natured exchanges with their representatives'; however, a growing number of candidates, 'tired of being baited by hooligans', had abandoned proper ward meetings, and were holding individual campaign meetings, 'where the rowdy element obtains much less latitude'. A further, 'curious', development was recorded: Labour candidates, previously the beneficiaries of the rowdies' interventions, were now beginning to be heckled by 'disgruntled opponents', who were drawn 'chiefly from their own ranks [i.e. the ILP] and those of the Communists'.[89]

At the general election of May 1929, which saw Labour returned as the largest party in the Commons for the first time, the distinction between Labour and Communist electioneering was well-established. Those who would attribute Labour's victory in 1929 to a rising nationwide class consciousness have overlooked the importance of Labour's adoption of respectable and constitutional methods of campaigning, and the extent to which this aided attempts to reject accusations of sectionalism.[90] This recalibration of Labour's canvassing style was most apparent at the constituency level. In Dundee, even the vehemently Unionist *Courier and Advertiser* was forced to accept that Labour speakers had now tuned 'their lyres to a minor key', casting aside 'the loud war cries natural to them'. A week later, the *Courier* found it 'difficult to believe that we are within three days of the general election . . . it remains to the last the quietest contest of the kind in living memory', a shift that was attributed to the expanded electorate, which, it was felt, contained a record number of undecided voters.[91] The only evidence of the old traditions was provided by the local Communists, who hosted a rally at the city's Caird Hall three days before polling. Approximately 1,500 supporters marched to the venue, carrying banners and singing 'The Red Flag'; the Labour *Dundee Free Press* had to admit that there was unlikely to be a better-attended or more enthusiastic meeting during the campaign.[92] But, in truth, the fervour on display at Communist events was testament to the party's impotence in national politics. While the CPGB remained committed to a model of electioneering that venerated the immediacy of volume and visibility, Labour was engaged in attempting to make new converts.

These contrasting approaches could be seen in the adverts for election meetings and rallies placed by both parties in the pages of the *Dundee Free Press*. Where the appeals of the CPGB in support of the party's candidate, Bob Stewart, were expressed in an uncompromising language of class, the Labour adverts were framed in terms designed to appeal to those who had not yet voted for the party, especially female voters. In the immediate postwar era, Labour election literature had tended to emphasise the working-class credentials of party nominees.[93] By 1929, this class-conscious rhetoric had been discarded, not just by the party leadership, but also by local Labour parties. Thus, in Dundee, Michael Marcus, the Labour candidate that year, made sure to distance himself from such traditional appeals. An indoor meeting to be addressed by Marcus in February 1929 was advertised in deliberate, formal terms; the bold typefaces and assertive slogans characteristic of earlier Labour notices had gone, and the emphasis was on Marcus's legal training.[94] A month later, another Labour meeting was publicised in the same measured language, and featured the invitation to 'come and hear Labour's case', suggesting that the intended audience was not the organised working class, but those yet to be convinced by the Labour Party. In May, an election rally at which Marcus was to speak was advertised: a 'cordial' invitation was extended to the 'ladies' of Dundee.[95]

The rhetoric of class was now employed solely by the Communists. The party's advertisement for the programme of meetings to be undertaken during the 1929 campaign called explicitly on the 'workers' to 'rally', while the use of the colloquial 'Bob' to refer to Stewart contrasted with the accent placed by Labour on Marcus's university education and record as a coun-cillor in Edinburgh. Even more strikingly, of the sixteen meetings listed in the advert, no fewer than eleven were to be held outdoors, either at street corners in the working-class districts of Hilltown and Lochee, or in the city centre at Albert Square: the very public spaces from which Labour was now conspicuously absent.[96] This confrontational language of class was main-tained in Communist notices throughout the campaign. The appearance at a rally in support of Stewart of Tom Mann, a founding member of the CPGB active in the socialist movement since the 1880s, was welcomed as the arrival of a 'veteran working-class fighter'.[97] Soon after, the 'workers' were implored to 'Rally! Rally!! Rally!!!', and to 'assure victory for YOUR class' by voting for Stewart at the coming election.[98] The Communist appeal to class was clear; but equally evident was that this was an identity and style with which Labour no longer wished to be identified. Labour's unwillingness to engage in the masculine platform traditions of public politics was articulated most clearly by Marcus himself when, during one election meeting, he refused to agree to a debate with Stewart, informing his Communist hecklers that a general election was 'not the equivalent of a debating society'. 'From previous experience', Marcus continued, 'debates of that kind generally resulted in pandemonium and endless noise', and were a 'sheer waste of time'. Despite Communist accusations that he had 'insulted' working-class voters, Marcus remained unconcerned, directing his attentions elsewhere.[99] His claim that Liberal and Unionist voters were approaching him in the street and declaring that they intended to vote Labour for the first time may have been typical campaign bluster, but it nonetheless highlighted where Labour's electoral priorities now lay.[100]

The conduct of the 1929 election in Dundee suggested that the con-tinued attempts of the Conservatives to condemn the Labour Party by associating it with rowdyism had lost their force. Accusations that Labour remained a 'party of disturbance', such as were peddled by Frederick Wallace, the Unionist candidate in Dundee, were faintly ludicrous given the respectable campaign waged by Marcus.[101] In Edinburgh, it was reported that the general election had 'been quiet and well-mannered to the point of dullness'.[102] And although in Leith the successful re-election campaign of the Liberal MP Ernest Brown was marred by disruption from disgruntled Labour and Communist supporters, in Edinburgh Central there was reportedly 'an almost remarkable freedom from any jarring or unpleasant note', and a Liberal meeting in the constituency drew an audience of just seventeen.[103] Similarly, in Glasgow apathy was considered to be the 'outstanding feature' of the campaign.[104]

The abrupt disappearance of traditions of rowdyism was equally pronounced at the municipal elections of that year, when across urban Scotland a lack of popular enthusiasm was recorded.[105] The greatest change in Edinburgh was felt to have occurred in George Square, a ward previously notorious for animated election campaigns, but which was now characterised by an absence of heckling and an increased number of women present at meetings. As the campaign approached its close, one meeting was considered 'extraordinary', since 'lively meetings and George Square audiences have [been] almost as synonymous. From beginning to end the meeting ran as smoothly as though on rails, and five speakers were heard, questions were asked and answered in little over an hour.'[106] The traditional election ardour was maintained only in the working-class ward of St Leonard's, where David Lesslie was standing for the Communist Party.[107] There was 'no stir' surrounding the elections in Glasgow, where it was felt that, if the public were aware 'that there are elections', then 'they are not very interested'. Perhaps, the *Evening Times* wondered, interest would be 'aroused if . . . candidates assaulted each other to the effusion of blood'; thankfully, however, nowadays they were 'too self-controlled to do that'.[108]

Excluding the interventions in Edinburgh of Communist and Unemployed Workers' Movement candidates, a similar lethargy was apparent at the municipal elections of 1930.[109] The *Dundee Courier and Advertiser* attributed this steep decline in popular engagement to the 1929 restructuring of local government, and the abolition of the local education authorities and parish councils.[110] There was certainly an element of truth in such claims: as discussed in Chapter 3, the growing centralisation of government weakened local political cultures and traditions, and the qualms expressed by the *Courier* over the impact of the reforms had been echoed in Aberdeen.[111] Still, the identity of central government was as important as its increasing authority, with the presence of a Labour government between 1929 and 1931 hastening the party's disengagement from local traditions of radical protest. As *The Labour Organiser* remarked in 1930 when dismissing the criticisms of the Labour government then emanating from the ILP left, 'for the best part of thirty years, criticisms of successive governments have been the daily joy and food of Labour propagandists and supporters'. Now, however, Labour was ready to 'inherit the estate'.[112] Popular protest was the remedy resorted to by those excluded from national office: if Labour could form a government, and the borders of the polity had been made congruous with those of the people, what need had Labour supporters now of the old methods?

After the failure of the CPGB to return a single candidate at the 1929 election, one letter writer to the Labour *Dundee Free Press* ascribed the divergent fortunes of Labour and the CPGB to the 'method' Communist speakers employed when 'delivering the goods at the street corner', which was 'more repellent than persuasive'. As they explained, this was not a question of ideology but of conduct: Communist tactics deterred 'many . . . who look upon Communism as the ultimate human ideal, but deplore the methods of the Communist Party in journalism, propaganda and election-eering'.[113] This interpretation was echoed by Arthur Woodburn, unsuccess-ful as the Labour candidate in the safe Unionist seat of Edinburgh South in 1929. Writing in the *Edinburgh Labour Standard* after the 1930 municipal elections, Woodburn suggested that in an era of public assistance com-mittees and complex legislation dealing with pensions and unemployment insurance, 'the old style of propaganda simply breaks down before the new task of making the people understand the job, and speeches of twenty minutes to three-quarters of an hour can barely explain one point effec-tively'. Election meetings were of little use, and activists needed to accept that the majority of the electorate did not attend them: what was required was that Labour take its message to the home of the voter, via canvassing and newsletters.[114]

Indeed, during the 1930 municipal campaign Woodburn argued that Labour would benefit from the emergence of this new, more rational, electoral culture, since in the past the party's candidates had suffered because they had 'been compelled to use the street corner as their publicity centre. Shouting [was] found necessary, and deliberation [was] sacrificed to fervour.' In a telling analogy, Woodburn counselled that Labour candidates should 'be deliberate . . . let them take their points one by one, and when they do so they will, like the most successful court pleaders, build a strong case'.[115] Woodburn was undoubtedly influenced by his personal experience during the 1929 contest: as he reflected in his memoirs, the audiences in Edinburgh South 'were mostly professional and executive types [and] I was subject to questions which called for reasoned and informed answers'.[116]

Yet his argument reflected a wider belief that the conduct of meetings held under Labour auspices was an important indication of the party's ability to govern the country.[117] By the time the second Labour government collapsed in August 1931, then, the conduct of Labour politics had changed dramatically.

LOCAL ELECTIONEERING IN THE 1930s

Historians of both Labour and the Conservatives have suggested that the formation of the National Government in 1931, and the subsequent implementation of cuts to unemployment benefit and imposition of the family means test, encouraged Labour to move sharply to the left.[118] Yet while the alleged 'banker's ramp', and the party's rout at the 1931 general election following the decision of Ramsay MacDonald and Philip Snowden to hold office at the head of a National Government dominated by the Conservatives, may have led to a greater theoretical commitment to socialism from a Labour Party more dependent on the TUC than at any time since 1918, it did not inspire what Philip Williamson has described as a 'socialist analysis . . . more confrontational than gradualist'.[119] Given that Labour had been reduced to a parliamentary rump of fifty-two MPs, but remained utterly committed to constitutional means, whatever the peripheral endeavours of Sir Stafford Cripps and his associates in the Socialist League, it is difficult to understand in what sense the party's approach could be construed as anything other than gradualist.

The reactions of Labour election agents to the 1931 defeat recorded in *The Labour Organiser* indicate that, if anything, the result strengthened the belief that the old methods of agitation were outdated, and that Labour needed to broaden its appeal still further. For one agent, 'unanimous meetings' attended by vociferous supporters were not evidence of success, but rather 'of our failure to attract the people we want to convert'.[120] The party's election agent in Wallsend went further, arguing that Labour lost 'because the Great Silent Electorate, who are attached to no political party, who attend no election meeting, who usually take no interest in politics and do not bother to vote, at this election did vote, and voted solidly National'.[121] Labour contested the claim of the National Government to speak for the nation; but it did not, as the Communists did, claim to speak for a class and not the nation; nor did it return to the politics of the street.[122] As Drummond Shiels argued at an election meeting in Edinburgh East in 1931 above the shouts of 'no confidence' from Communist hecklers, 'the issue was not that of a National Government or anti-National Government. The Labour Party claimed to be as patriotic . . . as any party in the state.' In Leith, Woodburn was adamant that Labour had 'never countenanced any interruption of the meetings of our opponents, and it is patent to all that our opponents gain votes by those disturbances and we lose them'.[123]

By 1931 electoral politics was largely segregated from any wider popular discontent. Although National Labour candidates were subjected to abuse during the campaign that year, this was almost certainly orchestrated by Communist supporters.[124] This was undoubtedly the case in Aberdeen North, where local Communists, having adopted Helen Crawfurd as a 'workers' candidate', targeted the meetings of the sitting Labour MP, Wedgwood Benn, who, although he did not join the National Government, was widely believed to have considered doing so, and as a result saw his meetings marred by cries of 'traitor'.[125] The meetings of Dingle Foot, the successful Liberal candidate in Dundee in 1931, were subject to similar interruption, with supporters of the Communist candidate Bob Stewart singing 'The Red Flag' throughout.[126] In Greenock, supporters of the Communist candidate Aitken Ferguson burned effigies of the Liberal and Labour candidates.[127] And while unrest was reported in Glasgow in the St Rollox, Bridgeton and Shettleston divisions, overall the election was felt to have been 'fought in a sporting way', with the three major parties grasping that the 'determined partisans' who attended public meetings represented an 'insignificant proportion of the electorate'; as a result, party officials placed little weight on election meetings, accepting that the country was not 'governed by noise or demonstrations'.[128] In Edinburgh Central, where William Graham battled unsuccessfully to retain a seat held by Labour since 1918, the only meetings marked by the oratory and fervour of previous campaigns were those of Fred Douglas, the Communist candidate. As the *Evening Dispatch* commented approvingly, 'in the immediate post-war years an election campaign in this division was one prolonged howl; time and the gravity of the national situation have wrought a change which is welcomed by the three parties'.[129] The final phrase was the most telling: despite the circumstances and outcome of the election, Labour was now a recognised presence in national politics alongside the Conservatives and Liberals. The parties may have disputed who was best placed to speak for the nation, but none doubted there was a nation that required such representation.

As the prevalence of disruption during elections declined, and as the doubts regarding Labour's motivations were assuaged, such isolated disturbances as still occurred ceased to be viewed with trepidation. During the 1932 local elections in Aberdeen, considered 'quiet and free from rowdyism', there was even space for nostalgia.[130] On the eve of polling, the

Press and Journal, rather than issuing the usual frenzied plea for readers to vote against the Labour candidates, published an article entitled 'Elections fights that shook the whole city: fiery campaigns of the past'. The elections in question were not those of the previous decades, but of a generation before: gone were the allegations that popular rowdiness was evidence of Bolshevism; instead, it was a harmless feature of the political past. The local election of 1869 was deemed worthy of specific mention, a contest in which 'every blackcoat voted for the Lord Provost . . . and every fustian and canvas jacket for the so-called party of progress'. That year voters did not require 'to be pulled out to the poll . . . by the cajolery and pleading of canvassers; they rolled up in their hundreds . . . marching . . . in a body headed by pipers . . . with a flag flying in the breeze'. The account not only bore a striking resemblance to the form of electioneering still favoured by local Communists: it made a mockery of complaints that Labour had introduced class and party politics into local affairs. Certainly, the author could remember no contest as bitter of those of 1895 and 1902, which were marred by a 'party feeling' that ensured that 'most of the speeches were hot stuff, with the heckling ditto'.[131]

Despite the widespread unrest in Dundee following the introduction of the means test, the 1932 local elections were quieter than in previous years, apart from the interventions of supporters of the six Communist candidates, who engaged in 'community singing' and the disruption of Labour ward meetings.[132] The following year in Aberdeen, Labour ward meetings were targeted by Communist supporters in the working-class wards of St Machar and St Clements.[133] Indeed, by the early 1930s there were even complaints at the apparent lack of public interest in local elections, reflected in the low levels of voter turnout. The *Glasgow Evening Times* issued an open letter to 'apathetic' electors, urging them to ignore other, more superficial attractions – such as those offered by the 'flaxen-haired sirens of Hollywood' – and ensure that they cast their votes.[134] In Aberdeen, the *Evening Express* demanded to know 'why on earth are so many reluctant to vote?'; the apathy of the 1930s was contrasted with the sentiments displayed when the franchise was reformed in 1832, and 'bonfires blazed and monuments were erected in celebration'.[135] It was, then, principally the Communists who reacted to the events of 1931 by pursuing confrontational forms of politics. At a meeting held by the independent candidate James Fraser during the 1934 municipal elections in Dundee, an estimated fifty Communists, led by James Littlejohn, commandeered the platform, aided by a megaphone; at subsequent ward meetings uniformed and plainclothes police were in attendance, and resort to the 1908 Act threatened. Yet such interventions aside, the election campaign was considered to have been 'singularly dull and uninteresting'. The *Courier and Advertiser* concluded that election meetings were of little import: voting was now the 'sole means' of expressing public opinion.[136]

The analysis of electoral culture should caution historians against writing the history of inter-war politics in ideological terms. For what it was worth, British Communism mined a deeper seam of class-based discontent and popular political tradition alongside an explicit identification with Soviet Russia. Equally, while the CPGB may well have retreated from the extremes of 'class against class' at a national level by 1934, this was not necessarily mirrored locally. At the Aberdeen South by-election of May 1935, local Communists were quite willing to wreck both Labour and Unionist meetings. The Labour candidate Joseph Duncan, founder of the Scottish Farm Servants' Union, was shouted down furiously when he responded to a question regarding the means test by stating that all governments, whatever their composition, had a duty to act responsibly when disbursing public money. Sir Douglas Thomson, contesting the seat on behalf of the Unionists following the death of his father, the previous MP, saw his platform seized by a Communist orator.[137] Viewed from this perspective, the ongoing popular depiction of the 1930s as a decade of heightened political awareness and competing ideologies appears questionable.[138] The 1935 general election was, in Dundee at least, said to be 'practically one of the dullest and least lively on record'.[139] Likewise, in Glasgow, besides the disruption endured by James Maxton in his Bridgeton seat at the hands of right-wing hecklers, the campaign was reportedly 'conducted with a gentle decorum', which had rendered it 'easily the quietest in recent years': it had, indeed, been 'singularly free from passion or excitement'.[140] In Aberdeen the municipal elections of that year were apparently 'practically featureless'.[141] The only evidence of heckling and disruption during the local elections in Edinburgh was provided by those who operated on the fringes of national politics. Supporters of John Cormack's Protestant Action Society targeted Moderate and Labour meetings, interrupting proceedings with shouts of 'no popery' and questions regarding the public subsidy granted to Roman Catholic schools.[142]

Ostensibly, the success of militant Protestantism in both Edinburgh and Glasgow suggests that the politics of the street retained some appeal during the 1930s. Cormack was undoubtedly an accomplished street-corner orator, who relied on the traditions of the platform to deliver his sectarian political message, and whose supporters happily employed physical intimidation against their religious and political opponents. Furthermore, the support Protestant Action attained in the municipal elections in Edinburgh, polling over 25 per cent in 1935 and over 30 per cent in 1936, was of a degree that local Communists could only envy.[143] However, we should not exaggerate the importance of Protestant Action. The organisation's success was relatively short-lived, with the Protestant vote falling to 12 per cent in 1938, and although Cormack survived as a councillor until 1962, he had long since exchanged the rough and tumble of street politics for the role of local institution.[144] If anything, the commitment of Protestant Action to a politics of physicality ensured that the Unionists, Orange Order and Protestant churches all refused to associate with Cormack, despite the shameful willingness of the Church of Scotland to indulge anti-Irish sentiment between the wars.[145] Support for Protestant Action was, then, akin to Communist support in the mining communities of West Fife: highly localised, maintained via the personal standing in the community of specific individuals, and ultimately unable to influence national politics. Protestant Action could not even reach an understanding with the Glasgow-based Scottish Protestant League; indeed, the chief political achievement of the latter organisation was to split the anti-socialist vote in Glasgow, and thereby hand control of the council to the Labour Party.

The limited success of militant Protestantism in fact reinforced the frontiers of acceptable political conduct, and encouraged the admittance of Labour to the political mainstream. As the *Edinburgh Evening Dispatch* argued after Protestant Action's emergence at the 1935 local elections, the question was now 'clearly not so much between Moderate or Progressive and their old enemies, the Socialists'. Accepting that it had never before supported the return of Labour candidates, the *Dispatch* nevertheless now chose to praise the contribution Labour councillors had made to the conduct of local government. The real political enemy were those responsible for the 'stormy scenes which have drowned the voice of the opposition and throttled that freedom of speech which should be the prerogative of every party'.[146] Conduct, not policy, was the key to membership of the political nation.[147]

CONCLUSION

During the 1932 municipal election campaign in Edinburgh, the three Moderate councillors in the ward of Portobello convened a meeting with the intention of reporting on their work on the town council in the previous year. After just thirty-five minutes, following the intervention of the Communist candidate Fred Douglas and his supporters, the meeting was abandoned. Douglas had demanded to be allowed to join the platform party, declaring that the audience had 'the right to hear all the candidates'. This appeal to electoral tradition was rejected: Douglas was informed that the hall had been hired by those on the platform, and he was welcome to do likewise; the chants of 'we want Douglas' continued until the meeting was declared closed. Triumphant, Douglas clambered atop a chair and began to speak; as he did so, however, the janitor turned off the lights, and Douglas and his followers exited the hall in darkness.[148]

The account offered of the meeting by an unsympathetic press is perhaps a little too neat, the metaphor provided by the caretaker's actions perhaps a little too obvious. Nevertheless, the sense remains of two mutually incomprehensible conceptions of politics in conflict, of a participatory, customary and communal understanding being dismissed by a more professional approach, of a victory for politics as administration. Had the meeting occurred a decade earlier Douglas could perhaps have celebrated a victory, having successfully seized an opponent's meeting. But the distance between the electoral culture of the early 1920s and that of the 1930s was vast, both in the behaviour of those seeking election, and the dwindling audiences they addressed.

This alteration took two forms: first, local ward meetings lost prestige as national and international issues came to dominate British politics. As is made abundantly clear by the local press across Scotland, the municipal elections of the early 1930s had, as a consequence of the increasing importance of Westminster in questions of social policy, lost status. There was, however, a second aspect apparent during both municipal and parliamentary election campaigns. This was the absence of the disruption that had characterised the contests of the early 1920s. Here the question of the relationship between the Labour and Communist parties is of vital importance, despite the seeming irrelevance of the latter. If, in Peter Clarke's phrase, the threat posed by Communism in Britain proved to be little more than a 'phantasm', it was nevertheless an exceedingly useful one, deployed first by Labour's opponents to portray the party as a threat to the constitution, and thereafter by Labour as a contrast to emphasise its commitment to that constitution.[149]

The conduct of elections provided a crucial means of distinguishing between Labour and Communist politics. Conservative and Liberal attempts to use electoral rowdyism to depict Labour as representative of a narrow class interest encouraged all three major parties to abandon the open election meeting and the traditions of the platform. This process was accelerated by the ongoing commitment of the CPGB to these traditions, and the targeting of Labour meetings by Communist supporters after 1928. The latter development granted a welcome plausibility to Labour's denials of any link between the two parties, so often hampered before 1926 by the support given to Labour candidates by local Communists. Moreover, it performed the central function of placing Labour on an equal footing alongside the Liberals and Conservatives as a national party of government, defending the constitution from political extremism. By the 1930s the crucial political division was not that suggested by the electoral contests of the early 1920s, of Labour and the broader left against the Liberal and Conservative establishment, but of the parties of the centre against the political extremes. While there were those in both Labour and Conservative ranks who were sympathetic to Communism and Fascism, the sense that engagement with political violence placed a party beyond the political pale remained powerful. Once rowdyism had become synonymous with extremism, as was largely the case by 1926, the Conservatives had, however cynical the initial intentions, bound their own party by the narrative they and their supporters in the media had constructed as much as they had Labour.[150] The Communists, alongside the ILP, Mosley's Fascists and the militant Protestants, were unable to contest this new political atmosphere, no matter their isolated local successes.

Prior to 1918, the theory of virtual representation had embraced multiple connections, linking parliament and MPs to the enfranchised, and the electorate to those beyond the franchise; in turn, this necessitated a variety of forums in which public opinion could be expressed. By the 1930s, however, this had been replaced by a single, direct link between individual voters and their representatives in parliament. As the *Glasgow Evening Times* opined in 1937 in a celebration of Britain's constitutional exceptionalism, 'we are a democratic people, and we had never more reason to be jealous of our principle of democracy than we have to-day': the only alternative visible elsewhere was the 'dictatorship of Fascism and Communism'. British politics was electoral politics, and elections were the sum of individual votes, and the sole legitimate measure of public opinion. As the constitution came to embrace the entire political nation, the belief in working-class exceptionalism declined, and the popular traditions of electoral rowdyism were at an end.

NOTES

1. *Dundee Courier*, 27 Oct. 1922.
2. On the culture surrounding election meetings prior to 1918, see: Good, 'Quit Ye Like Men'; Lawrence, *Electing Our Masters*, pp. 43–95.
3. Thompson, 'Pictorial Lies?'; Lawrence, *Electing Our Masters*. For the former view, see: O'Gorman, 'Campaign Rituals and Ceremonies'; Vernon, *Politics and the People*.
4. On this shift, see: Lawrence, 'Forging a Peaceable Kingdom', and 'The Transformation of British Public Politics'.

5. *The Labour Organiser*, vol. 96 (Jun. 1929), p. 106.
6. Beers, *Your Britain*, esp. pp. 11–26 and 199–204.
7. On this, see: Beers, 'Counter-Toryism', pp. 234–9.
8. *Glasgow Evening Times*, 11 Nov. 1922.
9. Gallacher, *Rolling of the Thunder*, pp. 44–6; Walker, 'Dundee's Disenchantment with Churchill', and *Juteopolis*, pp. 439–85.
10. *Aberdeen Evening Express*, 9 and 10 Nov. 1922.
11. *Aberdeen Daily Journal*, 17 Nov. 1922.
12. *Edinburgh Evening Dispatch*, 31 Oct. and 15 Nov. 1922. On the role of military service in enhancing a candidate's 'manly' appeal prior to 1918, see: Good, 'Quit Ye Like Men', pp. 158–9.
13. *Edinburgh Evening Dispatch*, 15 Nov. 1922.
14. *Glasgow Evening Times*, 4 Nov. 1922.
15. Lawrence, 'The Transformation of British Public Politics', pp. 189–90.
16. On such fears, see: Jarvis, 'British Conservatism and Class Politics', and 'The Shaping of Conservative Electoral Hegemony', esp. pp. 131–2; McKibbin, *Classes and Cultures*, pp. 50–9.
17. *Dundee Courier*, 4 Dec. 1923.
18. *Glasgow Herald*, 26 Nov. 1923.
19. *Glasgow Herald*, 27 Nov. 1923; *Glasgow Evening Times*, 30 Nov. 1923.
20. *Glasgow Herald*, 29 and 30 Nov. 1923.
21. *Glasgow Herald*, 1 Dec. 1923. See also: Lawrence, 'The Transformation of British Public Politics', p. 207.
22. *Glasgow Herald*, 5 Dec. 1923; *Glasgow Evening Times*, 30 Nov. 1923.
23. *Aberdeen Press and Journal*, 28 Nov. 1923.
24. *Dundee Advertiser*, 23 Nov. 1923.
25. *Edinburgh Evening Dispatch*, 28 and 30 Nov., 4 Dec. 1923.
26. *Glasgow Evening Times*, 3 Dec. 1923.
27. *Edinburgh Evening Dispatch*, 6 Dec. 1923.
28. *Aberdeen Press and Journal*, 6 Dec. 1923.
29. *Dundee Advertiser*, 23 Nov. 1923.
30. *Dundee Advertiser*, 29 Nov. 1923; *Glasgow Herald*, 1 Dec. 1923.
31. On the 1908 Act, see: Lawrence, *Electing Our Masters*, pp. 88–9.
32. *Dundee Advertiser*, 1 Dec. 1923. Similar accusations were made by the press in Aberdeen, see: *Aberdeen Evening Express*, 24 Nov. 1923.
33. *Dundee Advertiser*, 1 Dec. 1923.
34. On the wider context of sympathy with Italian Fascism in Britain during the 1920s, see: Bosworth, 'The British Press, the Conservatives, and Mussolini'; Pugh, *Hurrah for the Blackshirts*, pp. 37–50.
35. *Aberdeen Evening Express*, 30 Oct. 1922.
36. *Aberdeen Press and Journal*, 29 Oct. 1923.
37. *Aberdeen Press and Journal*, 24 Oct. 1924.
38. *Glasgow Evening Times*, 3 Dec. 1923; *Glasgow Herald*, 4 Dec. 1923.

39. *The Scotsman*, 27 Oct. 1924. On the British Fascisti, see: Pugh, *Hurrah for the Blackshirts*, pp. 51–74.
40. *Edinburgh Evening Dispatch*, 14, 15, 16 and 17 Oct. 1924.
41. *Edinburgh Evening Dispatch*, 18, 22 and 24 Oct. 1924.
42. *Aberdeen Press and Journal*, 21 Oct. 1924.
43. On the conduct of the 1924 election, see: Ramsden, *The Age of Balfour and Baldwin*, pp. 202–7.
44. *Dundee Courier*, 26 Sept. 1924.
45. See, for example, the comments of George Archibald, E. D. Morel and William Graham, the Labour candidates in, respectively, South Aberdeen, Dundee and Edinburgh Central in 1924: *Aberdeen Evening Express*, 16 Oct. 1924; *Dundee Advertiser*, 18 Oct. 1924; *Edinburgh Evening Dispatch*, 16 Oct. 1924.
46. *Dundee Courier*, 24 Oct. 1924.
47. *Aberdeen Evening Express*, 15, 17 and 24 Oct. 1924.
48. *Aberdeen Press and Journal*, 29 Oct. and 3 Nov. 1924.
49. *Glasgow Evening Times*, 20 Oct. 1924.
50. Thackeray, 'Building a Peaceable Party', pp. 663–6.
51. Jarvis, 'Mrs. Maggs and Betty'.
52. *Aberdeen Press and Journal*, 23 Oct. 1924.
53. See the reports of reactions to heckling in: *Dundee Advertiser*, 16 Oct. 1924; *Aberdeen Evening Express*, 18 Oct. 1924.
54. *Aberdeen Evening Express*, 15 and 17 Oct. 1924.
55. *Forward*, 8 Dec. 1923.
56. *Glasgow Evening Times*, 20 Oct. 1924.
57. On the rise of this 'constitutional Conservatism' see: McKibbin, 'Class and Conventional Wisdom'.
58. Schwarz, 'Language of Constitutionalism', p. 3.
59. *Glasgow Evening Times*, 22 Oct. 1924.
60. *Aberdeen Press and Journal*, 30 Oct. 1924.
61. *Dundee Advertiser*, 29 and 31 Oct. 1925.
62. Ramsden, *The Age of Balfour and Baldwin*, pp. 208–15; Schwarz, 'Language of Constitutionalism', pp. 11–14; McKibbin, 'Class and Conventional Wisdom'; Nicholas, 'The Construction of a National Identity'.
63. Williamson, *Stanley Baldwin*, pp. 207–8.
64. *Aberdeen Evening Express*, 17 Oct. 1924.
65. *Aberdeen Evening Express*, 27 and 31 Oct. 1924.
66. *Aberdeen Press and Journal*, 30 Oct. 1924.
67. *Aberdeen Evening Express*, 29 Oct. 1925; *Edinburgh Evening Dispatch*, 23 Oct. 1925.
68. *Dundee Courier*, 30 Oct. 1923.
69. *Dundee Advertiser*, 28 Oct. 1925.
70. *Aberdeen Press and Journal*, 28 Oct. 1926.
71. *Aberdeen Evening Express*, 2 Nov. 1926.

72. Griffiths, *Labour and the Countryside*.
73. *Edinburgh Evening Dispatch*, 22 and 29 Oct. 1926.
74. *The Labour Organiser*, vol. 67 (Sept. 1926), pp. 142 and 155.
75. *Aberdeen Citizen*, 22 Dec. 1927.
76. LHASC Labour Party NEC: E. Wake, *Leith By-Election Report*, 27 Apr. 1927.
77. On the transition to 'Class Against Class', see: Thorpe, *The British Communist Party and Moscow*, pp. 117–55. On the ILP during this period, and the publication of the Cook–Maxton manifesto, see: McKinlay and Smyth, 'The End of the "Agitator Workman"', pp. 184–9; Howell, *MacDonald's Party*, pp. 264–87.
78. H. Morrison, 'The ECCI's Lament', *The Labour Magazine*, vol. 7(1) (May 1928), p. 13.
79. *Aberdeen Press and Journal*, 10 Jan. 1928.
80. *Aberdeen Evening Express*, 10 and 15 Aug. 1928.
81. *Aberdeen Evening Express*, 8 and 14 Aug. 1928.
82. See the reports in: *Aberdeen Evening Express*, 8 Aug. 1928; *Aberdeen Press and Journal*, 8 Aug. 1928.
83. *Aberdeen Evening Express*, 16 Aug. 1928.
84. IWM Acc. 804: Interview with R. Cooney, Reel 1.
85. *Aberdeen Citizen*, 24 Aug. 1928.
86. *The Labour Organiser*, vol. 75 (Sept. 1927), pp. 97–9.
87. *Glasgow Evening Times*, 3 Nov. 1928.
88. *Aberdeen Press and Journal*, 5 Nov. 1928.
89. *Edinburgh Evening Dispatch*, 23 Oct. 1928.
90. See, for example: Todd, *The People*, pp. 62–5.
91. *Dundee Courier and Advertiser*, 21 and 27 May 1929.
92. *Dundee Free Press*, 28 May 1929.
93. See: Worley, *Labour Inside the Gate*, p. 71.
94. *Dundee Free Press*, 8 Feb. 1929.
95. *Dundee Free Press*, 29 May 1929.
96. *Dundee Free Press*, 17 May 1929.
97. *Dundee Free Press*, 23 May 1929.
98. *Dundee Free Press*, 24 May 1929. Capitalisation in original.
99. *Dundee Free Press*, 27 and 28 May 1929.
100. *Dundee Courier and Advertiser*, 29 May 1929.
101. *Dundee Free Press*, 24 May 1929.
102. *Edinburgh Evening Dispatch*, 18 May 1929.
103. *Edinburgh Evening Dispatch*, 16, 17, 24 and 28 May 1929.
104. *Glasgow Evening Times*, 20 May 1929.
105. See, for example, the various reports on the elections in: *Aberdeen Evening Express*, 6 Nov. 1929; *Aberdeen Press and Journal*, 5 and 6 Nov. 1929; *Dundee Courier and Advertiser*, 26 and 31 Oct. 1929; *Edinburgh Evening Dispatch*, 22 and 31 Oct. 1929; *Glasgow Evening Times*, 2 Nov. 1929.

106. *Edinburgh Evening Dispatch*, 22 and 31 Oct. 1929.

107. *Edinburgh Evening Dispatch*, 25 Oct. 1929.

108. *Glasgow Evening Times*, 2 Nov. 1929.

109. *Aberdeen Evening Express*, 3 and 4 Nov. 1930; *Aberdeen Press and Journal*, 29 Oct. 1930. On the CPGB in Edinburgh see: *Edinburgh Evening Dispatch*, 22, 25 and 30 Oct., 4 Nov. 1930.

110. *Dundee Courier and Advertiser*, 2 Nov. 1929 and 25 Oct. 1930.

111. *Aberdeen Evening Express*, 2 Jul. 1928.

112. *The Labour Organiser*, vol. 109 (Jul. 1930), p. 117.

113. *Dundee Free Press*, 9 Aug. 1929.

114. *Edinburgh Labour Standard*, 15 Nov. 1930.

115. *Edinburgh Labour Standard*, 25 Oct. 1930. This transition from oratory to canvassing in Labour campaigns is also highlighted by Ball, Thorpe and Worley, 'Elections, Leaflets and Whist Drives'.

116. NLS Acc. 7656/4/4: Arthur Woodburn, 'Living with History' (TS Unpublished Autobiography, n.d.), p. 62.

117. See the comments in: *The Labour Organiser*, vol. 98 (Aug. 1929), p. 161.

118. See, for example: Williamson, *National Crisis and National Government*, pp. 150–1.

119. Williamson, *National Crisis and National Government*, p. 458.

120. *The Labour Organiser*, vol. 125 (Nov. 1931), p. 205.

121. *The Labour Organiser*, vol. 126 (Dec. 1931), p. 234.

122. On this point see: Beers, 'Counter-Toryism', pp. 250–4.

123. *Edinburgh Evening Dispatch*, 13 and 22 Oct. 1931.

124. Thorpe, *The British General Election of 1931*, pp. 190–2.

125. *Aberdeen Evening Express*, 15 Oct. 1931; *Aberdeen Press and Journal*, 6, 8 and 9 Oct. 1931.

126. *Dundee Courier and Advertiser*, 21 Oct. 1931.

127. NRS HH55/670 Greenock Demonstrations and Disturbances: Chief Constable to Under-Secretary of State, 14 Oct. 1931.

128. *Glasgow Evening Times*, 26 Oct. 1931.

129. *Edinburgh Evening Dispatch*, 14 and 16 Oct. 1931.

130. *Aberdeen Evening Express*, 31 Oct. 1932.

131. *Aberdeen Press and Journal*, 1 Nov. 1932.

132. *Dundee Courier and Advertiser*, 25, 26 and 29 Oct., 1 and 2 Nov. 1932.

133. *Aberdeen Press and Journal*, 1 and 3 Nov. 1933.

134. *Glasgow Evening Times*, 28 Oct. 1932.

135. *Aberdeen Evening Express*, 3 Nov. 1934.

136. *Dundee Courier and Advertiser*, 30 Oct., 1 and 3 Nov. 1934.

137. *Aberdeen Press and Journal*, 9 and 18 May 1935.

138. See, for example, the account offered in: Overy, *The Morbid Age*, pp. 50–92 and 265–313.

139. *Dundee Courier and Advertiser*, 12 Nov. 1935.

140. *Glasgow Evening Times*, 7 and 14 Nov. 1935.

141. *Aberdeen Press and Journal*, 6, 13 and 14 Nov. 1935.
142. *Edinburgh Evening Dispatch*, 22, 24, 26 and 30 Oct., 2 Nov. 1935.
143. Bruce, *No Pope of Rome*, pp. 83–107; Gallagher, 'Protestant Extremism in Urban Scotland'.
144. On Cormack's later transformation, see: Gallagher, *Edinburgh Divided*, pp. 159–83.
145. Brown, 'Outside the Covenant'.
146. *Edinburgh Evening Dispatch*, 4 Nov. 1935.
147. For the contrary view that anti-Socialism remained central to municipal politics in the 1930s, see: Smyth, 'Resisting Labour'.
148. *Edinburgh Evening Dispatch*, 26 Oct. 1932; *The Scotsman*, 26 Oct. 1932.
149. Clarke, *Hope and Glory*, p. 106.
150. On the constraints on the relationship between the Conservatives and the British Union of Fascists, see: Lawrence, 'Fascist Violence and the Politics of Public Order'. This view has been challenged by Martin Pugh, see: 'The National Government, the British Union of Fascists and the Olympia Debate'. For Lawrence's reply, see: 'Why Olympia Mattered'.

Conclusion:
Popular Politics, Radicalism and Inter-war Democracy

In November 1933, the *Dundee Evening Telegraph and Post* reported the death, at the age of seventy-nine, of Sandy Gow. A member of the local parish council for more than thirty years, Gow was a renowned figure within Dundee politics over half a century. But his had also been a very public engagement with Dundee politics: a committed Radical Liberal, in 1884 Gow led a demonstration in the city in support of the third reform act that was estimated to number 20,000; he was responsible too for setting alight the effigy of the Liberal Unionist Joseph Chamberlain in the city's Albert Square four years later, once more before a crowd of 20,000. Gow was also a notorious presence at municipal and parliamentary election meetings, famed for his pointed questions and exquisitely timed interventions. Nonetheless, his obituarist acknowledged, in terms flecked with sorrow, that his passing had marked the severing of a 'venerable link with the bye-gone days when election meetings were battles of words', and 'heckling was heckling'.[1]

Gow's demise, and the accompanying acceptance that the political culture which he had embodied, with its amalgam of local personalities and bellicose forms of political participation, had drawn to a close, captures neatly the ways in which political identities and conduct altered in urban Scotland after 1918, especially among those on the political left who had inherited the radical tradition. To summarise (and, of course, to simplify), the Communists, and, after 1932, their peers in the ILP who chose to disaffiliate from the Labour Party, clung to the model of politics represented by Gow. The Labour Party, in contrast, traded the politics of place for those of the nation. Popular politics in Scotland and Britain were, then, reshaped during the inter-war decades. Local political identities, and especially those which had sustained the popular radical tradition, were integrated within a more uniform national political contest, while the mass franchise altered the way in which the relationship between the people and parliament was understood on the political left; politics was depicted in inclusive rather than oppositional terms. More than this, the means by which politics was pursued changed, and popular traditions of public involvement in politics came to be tarnished by association with political extremism in general, and Communism in particular. Of course, this is not to suggest that inter-war politics became entirely homogeneous: regional differences in political allegiance endured, and general elections still produced winners and losers. All the same, it remains the case that, by the 1930s if not before, British politics was carried out in the near-universal belief that the electorate, and the politicians who hoped to secure their votes, were participants in a democratic system capable of accommodating – within reason – all political creeds, no matter how keen the electoral contest became. There was, in effect, now a single forum in which political identities were to be expressed, and it was a shared national one; those who refused to adjust were left politically isolated.

A number of factors contributed to the fashioning of this new national politics. The consolidation of the press and the arrival of radio changed how politicians and parties communicated with the enlarged post-war electorate.[2] Further, the abolition of parish councils and education authorities in 1929, and the growing role of central government in welfare provision, reduced the standing of local government, leaving parliamentary elections as the pre-eminent political contest and measure of public opinion, with clear consequences for the cause of Scottish home rule. Equally, the scale of the inter-war economic crisis, particularly during the depression of the 1930s, ensured that local solutions appeared ineffective, and the focus of Labour politics moved to Westminster. But these structural and material factors were accompanied by a deeper cultural shift, one occasioned by the extension of the franchise, the apprehension caused by the rise of Communism in Europe, and the domestic upheaval that followed the end of the First World War.[3] It was this broader context that made the forceful public display of sectional, local political identities, a tactic deployed by Radicals such as Gow as well as their Tory opponents throughout the nineteenth and early twentieth centuries, appear now as a threat to social and political stability.[4] Rallies and demonstrations, heckling and disruption, militant banners and songs – all were interpreted differently after the arrival of mass democracy, the admission of women to the ranks of the electorate, Labour's ascent to government office, and the advance of Bolshevism overseas. The transformation of the franchise from a trust, held and exercised by propertied, independent male electors on behalf of the community, into something approaching an individual right challenged the very premise of virtual representation.

Competing sectional interests no longer required a voice within the political arena; neither was there any need now for vocal interventions from those outside the ranks of the electorate. And while the years from 1918 to 1926 were marked by political instability, especially during the three general elections held between November 1922 and October 1924, the tranquillity of British politics after 1926 is all the more conspicuous when contrasted with the intense political contests of the Edwardian era, and the rifts created by the questions of Irish home rule, free trade and House of Lords reform. We have, then, been tracing a change in the basis upon which British politics was conducted, as appeals to class largely disappeared from mainstream political debate, and the electoral contest between Labour and the Conservatives was remade as a question of competing images of the nation. Certainly, no major party dared run on a platform as brazenly populist and confrontational as that adopted by the Liberals in 1910, or felt able to challenge parliamentary sovereignty in the manner of the Unionist opponents of Irish home rule in 1912.[5] The extension of the franchise, by framing politics as an individual rather than collective pursuit, forced Labour to convert from being a sectional voice into being the representative of the 'people', the 'nation', and the 'community'. But this was not an automatic process: the reforms of 1918 and 1928 did not merely grant the vote to sections of the populace predisposed to vote Labour by virtue of their economic status: a similar, and more successful, process could also be discerned in Conservative politics.

It was local perceptions of the role of the Labour Party, and, more broadly, the popular radical tradition of which it was the chief inheritor, that changed most abruptly: the party, and its local institutions, ceased to be a vehicle for oppositional, outsider sentiment, but became rather one of three, and then in effect two, parties which claimed to speak for the interests of the nation. This shift in rhetoric, and in understandings of Labour's role, was accelerated by the identification of local class identities and public political traditions with a contentious politics of class. Labour, subjected to lurid accusations of Bolshevism by the Conservative press throughout the 1920s, abandoned these customary forms of political engagement, and adopted instead unambiguously constitutional methods. Labour politics moved indoors both metaphorically and literally, leaving the street corners and public squares of urban Scotland in the hands of the Communists and the disaffected ILP left. This physical distinction between an outmoded local politics of class and national electioneering was plainly understood: in December 1928, *The Labour Organiser*, in an article dispensing advice on how to properly plan and conduct election meetings, urged that only national figures and approved party candidates be used as speakers. That this would upset the local orators who had traditionally addressed such meetings was accepted; these characters were, it was noted, 'always a problem and sometimes a nuisance'. Still, Labour election agents were directed to exclude such personalities, who, it was suggested with just a hint of condescension, could 'retain a sense of [their] own importance by being asked to address an outdoor meeting'.[6] The hierarchies underpinning such a statement were clear; crucially, they were shared locally as well as nationally.

It is, therefore, chiefly in the domain of political practice that local relations on the political left in Scotland are of wider importance. The CPGB mattered during the inter-war decades not because of the particular ideology it promoted, but because the very presence of the party in British political life influenced the behaviour of others. If Liberals and Conservatives were keen to use Communism to label Labour as a class party, then Labour figures, both local and national, were convinced that, for their party to succeed in electoral terms, any suggestion of links with the CPGB had to be avoided. This required the distancing of Labour from local expressions of class identity and from the traditional sites of radical politics. By the 1930s these attempts had largely succeeded, and Labour had come to be an accepted actor in national politics, derided, to be sure, for its alleged financial incompetence, but no longer viewed seriously as the harbinger of Bolshevism. Too often, the scale of Labour's electoral rout in 1931, and the narratives of betrayal that surround the creation of the National Government, has ensured that the party's broader electoral success has been obscured: but even in defeat Labour received more than 6 million votes, and secured a share of the poll only marginally below that achieved in 1923. And although the result was distorted by the electoral system and the uncommon unity of the coalition confronting Labour, the party had, even with just fifty-two MPs, only exchanged government for opposition, and would retrieve its share of the vote, if not its place in office, by 1935. Even if we exclude the wartime coalition in place after 1940, the fourteen years Labour waited for an election victory after 1931 made the cost of defeat only marginally more ruinous than that suffered in 1951, and less disastrous than that of 1979.

British politics by the 1930s was a national electoral contest in which Labour, having cast off the trappings and traditions of class, was an acknowledged participant; it was, moreover, a contest that centred clearly on Westminster, even in the context of Scotland. This is the essential narrative of politics between the wars. A focus on individual parties, the policies they espoused and the electoral struggle between them, can overshadow the substantial practical agreement which existed among the major political parties, and which precluded opposing viewpoints. By the close of the inter-war decades, there existed in Britain a broad consensus regarding legitimate political identities, conduct and rhetoric. This consensus played a crucial role both in defining the boundaries of the political nation, and in shaping the particular appeals made by individual parties. If there were exceptions to this on the political left and right, then in truth these served only to illuminate the political harmony that faced, and excluded, them. This is the real purpose of examining the radical left in this period, and particularly the CPGB: to uncover what electoral failure reveals of the wider political culture within which the left operated. The travails of British Communists; their inability to cultivate a mass appeal; their exclusion from national politics except as a shadowy threat in the propaganda of others, which, humiliatingly, was not even directed at the CPGB: taken together these factors suggest that those who entered British politics after 1918 and sought to speak for a section of the electorate and not the whole were unlikely to succeed. The emergence of a more coherent national politics limited the appeals parties were able to make, and necessitated the construction of broad and inclusive political identities. While Labour and the Conservatives were, with varying degrees of success, able to achieve this, those on the radical left, with their focus on class and the virtues of the locality, appeared in public only as a reminder of what British politics was not.

The origins of the two-party political contest of the post-1945 era, and the so-called politics of consensus, are, then, to be found in the remodel-ling of British political culture during the 1920s, and extend beyond an acceptance of the mixed economy and a degree of economic planning to encompass a range of assumptions regarding the nature of democracy, political engagement, and membership of the polity. Similarly, the cross-class appeal associated with the 'new' Labour project of the late twentieth century was, as we have seen, far from novel: its proponents were heirs to a deep-rooted strand in Labour thought, one that understood the necessity of compromise in securing electoral success, and which was alive to the dangers of being identified with a narrow appeal to class. Those lessons have, of course, been unlearnt at various points in the party's history. Equally, the political consensus that arose during the 1920s and 1930s, with its acceptance of Westminster as the guarantor of British liberty and faith in the potential of parliamentary democracy, did not endure without complication, and by the 1970s it was once more possible to speak for a part of the whole, as the rise of political nationalism in Scotland and Wales, and the recrudescence of Irish republicanism, make clear. If this study has explored the creation of a democratic British political nation in the context of Scotland, then the cause of the fragmentation of that nation, as the boundaries, rules and expectations that had sustained popular faith in it were eroded, remains open to discussion.

This is what an examination of the radical left in urban Scotland offers: an indication of the particular course followed by British politics after 1918. Across Europe, and especially in France and Germany, the inter-war decades witnessed an increased use of public space as a means of shaping political identities, and a rise in political violence as competing factions fought for control of specific sites.[7] Political convictions were, as a result, transferred from private to public spaces such as streets, squares and taverns, politicising the everyday; politics became about more than just elections, as dominance in the streets, achieved via processions and demonstrations, became a vital objective, and the crowd came to be viewed as a source of political legitimacy.[8] Yet in Britain, trust in parliament, and a popular reading of franchise reform as the resolution of class conflict, strengthened a self-fulfilling belief in British constitutional and political exceptionalism, and created a sense of distance from (and complacency about) events in continental Europe. The result was that, unlike elsewhere in Europe, politics in Britain was not a communal activity, and political allegiances were not something to be displayed physically in public spaces. Instead, the reverse was true: rather than the politicisation of pubs, streets and neighbourhoods, public space in inter-war Britain was depoliticised, and politics remade as a private, individual act, executed by members of an electorate who were, whatever the social and economic realities, in this regard at least, theoretically equal. There was no room within this conception of politics for those who clung to models of representation and participation that granted primacy to the local, the collective and the sectional. By the 1930s, and for at least a generation after, popular politics in Scotland and Britain was moulded by the centripetal force of the mass franchise and the untrammelled prestige of parliamentary democracy, which discredited alternative understandings of political action and largely removed legitimate politics from public sight. This distinguished inter-war politics in Scotland and Britain from that witnessed elsewhere in Europe, as well as from the domestic political culture which preceded and followed it.

NOTES

1. *Dundee Evening Telegraph and Post*, 23 Nov. 1933.
2. Beers, *Your Britain*.
3. Lawrence, 'Forging a Peaceable Kingdom'.
4. On the political culture of Scottish radicalism in the nineteenth century, see: Nixon, Pentland and Roberts, 'The Material Culture of Scottish Reform Politics'.

5. Beers and Thomas, 'Introduction'; Lawrence, 'Labour and the Politics of Class'.
6. *The Labour Organiser*, vol. 90 (Dec. 1928), pp. 233–4.
7. On France, see: Dell, *The Image of the Popular Front*, pp. 44–91; Jackson, *The Popular Front in France*, pp. 114–21; Millington, 'Street-fighting Men'; Wardhaugh, *In Pursuit of the People*. On Germany, see: Brown, *Weimar Radicals*; Epstein, *The Last Revolutionaries*; Fischer, 'Unemployment and Left-Wing Radicalism in Weimar Germany'; Fischer, *The German Communists and the Rise of Nazism*, pp. 138–61; Rosenhaft, 'The Unemployed in the Neighbourhood'; Rosenhaft, *Beating the Fascists?*; Stibbe, *Germany: Politics, Society and Culture, 1914–1933*, pp. 67–97 and 173–80; Swett, *Neighbors and Enemies*; Weitz, *Creating German Communism*, pp. 160–87.
8. On this process, see esp.: Swett, *Neighbors and Enemies*, pp. 1–29.

Bibliography

MANUSCRIPT SOURCES

Dundee City Council Archives

GD/Mus 34/2, Amalgamated Society of Boilermakers (Dundee Branch, No. 1) Minutes, 1909–1926.
GD/JF, Records of the Dundee and District Jute and Flax Workers' Union.
GD/x199, Railway Clerks' Association (Dundee and District Branch) Minutes, 1915–1937.

Dundee Public Library, Local History Centre

Dundee Trades Council and City Labour Party Collection.
Lamb Collection.
Scottish Painters' Society (Dundee Branch) Minute Books.

Imperial War Museum

Acc. 804, Interview with Robert Cooney.
Acc. 11384, Interview with John Londragon.

Labour History Archive and Study Centre, People's History Museum, Manchester

Communist Party of Great Britain
CP/CENT/PC/1/1–15, Political Committee Minutes, 1924, Organisation Committee Minutes, 1924–25.
CP/CENT/PERS/1–8, Personal Files.
CP/HIST/2/7, Interviews conducted by Kevin Morgan.
CP/HIST/6/3, Interviews conducted by Sue Bruley.
CP/IND/GALL, William Gallacher Papers.
CP/IND/GOLL, John Gollan Papers.
CP/IND/KETT, Margot Kettle Papers.
CP/IND/MISC/9/8–9, Robert Stewart Papers.
CP/IND/MISC/10/1, Helen Crawfurd Papers.

CP/IND/MISC/18/6–7; 19/1, Peter Kerrigan Papers.
CP/LOC/SCOT/1/1 3, Scottish Meeting 1922, Scottish Bulletin 1929.
CP/LOC/SCOT/1/7–11, Dundee Branch Collection.

Labour Party
National Executive Committee Minutes and Papers.
Scottish Executive Committee Minutes, 1915–43.

Marx Memorial Library, London

Acc. 4350, Robert Cooney Papers.

Mitchell Library, Glasgow

Records of Glasgow Trades and Labour Council.

National Library of Scotland

Acc. 4068, Records of the Edinburgh Typographical Society (a member of the Scottish Typographical Association), Press and Machinemen's Section records, 1873–1955.
Acc. 4050, Records of the Edinburgh No. 1 Branch of the National Union of Sheet Metal Workers and Braziers.
Acc. 4251, John Maclean Papers.
Acc. 4313, Records of Edinburgh Branch No. 1 of the National Union of Railwaymen.
Acc. 4516, Records of the Edinburgh District Committee of the Amalgamated Engineering Union.
Acc. 4676, Minutes and Annual Reports of Edinburgh and District Trades Council.
Acc. 5421, Minutes of Edinburgh Central Independent Labour Party.
Acc. 4977/6, Minute book of Edinburgh Central Socialist Sunday School, 1924–30.
Acc. 4977/8, Minute book of the Edinburgh Fabian Society, 1926–34.
Acc. 5120, Records of the National Council of Labour Colleges.
Acc. 5641, Social Democratic Federation: Minutes of the Executive Committee, 1931–41.
Acc. 5862, Thomas Johnston Papers.
Acc. 6471, Ben Shaw Papers.
Acc. 7656, Arthur Woodburn Papers.
Acc. 9083, Thomas Murray Papers.
Acc. 11177, Records of Edinburgh and District Trades Council.

National Records of Scotland

HH16/515–19 and 18/167–8, Albert Percival Gow Papers, 1933–50.

HH55/661–3, Demonstrations and Disturbances (Unemployed in Dundee), 1931–39.
HH55/664, Demonstrations and Disturbances (Glasgow), 1931–32.
HH55/670, Demonstrations and Disturbances (Greenock), 1931–35.
HH55/673–9, Demonstrations and Disturbances (Edinburgh), 1931–39.
HH55/682–92 and 694, Demonstrations and Disturbances (Glasgow), 1931–40.
HH55/704, Demonstrations and Disturbances (Aberdeen), 1937–38.

Parliamentary Archives

ST, Viscount Stansgate Papers.

University of Aberdeen Library, Special Collections

MS 950–1, General Strike Newspaper Editions.
MS 2270, Aberdeen Trades and Labour Council Collection.
MS 2640, Amalgamated Engineering Union (Aberdeen Branch) Minutes.
MS 2657, Scottish Painters' Society (Aberdeen Branch) Minutes.
MS 2664, Aberdeen Communist Party Collection.
MS 2669, United Society of Boilermakers and Iron and Steel Shipbuilders (Aberdeen Branch) Minutes.

PRINTED PRIMARY SOURCES

Newspapers and periodicals

Aberdeen Citizen
Aberdeen Daily Journal
Aberdeen Evening Express
Aberdeen Free Press
Aberdeen Press and Journal
The Communist
The Communist Review
Daily Herald
Daily Worker
Dundee Advertiser
Dundee Courier
Dundee Courier and Advertiser
Dundee Evening Telegraph and Post
Dundee Free Press
Edinburgh Evening Dispatch
Edinburgh Evening News
Edinburgh Labour Standard
Forward

Glasgow Evening Times
Glasgow Herald
Labour Magazine
Labour Monthly
The Labour Organiser
The Manchester Guardian
The Observer
Plebs
The Scotsman
The Sunday Times
The Sunday Worker
The Times
The Weekly Worker
The Worker
Workers' Life
Workers' Weekly

Contemporary publications

Anon., 'It': *Dundee's Labour Monthly, A Journal of Labour News and Views*, No 1, December 1920 (Dundee, 1920).

Anon., *Labour Party Parish Council Election Address Ward One 1928: G. S. Ireland, R. M. Smith, H. Hird* (Dundee, 1928).

Arnot, R. P., *Twenty Years: The Policy of the Communist Party of Great Britain from its Foundation, July 31st, 1920* (London, 1940).

Bell, Thomas, *Communist Party Training*, 2nd edn (London, 1927).

Bell, Thomas, *The British Communist Party: A Short History* (London, 1937).

Burns, Emile, *The General Strike 1926: Trades Councils in Action* (London, 1926).

Burns, Emile, *Communist Affiliation* (London, 1936).

Campbell, J. R., *Communism and Industrial Peace* (London, 1928).

Campbell, J. R., *Is Labour Lost? The New Labour Party Programme Examined* (London, 1928).

Campbell, J. R., *Red Politics in the Trade Unions: Who Are the Disrupters?* (London, 1928).

Communist Party of Great Britain, *Course for New Members* (London, 1920).

Communist Party of Great Britain, *The Militant Trades Council: A Model Constitution for Trades Councils* (London, 1926).

Communist Party of Great Britain, *Communist Party Training* (London, 1927).

Communist Party of Great Britain, *The Plebs League and the NCLC* (London, 1927).

Communist Party of Great Britain, *Mondism and MacDonaldism* (London, 1928).

Communist Party of Great Britain, *The Scottish TUC and the United Front: Where the Scottish Workers Stand* (Glasgow, 1935).

Communist Party of Great Britain, *Four Lesson Course for the Use of Communist Party Branches and Training Groups* (London, 1937).

Communist Party of Great Britain, *Programme of the Communist Pageant of Scottish History* (Aberdeen, 1938).

Douglas, Fred, *The Protestant Movement X-Rayed: The Balance Sheet (Political and Financial) and an Appeal to Protestant Workers* (Edinburgh, 1937).

Douglas, Fred, *Let's Spend a Million! The Communist Plan for building a better Edinburgh* (Edinburgh, 1938).

Edinburgh Labour College, *Organised Labour's Educational Needs: Being a statement submitted by the Scottish Labour College (Edinburgh District) to the Executive of the Edinburgh Trades and Labour Council* (Edinburgh, 1922).

Edinburgh Trades and Labour Council, *Annual Reports* (Edinburgh, 1922–39).

Edinburgh Trades and Labour Council, *Our Unseen City Revealed, a tale of housing atrocities: Report by the Executive Committee of Edinburgh and District Trades and Labour Council on the condition of housing in Edinburgh, as revealed by the annual report of the Medical Officer of Health for the year 1921* (Edinburgh, 1922).

Ellis, Albert, *A Secret History of the NCLC* (Birmingham, 1937).

'Espoir' and others, *Communist Cartoons* (London, 1922).

Ferguson, Aitken, *Scotland* (Glasgow, 1938).

Gollan Defence Committee and Edinburgh Friends of the Soviet Union, *The Workers' Voice No. 1: Against the Next War for Capitalism, For the Fight – How to Win Socialism* (Edinburgh, 1931).

Kerrigan, Peter, *Scotland's March to Peace and Progress* (Glasgow, 1939).

Labour Party, *Labour and the Nation* (London, 1928).

Labour Party, *Scottish Council: Report of the 14th Annual Conference, 6th April 1929* (1929).

Labour Party, *Statement of the NEC: Labour and the Popular Front* (London, 1937).

MacDiarmid, Hugh and Lewis Grassic Gibbon, *Scottish Scene or: the Intelligent Man's Guide to Albyn* (London, 1934).

Maclean, John, *A Plea for a Labour College in Scotland* (Glasgow, 1916).

McShane, Harry, *Three Days that Shook Edinburgh* (Edinburgh, 1933, repr. 1994).

Mackie, R. L. (ed.), *A Scientific Survey of Dundee and District* (London, 1939).

Murphy, J. T., *The Political Meaning of the General Strike* (London, 1926).

Niccolls, Charles, *Mr Charles Niccolls: Communist Candidate Parish Council Election, Ward One* (Dundee, 1928).

Paul, William, *The Path to Power: The Communist Party on Trial* (London, 1925).

Scottish Labour College, *To the Toilers of Scotland* (Glasgow, 1920).

Scottish Labour College: Dundee and District Committee, *Circular to Trade Union Branches* (Dundee, 1922).

Woodburn, Arthur, *An Outline of Finance* (London, 1931).

Memoirs and autobiographies

Bell, Thomas, *Pioneering Days* (London: Lawrence & Wishart, 1941).

Brooksbank, Mary, *No Sae Lang Syne: A Tale of this City* (Dundee: Dundee Printers, 1968).

Brooksbank, Mary, *Sidlaw Breezes* (Dundee: David Winter & Son, 1982).

Cooney, Robert, *Proud Journey: A Spanish Civil War Memoir* (London: Marx Memorial Library, 2015).

Docherty, Mary, *A Miner's Lass* (Cowdenbeath: Mary Docherty, 1992).

Docherty, Mary, *Auld Bob: A Man in a Million* (Cowdenbeath: Mary Docherty, 1996).

Gallacher, William, *Revolt on the Clyde: An Autobiography* (London: Lawrence & Wishart, 1936).

Gallacher, William, *The Rolling of the Thunder* (London: Lawrence & Wishart, 1947).

Gallacher, William, *Last Memoirs* (London: Lawrence & Wishart, 1966).

Hannington, Wal, *Unemployed Struggles, 1919–1936* (London: Lawrence & Wishart, 1936).

Hannington, Wal, *Never On Our Knees* (London: Lawrence & Wishart, 1967).

Jackson, T. A., *Solo Trumpet* (London: Lawrence & Wishart, 1953).

Lee, Jennie, *Tomorrow Is a New Day* (London: Cresset Press, 1939).

MacCarthy, Margaret, *Generation in Revolt* (London: Heinemann, 1953).

MacDiarmid, Hugh, *The Company I've Kept: Essays in Autobiography* (London: Hutchinson, 1966).

McGovern, John, *Neither Fear nor Favour* (London: Blandford, 1960).

McShane, Harry and Joan Smith, *No Mean Fighter* (London: Pluto Press, 1978).

Moffat, Abe, *My Life with the Miners* (London: Lawrence & Wishart, 1965).

Muir, Edwin, *Scottish Journey* (London: Heinemann, 1935).

Murphy, J. T., *New Horizons* (London: Bodley Head, 1941).

Paton, John, *Left Turn!* (London: Secker and Warburg, 1936).

Paton, John, *Proletarian Pilgrimage* (London: Routledge, 1935).

Phillips, David, *I Never Fell into a Midden* (Dundee: David Winter & Son, 1978).

Selkirk, Robert, *Life of a Worker* (Dundee: Dundee Printers, 1967).

Stewart, Robert J., *Breaking the Fetters* (London: Lawrence & Wishart, 1967).

SECONDARY SOURCES

Books

Abrams, Lynn and Callum G. Brown (eds), *A History of Everyday Life in Twentieth Century Scotland* (Edinburgh: Edinburgh University Press, 2010).

Aitken, Keith, *The Bairns o' Adam: The Story of the STUC* (Edinburgh: Polygon, 1997).

Almond, Gabriel, *The Appeals of Communism* (Princeton, NJ: Princeton University Press, 1954).

Anderson, Benedict, *Imagined Communities: Reflections on the Origin and Spread of Nationalism* (London: Verso, 1983).

Andrews, Geoff, Nina Fishman and Kevin Morgan (eds), *Opening the Books: Essays on the Social and Cultural History of British Communism* (London: Pluto Press, 1995).

Arnot, Robin Page, *A History of the Scottish Miners from the Earliest Times* (London: Allen & Unwin, 1955).

Arnot, Robin Page, *The Impact of the Russian Revolution in Britain* (London: Lawrence & Wishart, 1967).

Arnott, Mike, *Dundee and the Spanish Civil War: The Contribution of a City and Its People* (Dundee: Dundee Trades Union Council, 2008).

Atherton, David (ed.), *We're Far Fae Hame Now! Aberdeen and the North East's Experience of Military Service Abroad* (Aberdeen: Aberdeen City Council, 1998).

Ball, Stuart, *Baldwin and the Conservative Party: The Crisis of 1929–1931* (New Haven, CT: Yale University Press, 1988).

Ball, Stuart, *The Conservative Party and British Politics, 1902–1951* (London: Longman, 1995).

Ball, Stuart and Ian Holliday (eds), *Mass Conservatism: The Conservatives and the Public since the 1880s* (London: Frank Cass, 2002).

Barclay, J. B., *When Work Is Done* (Edinburgh: University of Edinburgh, 1971).

Baxell, Richard, *British Volunteers in the Spanish Civil War: The British Battalion in the International Brigades, 1936–1939* (London: Routledge, 2004).

Baxendale, John and Christopher Pawling, *Narrating the Thirties: 1930 to the Present* (London: Macmillan, 1995).

Beckett, Francis, *Enemy Within: The Rise and Fall of the British Communist Party* (London: John Murray, 1995).

Beers, Laura, *Your Britain: Media and the Making of the Labour Party* (Cambridge, MA: Harvard University Press, 2010).

Beers, Laura and Geraint Thomas (eds), *Brave New World: Imperial and Democratic Nation-Building in Britain between the Wars* (London: Institute of Historical Research, 2011).

Bennett, Gillian, '*A Most Extraordinary and Mysterious Business*': The Zinoviev Letter of 1924 (London: Foreign and Commonwealth Office, 1999).

Ben-Ze'ev, Efrat, Ruth Ginio and Jay Winter (eds), *Shadows of War: A Social History of Silence in the Twentieth Century* (Cambridge: Cambridge University Press, 2010).

Biagini, Eugenio and Alastair J. Reid (eds), *Currents of Radicalism: Popular Radicalism, Organised Labour and Party Politics in Britain, 1850–1914* (Cambridge: Cambridge University Press, 1991).

Blaazer, David, *The Popular Front and the Progressive Tradition: Socialists, Liberals, and the Quest for Unity, 1884–1939* (Cambridge: Cambridge University Press, 1992).

Black, Lawrence, *The Political Culture of the Left in Affluent Britain, 1951–64: Old Labour, New Britain?* (Basingstoke: Palgrave Macmillan, 2003).

Borkenau, Franz, *World Communism: A History of the Communist International* (Ann Arbor, MI: University of Michigan, 1962).

Branson, Noreen, *Britain in the Nineteen Twenties* (London: Weidenfeld & Nicolson, 1975).

Branson, Noreen, *History of the Communist Party of Great Britain, 1927–41* (London: Lawrence & Wishart, 1985).

Braunthal, Julius, *History of the International: Volume 2, 1914–1943* (London: Nelson, 1967).

Briggs, Asa and John Saville (eds), *Essays in Labour History, 1918–1939* (London: Croom Helm, 1977).

Brotherstone, Terry (ed.), *Covenant, Charter and Party: Traditions of Revolt and Protest in Modern Scottish History* (Aberdeen: Aberdeen University Press, 1989).

Brotherstone, Terry and Donald J. Withrington (eds), *The City and Its Worlds: Aspects of Aberdeen's History since 1794* (Glasgow: Cruithne Press, 1996).

Brown, Timothy S., *Weimar Radicals: Nazis and Communists between Authenticity and Performance* (New York: Berghahn, 2009).

Bruce, Steve, *No Pope of Rome* (Edinburgh: Mainstream Publishing, 1985).

Bruley, Sue, *Leninism, Stalinism and the Women's Movement in Britain, 1920–1939* (London: Routledge, 2013).

Buchanan, Tom, *The Spanish Civil War and the British Labour Movement* (Cambridge: Cambridge University Press, 1991).

Buchanan, Tom, *Britain and the Spanish Civil War* (Cambridge: Cambridge University Press, 1997).

Buchanan, Tom, *The Impact of the Spanish Civil War on Britain* (Brighton: Sussex Academic Press, 2007).

Bulaitis, John, *Communism in Rural France: French Agricultural Workers and the Popular Front* (London: I. B. Tauris, 2008).

Cairncross, Alec (ed.), *The Scottish Economy* (Cambridge: Cambridge University Press, 1954).

Calhoun, Craig (ed.), *Habermas and the Public Sphere* (Cambridge, MA: MIT Press, 1992).

Calhoun, Daniel F., *The United Front: The TUC and the Russians, 1923–1928* (Cambridge: Cambridge University Press, 1976).

Cameron, Ewen A., *Impaled upon a Thistle: Scotland Since 1880* (Edinburgh: Edinburgh University Press, 2010).

Campbell, Alan, *The Scottish Miners, 1874–1939: Volume 1 Industry, Work and Community* (Aldershot: Ashgate, 2000).

Campbell, Alan, *The Scottish Miners, 1874–1939: Volume 2 Trade Unions and Politics* (Aldershot: Ashgate, 2000).

Campbell, Alan, Nina Fishman and David Howell (eds), *Miners, Unions, and Politics, 1910–1947* (Aldershot: Scolar Press, 1996).

Campbell, J. R., *Forty Fighting Years* (London: CPGB, 1960).

Campbell, Roy H., *The Rise and Fall of Scottish Industry, 1707–1939* (Edinburgh: John Donald, 1980).

Carr, E. H., *The Twilight of Comintern, 1930–35* (London: Macmillan, 1982).

Challinor, Raymond, *The Origins of British Bolshevism* (London: Croom Helm, 1977).

Clarke, Peter, *Lancashire and the New Liberalism* (Cambridge: Cambridge University Press, 1971).

Clarke, Peter, *Hope and Glory: Britain, 1900–2000* (London: Penguin, 2004).

Clegg, Hugh, *A History of British Trade Unionism: Volume 2, 1911–1933* (Oxford: Clarendon Press, 1985).

Clinton, Alan, *The Trade Union Rank and File: Trades Councils in Britain, 1900–1940* (Manchester: Manchester University Press, 1977).

Cohen, Gidon, *The Failure of a Dream: The ILP from Disaffiliation to World War Two* (London: I. B. Tauris, 2007).

Corkill, David and Stuart Rawnsley (eds), *The Road to Spain: Anti-Fascists at War, 1936–1939* (Dunfermline: Borderline, 1981).

Cornwall, Mark and Murray Frame (eds), *Scotland and the Slavs: Cultures in Contact 1500–2000* (Newtonville, MA: ORP, 2001).

Corthorn, Paul, *In the Shadow of the Dictators: The British Left in the 1930s* (London: I. B. Tauris, 2006).

Corthorn, Paul and Jonathan Davis (eds), *The British Labour Party and the Wider World: Domestic Politics, Internationalism and Foreign Policy* (London: I. B. Tauris, 2008).

Cowan, Edward J. and Richard J. Finlay (eds), *Scottish History: The Power of the Past* (Edinburgh: Edinburgh University Press, 2002).

Cowling, Maurice, *The Impact of Labour, 1920–1924: The Beginning of Modern British Politics* (Cambridge: Cambridge University Press, 1971).

Craig, F. W. S. (ed.), *British Parliamentary Election Results, 1918–1949* (Glasgow: Political Reference Publications, 1969).

Crick, Martin, *The History of the Social-Democratic Federation* (Keele: Ryburn Publishing, 1994).

Croft, Andy (ed.), *A Weapon in the Struggle: The Cultural History of the Communist Party in Britain* (London: Pluto Press, 1998).

Croucher, Richard, *We Refuse to Starve in Silence: A History of the National Unemployed Workers' Movement, 1920–1946* (London: Lawrence & Wishart, 1987).

Cunnison, J. and J. B. S. Gilfillan (eds), *The Third Statistical Account of Scotland: Volume Five, Glasgow* (Glasgow: Collins, 1958).

Darlington, Ralph, *The Political Trajectory of J. T. Murphy* (Liverpool: Liverpool University Press, 1998).

Degras, Jane (ed.), *The Communist International, 1919–1943: Documents* (3 vols) (Oxford: Oxford University Press, 1956–65).

Dell, Simon, *The Image of the Popular Front: The Masses and the Media in Interwar France* (Basingstoke. Palgrave Macmillan, 2007).

Devine, T. M., *The Scottish Nation, 1700–2000* (London: Penguin, 2000).

Devine, T. M., *To the Ends of the Earth: Scotland's Global Diaspora, 1750–2010* (London: Allen Lane, 2011).

Devine, T. M. and Richard J. Finlay (eds), *Scotland in the Twentieth Century* (Edinburgh: Edinburgh University Press, 1996).

Devine, T. M., C. H. Lee and G. C. Peden (eds), *The Transformation of Scotland: The Economy since 1700* (Edinburgh: Edinburgh University Press, 2005).

Dewar, Hugo, *Communist Politics in Britain: The CPGB from its Origins to the Second World War* (London: Pluto Press, 1976).

Diack, William, *History of the Trades Council and the Trade Union Movement in Aberdeen* (Aberdeen: Aberdeen Trades Council, 1939).

Dickson, Tony (ed.) *Capital and Class in Scotland* (Edinburgh: John Donald, 1982).

Dickson, Tony and James H. Treble (eds), *People and Society in Scotland: Volume III, 1914–1990* (Edinburgh: John Donald, 1992).

Dickson, T. (ed.) *Scottish Capitalism: Class, State and Nation from before the Union to the Present* (London: Lawrence & Wishart, 1980).

Donnachie, Ian, Christopher Harvie and Ian S. Wood (eds), *Forward! Labour Politics in Scotland 1888–1988* (Edinburgh: Polygon, 1989).

Duncan, Robert, *James Leatham, 1865–1945: Portrait of a Socialist Pioneer* (Aberdeen: Aberdeen People's Press, 1978).

Duncan, Robert and Arthur McIvor (eds), *Militant Workers: Labour and Class Conflict on the Clyde, 1900–1950* (Edinburgh: John Donald, 1992).

Dyer, Michael, *Capable Citizens and Improvident Democrats: The Scottish Electoral System, 1884–1929* (Aberdeen: Scottish Cultural Press, 1996).

Eaden, James and David Renton, *The Communist Party of Great Britain since 1920* (Basingstoke: Palgrave Macmillan, 2002).

Epstein, Catherine, *The Last Revolutionaries: German Communists and Their Century* (Cambridge, MA: Harvard University Press, 2003).

Epstein, James, *Radical Expression: Political Language, Ritual and Symbol in England, 1790–1850* (Oxford: Oxford University Press, 1994).

Epstein, James, *In Practice: Studies in the Language and Culture of Popular Politics in Modern Britain* (Stanford, CA: Stanford University Press, 2003).

Evans, Richard J. and Dick Geary (eds), *The German Unemployed: Experiences and Consequences of Mass Unemployment from the Weimar Republic to the Third Reich* (London: Croom Helm, 1987).

Ewing, K. D. and C. A. Gearty, *The Struggle for Civil Liberties: Political Freedom and the Rule of Law in Britain, 1914–1945* (Oxford: Clarendon Press, 2000).

Feldman, David and Jon Lawrence (eds), *Structures and Transformations in Modern British History* (Cambridge: Cambridge University Press, 2011).

Fentress, James and Chris Wickham, *Social Memory* (Oxford: Blackwell, 1992).

Finlay, Richard J., *Independent and Free: Scottish Politics and the Origins of the Scottish National Party, 1918–1945* (Edinburgh: John Donald, 1994).

Finlay, Richard J., *Modern Scotland 1914–2000* (London: Profile, 2004).

Fischer, Conan, *The German Communists and the Rise of Nazism* (Basingstoke: Palgrave Macmillan, 1991).

Fischer, Conan (ed.), *The Rise of National Socialism and the Working Classes in Weimar Germany* (Providence, RI: Berghahn, 1996).

Fishman, Nina, *The British Communist Party and the Trade Unions, 1933–45* (Aldershot: Scolar Press, 1995).

Flanagan, Richard, *'Parish-Fed Bastards': A History of the Politics of the Unemployed in Britain, 1884–1939* (New York: Greenwood Press, 1991).

Floud, Roderick and Paul Johnson (eds), *The Cambridge Economic History of Modern Britain, Volume 2: Economic Maturity, 1860–1939* (Cambridge: Cambridge University Press, 2003).

Francis, Martin and Ina Zweiniger-Bargielowska (eds), *The Conservatives and British Society, 1880–1990* (Cardiff: University of Wales Press, 1996).

Fraser, W. Hamish, *Scottish Popular Politics: From Radicalism to Labour* (Edinburgh: Polygon, 2000).

Fraser, W. Hamish and Clive H. Lee (eds), *Aberdeen, 1800–2000: A New History* (East Linton: Tuckwell Press, 2000).

Fry, Michael, *Patronage and Principle: A Political History of Modern Scotland* (Aberdeen: Aberdeen University Press, 1987).

Fyrth, Jim, *The Signal Was Spain: The Aid Spain Movement in Britain, 1936–39* (London: Lawrence & Wishart, 1986).

Fyrth, Jim (ed.), *Britain, Fascism and the Popular Front* (London: Lawrence & Wishart, 1985).

Gall, Gregor, *The Political Economy of Scotland: Red Scotland? Radical Scotland?* (Cardiff: University of Wales Press, 2005).

Gallagher, Tom, *Edinburgh Divided: John Cormack and 'No Popery' in the 1930s* (Edinburgh: Polygon, 1987).

Gardiner, Juliet, *The Thirties: An Intimate History* (London: HarperCollins, 2011).

Garside, William R., *British Unemployment, 1919–1939: A Study in Public Policy* (Cambridge: Cambridge University Press, 1990).

Gibbon, Lewis Grassic, *Cloud Howe* (London: Pan, 1973, first published 1933).

Gibbon, Lewis Grassic, *A Scots Hairst: Essays and Short Stories* (London: Hutchison, 1967).

Gibbon, Lewis Grassic, *A Scots Quair* (Edinburgh: Canongate, 1998).

Gloversmith, Frank (ed.), *Class, Culture and Social Change: A New View of the 1930s* (Brighton: Harvester Press, 1980).

Graham, Thomas N., *Willie Graham: The Life of the Right Honourable W. Graham* (London: Hutchinson, 1948).

Graubard, Stephen, *British Labour and the Russian Revolution, 1917–1924* (Cambridge, MA: Harvard University Press, 1956).

Graves, Pamela, *Labour Women: Women in British Working-Class Politics, 1918–1939* (Cambridge: Cambridge University Press, 1994).

Gray, Daniel, *Homage to Caledonia: Scotland and the Spanish Civil War* (Edinburgh: Luath Press, 2008).

Gray, Nigel (ed.), *The Worst of Times: An Oral History of the Great Depression in Britain* (London: Wildwood House, 1985).

Green, E. H. H., *Ideologies of Conservatism: Conservative Political Ideas in the Twentieth Century* (Oxford: Oxford University Press, 2002).

Gregory, Adrian, *The Silence of Memory: Armistice Day, 1919–1946* (Oxford: Berg, 1994).

Gregory, Adrian, *The Last Great War: British Society and the First World War* (Cambridge: Cambridge University Press, 2008).

Griffiths, Clare V. J., *Labour and the Countryside: The Politics of Rural Britain* (Oxford: Oxford University Press, 2007).

Gunn, Simon and Robert J. Morris (eds), *Identities in Space: Contested Terrains in the Western City since 1850* (Aldershot: Ashgate, 2001).

Gunn, Simon and James Vernon (eds), *The Peculiarities of Liberal Modernity in Imperial Britain* (Berkeley, CA: University of California Press, 2011).

Habermas, Jürgen, *The Structural Transformation of the Public Sphere: An Inquiry into a Category of Bourgeois Society* (London: Polity Press, 1989).

Harper, Marjory, *Emigration from Scotland between the Wars: Opportunity or Exile?* (Manchester: Manchester University Press, 1998).

Harrison, Royden (ed.), *Independent Collier: The Coal Miner as Archetypal Proletarian Reconsidered* (Hassocks: Harvester Press, 1978).

Harvie, Christopher, *No Gods and Precious Few Heroes: Scotland, 1914–1980* (London: Arnold, 1981).

Hinton, James, *The First Shop Stewards' Movement* (London: Allen & Unwin, 1973).

Hinton, James, *Labour and Socialism: A History of the British Labour Movement, 1867–1974* (Brighton: Wheatsheaf, 1983).

Hinton, James and Richard Hyman, *Trade Unions and Revolution: The Industrial Politics of the Early British Communist Party* (London: Pluto Press, 1975).

Hobsbawm, Eric J., *Labouring Men: Studies in the History of Labour* (London: Weidenfeld & Nicolson, 1964).

Hobsbawm, Eric J., *Primitive Rebels: Studies in Archaic Forms of Social Movement in the 19th and 20th Centuries* (Manchester: Manchester University Press, 1971).

Hobsbawm, Eric J., *Revolutionaries* (London: Weidenfeld & Nicolson, 1982).

Hobsbawm, Eric J., *The Age of Extremes, 1914–1991* (London: Abacus, 1995).

Hobsbawm, Eric J., *Uncommon People: Resistance, Rebellion and Jazz* (London: Weidenfeld & Nicolson, 1999).

Hobsbawm, Eric J., *Industry and Empire: From 1750 to the Present Day* (London: Penguin, 1999).

Hobsbawm, Eric J. and Terence Ranger (eds), *The Invention of Tradition* (Cambridge: Cambridge University Press, 1983).

Hoggart, Richard, *The Uses of Literacy* (London: Chatto & Windus, 1957).

Holford, John, *Reshaping Labour – Organisation, Work and Politics: Edinburgh in the Great War and After* (London: Chatto & Windus, 1988).

Hopkins, James K., *Into the Heart of the Fire: The British in the Spanish Civil War* (Stanford, CA: Stanford University Press, 1998).

Howell, David, *British Workers and the Independent Labour Party, 1888–1906* (Manchester: Manchester University Press, 1983).

Howell, David, *MacDonald's Party: Labour Identities and Crisis, 1922–1931* (Oxford: Oxford University Press, 2002).

Hughes, Annmarie, *Gender and Political Identities in Scotland, 1919–1939* (Edinburgh: Edinburgh University Press, 2010).

Hutchison, I. G. C., *A Political History of Scotland, 1832–1924: Parties, Elections and Issues* (Edinburgh: John Donald, 1986).

Hutchison, I. G. C., *Scottish Politics in the Twentieth Century* (Basingstoke: Palgrave Macmillan, 2001).

Jackson, J. M. (ed.), *The Third Statistical Account of Scotland: Volume Twenty-Five, The City of Dundee* (Arbroath: Herald Press, 1979).

Jackson, Julian, *The Politics of Depression in France, 1932–1936* (Cambridge: Cambridge University Press, 1985).

Jackson, Julian, *The Popular Front in France: Defending Democracy, 1934–1938* (Cambridge: Cambridge University Press, 1988).

Jeffreys, J. B., *The Story of the Engineers* (London: Lawrence & Wishart, 1945).

Jones, Gareth Stedman, *Languages of Class: Studies in English Working Class History, 1832–1982* (Cambridge: Cambridge University Press, 1983).

Joyce, Patrick, *Visions of the People: Industrial England and the Question of Class* (Cambridge: Cambridge University Press, 1990).

Joyce, Patrick, *The Rule of Freedom: Liberalism and the Modern City* (London: Verso, 2003).

Jupp, James, *The Radical Left in Britain, 1931–1941* (London: Cass, 1982).

Katz, Philip, *The Long Weekend: Combating Unemployment during the Interwar Years* (London: Hetherington Press, 2001).

Kay, Billy (ed.), *Odyssey: Voices from Scotland's Recent Past* (Edinburgh: Polygon, 1980).

Kay, Billy (ed.), *Odyssey: Voices from Scotland's Recent Past, the Second Collection* (Edinburgh: Polygon, 1982).

Keir, David (ed.), *The Third Statistical Account of Scotland: The City of Edinburgh* (Glasgow: Collins, 1966).

Kendall, Walter, *The Revolutionary Movement in Britain, 1900–21: The Origins of British Communism* (London: Weidenfeld & Nicolson, 1969).

Kenefick, William, *Red Scotland! The Rise and Fall of the Radical Left c.1872 to 1932* (Edinburgh: Edinburgh University Press, 2007).

Kent, Susan K. *Making Peace: The Reconstruction of Gender in Interwar Britain* (Princeton, NJ: Princeton University Press, 1993).

Kibblewhite, Liz and Andy Rigby, *Aberdeen in the General Strike* (Aberdeen: Aberdeen People's Press, 1977).

Kibblewhite, Liz and Andy Rigby, *Fascism in Aberdeen: Street Politics in the 1930s* (Aberdeen: Aberdeen People's Press, 1978).

King, Alex, *Memorials of the Great War in Britain: The Symbolism and Politics of Remembrance* (Oxford: Berg, 1998).

Kingsford, Paul, *The Hunger Marchers in Britain 1920–1939* (London: Lawrence & Wishart, 1982).

Kirk, Neville, *Change, Continuity and Class: Labour in British Society, 1850–1920* (Manchester: Manchester University Press, 1998).

Klugmann, James, *History of the Communist Party of Great Britain, 1919–24* (London: Lawrence & Wishart, 1969).

Klugmann, James, *History of the Communist Party of Great Britain, 1925–27* (London: Lawrence & Wishart, 1969).

Knox, William W., *James Maxton* (Manchester: Manchester University Press, 1987).

Knox, William W., *Industrial Nation: Work, Culture and Society in Scotland, 1800–Present* (Edinburgh: Edinburgh University Press, 1999).

Knox, William W., *Lives of Scottish Women: Women and Scottish Society, 1800–1980* (Edinburgh: Edinburgh University Press, 2006).

Knox, William W. (ed.), *Scottish Labour Leaders 1918–1939: A Bibliographical Dictionary* (Edinburgh: Mainstream, 1984).

LaPorte, Norman, Kevin Morgan and Matthew Worley (eds), *Bolshevism, Stalinism and the Comintern: Perspectives on Stalinization, 1917–1953* (Basingstoke: Palgrave Macmillan, 2008).

Lawrence, Jon, *Speaking for the People: Party, Language and Popular Politics in England, 1867–1914* (Cambridge: Cambridge University Press, 1998).

Lawrence, Jon, *Electing Our Masters: The Hustings in British Politics from Hogarth to Blair* (Oxford: Oxford University Press, 2009).

Lawrence, Jon and Miles Taylor (eds), *Party, State and Society: Electoral Behaviour in Britain since 1820* (Aldershot: Scolar Press, 1997).

Laybourn, Keith and Dylan Murphy, *Under the Red Flag: A History of Communism in Britain* (Stroud: Sutton Publishing, 1999).

LeMahieu, D. L., *A Culture for Democracy: Mass Communication and the Cultivated Mind in Britain between the Wars* (Oxford: Clarendon Press, 1988).

Lenman, Bruce, *An Economic History of Modern Scotland, 1660–1976* (London: Batsford, 1977).

Levitt, Ian, *Poverty and Welfare in Scotland, 1890–1948* (Edinburgh: Edinburgh University Press, 1988).

Light, Alison, *Forever England: Femininity, Literature, and Conservatism between the Wars* (London: Routledge, 1991).

Linehan, Thomas, *Communism in Britain, 1920–1939: From the Cradle to the Grave* (Manchester: Manchester University Press, 2007).

Livingstone, Sheila, *Bonnie Fechters: Women in Scotland, 1900–1950* (Motherwell: Scottish Library Association, 1994).

McCarthy, Helen, *The British People and the League of Nations: Democracy, Citizenship and Internationalism, c. 1918–45* (Manchester: Manchester University Press, 2011).

McCormack, Matthew (ed.), *Public Men: Masculinity and Politics in Modern Britain* (Basingstoke: Palgrave Macmillan, 2007).

McDermott, Kevin and Jeremy Agnew, *The Comintern: A History of International Communism from Lenin to Stalin* (Basingstoke: Palgrave Macmillan, 1996).

MacDonald, Catriona M. M., *The Radical Thread: Political Change in Scotland, Paisley Politics 1885–1924* (East Linton: Tuckwell Press, 2000).

MacDonald, Catriona M. M., *Whaur Extremes Meet: Scotland's Twentieth Century* (Edinburgh: John Donald, 2009).

MacDonald, Catriona M. M. (ed.), *Unionist Scotland, 1800–1997* (Edinburgh: John Donald, 1998).

MacDougall, Ian (ed.), *Essays in Scottish Labour History* (Edinburgh: John Donald, 1978).

MacDougall, Ian (ed.), *A Catalogue of Some Labour Records in Scotland* (Edinburgh: Scottish Labour History Society, 1978).

MacDougall, Ian (ed.), *Militant Miners* (Edinburgh: Polygon, 1981).

MacDougall, Ian (ed.), *Voices from the Spanish Civil War: Personal Recollections of Scottish Volunteers in Republican Spain, 1936–39* (Edinburgh: Polygon, 1986).

MacDougall, Ian (ed.), *Voices from the Hunger Marches, Volume 1* (Edinburgh: Polygon, 1990).

MacDougall, Ian (ed.), *Voices from the Hunger Marches, Volume 2* (Edinburgh: Polygon, 1991).

MacDougall, Ian (ed.), *Voices from Work and Home: Personal Recollections of Working Life and Labour Struggles in the Twentieth Century by Scots Men and Women* (Edinburgh: Mercat Press, 2000).

MacFarlane, Leslie J., *The British Communist Party: Its Origin and Development until 1929* (London: MacGibbon & Kee, 1966).

Macintyre, Stuart, *Little Moscows: Communism and Working Class Militancy in Inter-War Britain* (London: Croom Helm, 1980).

Macintyre, Stuart, *A Proletarian Science: Marxism in Britain 1917–1933* (Cambridge: Cambridge University Press, 1980).

MacKenzie, Hugh, *The Third Statistical Account of Scotland: Volume Four, The City Of Aberdeen* (Edinburgh: Oliver & Boyd, 1953).

McKibbin, Ross, *The Evolution of the Labour Party, 1910–1924* (Oxford: Oxford University Press, 1974).

McKibbin, Ross, *The Ideologies of Class: Social Relations in Britain, 1880–1950* (Oxford: Clarendon Press, 1990).

McKibbin, Ross, *Classes and Cultures: England, 1918–1951* (Oxford: Oxford University Press, 1998).

McKibbin, Ross, *Parties and People: England, 1914–1951* (Oxford: Oxford University Press, 2010).

McKinlay, Alan and Robert J. Morris (eds), *The Independent Labour Party on Clydeside, 1892–1932: From Foundation to Disintegration* (Manchester: Manchester University Press, 1991).

McLean, Iain, *The Legend of Red Clydeside* (Edinburgh: John Donald, 1983).

Malcolm, William K., *A Blasphemer and Reformer: A Study of James Leslie Mitchell/Lewis Grassic Gibbon* (Aberdeen: Aberdeen University Press, 1984).

Martin, Roderick, *Communism and the Trade Unions 1924–1933: A Study of the National Minority Movement* (Oxford: Clarendon Press, 1969).

Marwick, Arthur, *The Deluge: British Society and the First World War* (London: Macmillan, 1973).

Marwick, William H., *A Short History of Labour in Scotland* (Edinburgh: Chambers, 1967).

Melling, Joseph (ed.), *Housing, Social Policy and the State* (London: Croom Helm, 1980).

Miliband, Ralph, *Parliamentary Socialism: A Study in the Politics of Labour*, 2nd edn (London: Merlin Press, 1973).

Millar, J. P. M., *The Labour College Movement* (London: NCLC Publishing, 1980).

Milton, Nan, *John Maclean* (London: Pluto Press, 1973).

Milton, Nan (ed.), *John Maclean: In the Rapids of Revolution – Essays, Articles and Letters, 1902–1923* (London: Allison & Busby, 1978).

Minkin, Lewis, *The Contentious Alliance: Trade Unions and the Labour Party* (Edinburgh: Edinburgh University Press, 1991).

Morgan, Kevin, *Against Fascism and War: Ruptures and Continuities in British Communist Politics 1935–1941* (Manchester: Manchester University Press, 1989).

Morgan, Kevin, *Bolshevism and the British Left Part 1: Labour Legends and Russian Gold* (London: Lawrence & Wishart, 2006).

Morgan, Kevin, *Bolshevism and the British Left Part 2: The Webbs and Soviet Communism* (London: Lawrence & Wishart, 2006).

Morgan, Kevin, *Bolshevism and the British Left Part 3: Bolshevism, Syndicalism and the General Strike, the Lost Internationalist world of A. A. Purcell* (London: Lawrence & Wishart, 2013).

Morgan, Kevin, John McIlroy and Alan Campbell (eds), *Party People, Communist Lives: Explorations in Biography* (London: Lawrence & Wishart, 2001).

Morgan, Kevin, Gidon Cohen and Andrew Flinn (eds), *Agents of the Revolution: New Biographical Approaches to the History of International Communism in the Age of Lenin and Stalin* (London: Peter Lang, 2005).

Morgan, Kevin, Gidon Cohen and Andrew Flinn, *Communists and British Society, 1920–1991* (London: Rivers Oram, 2007).

Morris, M., *The General Strike* (London: Journeyman, 1980).

Mosse, George L., *Fallen Soldiers: Reshaping the Memory of the World Wars* (New York: Oxford University Press, 1990).

Mowat, C. L., *Britain between the Wars, 1918–1940* (London: Methuen, 1968).

Newton, Kenneth, *The Sociology of British Communism* (London: Allen Lane, 1969).

O'Gorman, Frank, *The Emergence of the British Two-Party System, 1760–1832* (London: Edward Arnold, 1982).

O'Gorman, Frank, *Voters, Patrons and Parties: The Unreformed Electorate of Hanoverian England, 1734–1832* (Oxford: Clarendon Press, 1989).

Orwell, George, *The Road to Wigan Pier* (London: Gollancz, 1937).

Overy, Richard, *The Morbid Age: Britain and the Crisis of Civilization, 1919–1939* (London: Penguin, 2010).

Peele, Gillian and Chris Cook (eds), *The Politics of Reappraisal, 1918–1939* (London: Macmillan, 1975).

Pelling, Henry M., *The British Communist Party: A Historical Profile* (London: A. & C. Black, 1958).

Pelling, Henry M., *Popular Politics and Society in Late Victorian Britain* (London: Macmillan, 1968).

Pelling, Henry M., *A History of British Trade Unionism*, 5th edn (London: Penguin, 1992).

Perry, Matt, *Bread and Work: Social Policy and the Experience of Unemployment, 1918–39* (London: Pluto Press, 2000).

Perry, Matt, *Prisoners of Want: The Experience and the Protest of the Unemployed in France, 1921–45* (Aldershot: Ashgate, 2007).

Phillips, David, *The Hungry Thirties: Dundee between the Wars* (Dundee: David Winter & Son, 1981).

Phillips, G. A., *The General Strike: The Politics of Industrial Conflict* (London: Weidenfeld & Nicolson, 1976).

Pickering, Paul A. and Alex Tyrrell (eds), *Contested Sites: Commemoration, Memorial and Popular Politics in Nineteenth-Century Britain* (Aldershot: Ashgate, 2004).

Pimlott, Ben, *Labour and the Left in the 1930s* (London: Allen & Unwin, 1986).

Pugh, Martin, *The Tories and the People, 1880–1935* (Oxford: Blackwell, 1985).

Pugh, Martin, *Hurrah for the Blackshirts! Fascists and Fascism in Britain between the Wars* (London: Pimlico, 2006).

Pugh, Martin, *We Danced All Night: A Social History of Britain between the Wars* (London: Vintage, 2009).

Pugh, Martin, *Speak for Britain! A New History of the Labour Party* (London: Vintage, 2011).

Rafeek, Neil, *Communist Women in Scotland: Red Clydeside from the Russian Revolution to the End of the Soviet Union* (London: I. B. Tauris, 2008).

Ramsden, John, *The Age of Balfour and Baldwin, 1902–1940* (London: Longman, 1978).

Raymond, John (ed.), *The Baldwin Age* (London: Eyre & Spottiswoode, 1960).

Redfern, Neil, *Class or Nation: Communism, Imperialism and Two World Wars* (London: I. B. Tauris, 2005).

Rée, Jonathan, *Proletarian Philosophers: Problems in Socialist Culture, 1900–1940* (Oxford: Oxford University Press, 1984).

Rees, Tim and Andrew Thorpe (eds), *International Communism and the Communist International, 1919–1943* (Manchester: Manchester University Press, 1998).

Reid, Alastair J., *United We Stand: A History of Britain's Trade Unions* (London: Allen Lane, 2004).

Reiss, Matthias (ed.), *The Street as Stage: Protest Marches and Public Rallies since the Nineteenth Century* (Oxford: Oxford University Press, 2007).

Reiss, Matthias and Matt Perry (eds), *Unemployment and Protest: New Perspectives on Two Centuries of Contention* (Oxford: Oxford University Press, 2011).

Roberts, Matthew, *Political Movements in Urban England, 1832–1914* (Basingstoke: Palgrave Macmillan, 2009).

Rodger, Richard (ed.), *Scottish Housing in the Twentieth Century* (Leicester: Leicester University Press, 1989).

Rose, Jonathan, *The Intellectual Life of the British Working Classes*, 2nd edn (New Haven, CT: Yale University Press, 2010).

Rosenhaft, Eve, *Beating the Fascists? The German Communists and Political Violence, 1929–1933* (Cambridge: Cambridge University Press, 1983).

Rosenhaft, Eve, *German Communism and the Popular Front* (Loughborough: Loughborough University, 1991).

Samuel, Raphael (ed.), *People's History and Socialist Theory* (London: Routledge & Kegan Paul, 1981).

Savage, Michael, *The Dynamics of Working Class Politics: The Labour Movement in Preston, 1880–1940* (Cambridge: Cambridge University Press, 1987).

Savage, Michael and Andrew Miles, *The Remaking of the British Working Class, 1840–1940* (London: Routledge, 1994).

Saville, John, *The Labour Movement in Britain* (London: Faber, 1988).

Scott, George (ed.), *Remembering the Spanish Civil War, 1936–39* (Aberdeen: Aberdeen Trades Council, 1996).

Seldon, Anthony and Stuart Ball (eds), *The Conservative Century: The Conservative Party since 1900* (Oxford: Oxford University Press, 1994).

Simon, Brian, *Education and the Labour Movement, 1870–1920* (London: Lawrence & Wishart, 1965).

Simon, Brian (ed.), *The Search for Enlightenment: The Working Class and Adult Education in the Twentieth Century* (Leicester: National Institute of Adult Continuing Education, 1992).

Skelley, Jeffrey (ed.), *The General Strike 1926* (London: Lawrence & Wishart, 1976).

Skidelsky, Robert, *Politicians and the Slump: The Labour Government of 1929–1931* (London: Macmillan, 1967).

Smout, T. C., *A Century of the Scottish People, 1830–1950* (London: Collins, 1986).

Smyth, J. J., *Labour in Glasgow, 1896–1936* (East Lothian: Tuckwell Press, 2000).

Stachura, Peter D. (ed.), *Unemployment and the Great Depression in Weimar Germany* (Basingstoke: Palgrave Macmillan, 1986).

Stevenson, John, *British Society, 1914–1945* (Harmondsworth: Penguin, 1984).

Stevenson, John and Chris Cook, *The Slump: Society and Politics during the Depression* (London: Quartet, 1979).

Stibbe, Matthew, *Germany, 1914–1933: Politics, Society and Culture* (Harlow: Longman, 2010).

Swett, Pamela E., *Neighbors and Enemies: The Culture of Radicalism in Berlin, 1929–1933* (Cambridge: Cambridge University Press, 2004).

Szajkowski, Bogdan (ed.), *Marxist Local Governments in Western Europe and Japan* (London: Pinter, 1985).

Tanner, Duncan, *Political Change and the Labour Party, 1900–18* (Cambridge: Cambridge University Press, 1990).

Tanner, Duncan, Pat Thane and Nick Tiratsoo (eds), *Labour's First Century* (Cambridge: Cambridge University Press, 2000).

Thompson, James, *British Political Culture and the Idea of 'Public Opinion', 1867–1914* (Cambridge: Cambridge University Press, 2013).

Thompson, Willie, *The Good Old Cause: British Communism 1920–1991* (London: Pluto Press, 1991).

Thomson, George M., *Scotland: That Distressed Area* (Edinburgh: Porpoise Press, 1935).

Thorpe, Andrew, *The British General Election of 1931* (Oxford: Clarendon Press, 1991).

Thorpe, Andrew, *Britain in the 1930s* (Oxford: Blackwell, 1992).

Thorpe, Andrew, *The British Communist Party and Moscow, 1920–43* (Manchester: Manchester University Press, 2000).

Thorpe, Andrew (ed.), *The Failure of Political Extremism in Inter-war Britain* (Exeter: University of Exeter, 1989).

Todd, Selina, *The People: The Rise and Fall of the Working Class, 1910–2010* (London: John Murray, 2014).

Tomlinson, Jim and Christopher Whatley (eds), *Jute No More: Transforming Dundee* (Dundee: Dundee University Press, 2011).

Torrance, David (ed.), *Great Scottish Speeches* (Edinburgh: Luath Press, 2011).

Tuckett, Angela, *The Scottish Trades Union Congress: The First 80 Years* (Edinburgh: Mainstream, 1986).

Vernon, James, *Politics and the People: A Study in English Political Culture c.1815–1867* (Cambridge: Cambridge University Press, 1993).

Vernon, James, *Hunger: A Modern History* (Cambridge, MA: Harvard University Press, 2007).

Vernon, James (ed.), *Re-reading the Constitution: New Narratives in the Political History of England's Long Nineteenth Century* (Cambridge: Cambridge University Press, 1996).

Walker, Graham and Tom Gallagher (eds), *Sermons and Battle Hymns: Protestant Popular Culture in Modern Scotland* (Edinburgh: Edinburgh University Press, 1990).

Walker, W. M., *Juteopolis: Dundee and its Textile Workers, 1885–1923* (Edinburgh: Scottish Academic Press, 1979).

Waller, P. J. (ed.), *Politics and Social Change in Modern Britain* (Brighton: Harvester, 1987).

Wardhaugh, Jessica, *In Pursuit of the People: Political Culture in France, 1934–9* (Basingstoke: Palgrave Macmillan, 2009).

Warf, Barney and Santa Arias, *The Spatial Turn: Interdisciplinary Perspectives* (London: Routledge, 2009).

Weitz, Eric D., *Creating German Communism, 1890–1980: From Popular Protests to Socialist State* (Princeton, NJ: Princeton University Press, 1997).

West, Nigel, *MASK: MI5's Penetration of the Communist Party of Great Britain* (London: Routledge, 2005).

Whitney, S. B., *Mobilizing Youth: Communists and Catholics in Inter-War France* (Durham, NC: Duke University Press, 2009).

Williamson, Philip, *National Crisis and National Government: British politics, the economy and Empire, 1926–32* (Cambridge: Cambridge University Press, 1992).

Williamson, Philip, *Stanley Baldwin: Conservative Leadership and National Values* (Cambridge: Cambridge University Press, 1999).

Winter, Jay, *Sites of Memory, Sites of Mourning: The Great War in European Cultural History* (Cambridge: Cambridge University Press, 1998).

Winter, Jay (ed.), *The Working Class in Modern British History: Essays in honour of Henry Pelling* (Cambridge: Cambridge University Press, 1983).

Woodhouse, Michael and Brian Pearce (eds), *Essays on the History of Communism in Britain* (London: New Park Publications, 1975).

Worley, Matthew, *Class Against Class: The Communist Party in Britain between the Wars* (London: I. B. Tauris, 2002).

Worley, Matthew, *Labour Inside the Gate: A History of the British Labour Party between the Wars* (London: I. B. Tauris, 2005).

Worley, Matthew (ed.), *In Search of Revolution: International Communist Parties and the Third Period* (London: I. B. Tauris, 2004).

Worley, Matthew (ed.), *Labour's Grass Roots: Essays on the Activities of Local Labour Parties and Members, 1918–1945* (Aldershot: Ashgate, 2005).

Worley, Matthew (ed.), *The Foundations of the British Labour Party: Identities, Cultures and Perspectives, 1900–1939* (Farnham: Ashgate, 2009).

Wrigley, Chris (ed.), *A History of British Industrial Relations: Volume 2, 1914–1939* (Aldershot: Ashgate, 1993).

Chapters in edited collections

Ball, Stuart, Andrew Thorpe and Matthew Worley, 'Elections, Leaflets and Whist Drives: Constituency Party Members in Britain between the Wars' in Worley (ed.), *Labour's Grass Roots*, pp. 7–32.

Baxter, Kenneth and William Kenefick, 'Labour Politics and the Dundee Working Class, c. 1895–1936' in Tomlinson and Whatley (eds), *Jute no More*, pp. 191–219.

Beers, Laura, 'Counter-Toryism: Labour's Response to Anti-Socialist Propaganda, 1918–39' in Worley (ed.), *The Foundations of the British Labour Party*, pp. 231–54.

Beers, Laura and Geraint Thomas, 'Introduction' in Beers and Thomas (eds), *Brave New World*, pp. 1–38.

Biagini, Eugenio and Alastair J. Reid, 'Currents of Radicalism, 1850–1914' in Biagini and Reid (eds), *Currents of Radicalism*, pp. 1–19.

Brims, John, 'The Covenanting Tradition and Scottish Radicalism in the 1790s' in Brotherstone (ed.), *Covenant, Charter and Party*, pp. 50–62.

Clark, Anna, 'Gender, Class, and the Constitution: Franchise reform in England, 1832–1928' in Vernon (ed.), *Re-reading the Constitution*, pp. 230–53.

Cowan, Edward J., 'The Covenanting Tradition in Scottish History' in Cowan and Finlay (eds), *Scottish History: The Power of the Past*, pp. 121–45.

Davis, Jonathan, 'Labour's Political Thought: The Soviet Influence in the Inter-war Years' in Corthorn and Davis (eds), *The British Labour Party and the Wider World*, pp. 64–85.

Duncan, Robert, 'Independent Working-Class Education and the Formation of the Labour College Movement in Glasgow and the West of Scotland, 1915–1922' in Duncan and McIvor (eds), *Militant Workers*, pp. 106–28.

Dyer, Michael, 'Twentieth-Century Politics' in Fraser and Lee (eds), *Aberdeen 1800–2000*, pp. 204–35.

Eley, Geoff, 'Nations, Publics, and Political Cultures: Placing Habermas in the Nineteenth Century' in Calhoun (ed.), *Habermas and the Public Sphere*, pp. 289–339.

Fischer, Conan, 'Unemployment and Left-Wing Radicalism in Weimar Germany, 1930–33' in Stachura (ed.), *Unemployment and the Great Depression in Weimar Germany*, pp. 209–25.

Fraser, William, 'Trades Councils in the Labour Movement in Nineteenth-Century Scotland' in MacDougall (ed.), *Essays in Scottish Labour History*, pp. 1–28.

Good, Kit, '"Quit Ye Like Men": Platform Manliness and Electioneering, 1895–1939' in McCormack (ed.), *Public Men*, pp. 143–64.

Gunn, Simon, 'The Spatial Turn: Changing Histories of Space and Place' in Gunn and Morris (eds), *Identities in Space*, pp. 1–14.

Harmer, Harry, 'The Failure of the Communists: The National Unemployed Workers' Movement, 1921–1939: A Disappointing Success?' in Thorpe (ed.) *The Failure of Political Extremism in Inter-War Britain*, pp. 29–47.

Hobsbawm, Eric J., 'Birth of a Holiday: The First of May' in *Uncommon People: Resistance, Rebellion and Jazz* (London, 1999), pp. 150–70.

Howkins, Alun, 'Class Against Class: The Political Culture of the CPGB, 1930–35' in Gloversmith (ed.), *Class, Culture and Social Change*, pp. 240–57.

Hutchison, I. G. C., 'Unionism between the Two World Wars' in MacDonald (ed.), *Unionist Scotland*, pp. 73–99.

Jarvis, David, 'The Conservative Party and the Politics of Gender' in Francis and Zweiniger-Bargielowska, *The Conservatives and British Society*, pp. 172–93.

Jarvis, David, 'The Shaping of Conservative Electoral Hegemony, 1918–39' in Lawrence and Taylor, *Party, State and Society*, pp. 131–52.

Jones, Gareth Stedman, 'Rethinking Chartism' in *Languages of Class*, pp. 90–178.

Knox, William W., 'The Red Clydesiders and the Scottish Political Tradition' in Brotherstone (ed.), *Covenant, Charter and Party*, pp. 92–104.

Knox, William W., '"Ours Is Not an Ordinary Parliamentary Movement": 1922–1926' in McKinlay and Morris (eds), *The ILP on Clydeside*, pp. 154–76.

Knox, William W., 'Working Life in the City' in Fraser and Lee (eds), *Aberdeen 1800–2000*, pp. 153–75.

Lawrence, Jon, 'The Dynamics of Urban Politics' in Lawrence and Taylor (eds), *Party, State and Society*, pp. 79–105.

Lawrence, Jon, 'Labour and the Politics of Class, 1900–1940' in Feldman and Lawrence (eds), *Structures and Transformations in Modern British History*, pp. 237–60.

Lawrence, Jon, 'Paternalism, Class, and the British Path to Modernity' in Gunn and Vernon (eds), *The Peculiarities of Liberal Modernity in Imperial Britain*, pp. 147–64.

MacDonald, Catriona M. M., '"Their Laurels Wither'd and their Name Forgot": Women and the Scottish Radical Tradition' in Cowan and Finlay (eds), *Scottish History: The Power of the Past*, pp. 225–52.

McKibbin, Ross, 'The Economic Policy of the Second Labour Government' in *Ideologies of Class*, pp. 197–227.

McKibbin, Ross, 'The "Social Psychology" of Unemployment in Inter-war Britain' in *The Ideologies of Class*, pp. 228–58.

McKibbin, Ross, 'Class and Conventional Wisdom: The Conservative Party and the "Public" in Inter-war Britain' in *The Ideologies of Class*, pp. 259–93.

McKinlay, Alan and J. J. Smyth, 'The End of "The Agitator Workman": 1926–32' in McKinlay and Morris (eds), *The ILP on Clydeside*, pp. 177–203.

Matthew, H. C. G., 'Rhetoric and Politics in Britain, 1860–1950' in Waller (ed.), *Politics and Social Change in Modern Britain*, pp. 34–58.

Nicholas, Sian, 'The Construction of a National Identity: Stanley Baldwin, "Englishness" and the Mass Media in Inter-war Britain' in Francis and Zweiniger-Bargielowska (eds), *The Conservatives and British Society*, pp. 127–46.

Reiss, Matthias, 'Marching on the Capital: National Protest Marches of the British Unemployed in the 1920s and 1930s' in Reiss (ed.), *The Street as Stage*, pp. 147–68.

Riddell, D. S., 'Social Structure and Relations' in Jackson (ed.), *The Third Statistical Account of Scotland: The City of Dundee*, pp. 459–514.

Rosenhaft, Eve, 'The Unemployed in the Neighbourhood: Social Dislocation and Political Mobilisation in Germany, 1929–33' in Evans and Geary (eds), *The German Unemployed*, pp. 194–227.

Tanner, Duncan, 'Class Voting and Radical Politics: The Liberal and Labour Parties, 1910–31', in Lawrence and Taylor (eds), *Party, State and Society*, pp. 106–30.

Taylor, Andrew, 'Speaking to Democracy: The Conservative Party and Mass Opinion from the 1920s to the 1950s' in Ball and Holliday (eds) *Mass Conservatism*, pp. 78–99.

Thomas, Geraint, 'Political Modernity and "Government" in the Construction of inter-war Democracy: Local and National Encounters' in Beers and Thomas (eds), *Brave New World*, pp. 39–65.

Thorpe, Andrew, '"The Only Effective Bulwark against Reaction": Labour and the Frustration of the Extreme Left' in Thorpe (ed.), *The Failure of Political Extremism in Inter-War Britain*, pp. 11–28.

Tsuzuki, Chushici, 'Anglo-Marxism and Working-Class Education' in Winter (ed.), *The Working Class in Modern British History: Essays in Honour of Henry Pelling*, pp. 187–99.

Walker, Graham and Tom Gallagher, 'Protestantism and Scottish Politics' in Walker and Gallagher (eds), *Sermons and Battle Hymns*, pp. 86–111.

Journal articles

Beaven, Brad and Griffiths, John, 'Creating the Exemplary Citizen: The Changing Notion of Citizenship in Britain, 1870–1939', *Contemporary British History* 22(2) (2008), pp. 203–25.

Beers, Laura, 'Education or Manipulation? Labour, Democracy, and the Popular Press in Interwar Britain', *Journal of British Studies* 48(1) (2009), pp. 129–52.

Booth, Alan E. and Sean Glynn, 'Unemployment in the Interwar Period: A Multiple Problem', *Journal of Contemporary History* 10(4) (1975), pp. 611–36.

Bosworth, R. J. B., 'The British Press, the Conservatives, and Mussolini, 1920–34', *Journal of Contemporary History* 5(1) (1970), pp. 163–82.

Bowlby, Chris, 'Blutmai 1929: Police, Parties and Parliamentarians in a Berlin Confrontation', *Historical Journal* 29(1) (1986), pp. 137–58.

Brown, S. J., '"A Victory for God": The Scottish Presbyterian Churches and the General Strike of 1926', *Journal of Ecclesiastical History* 42(4) (1991), pp. 596–617.

Brown, S. J., '"Outside the Covenant": the Scottish Presbyterian Churches and Irish immigration', *Innes Review* 42(1) (1991), pp. 19–45.

Buchanan, Tom, 'The Politics of Internationalism: The Amalgamated Engineering Union and the Spanish Civil War', *Bulletin of the Society for the Study of Labour History* 53(3) (1988), pp. 47–55.

Buchanan, Tom, 'The Role of the British Labour Movement in the Origins and Work of the Basque Children's Committee, 1937–39', *European History Quarterly* 18(2) (1988), pp. 155–74.

Buchanan, Tom, 'Britain's Popular Front?: Aid Spain and the British Labour Movement', *History Workshop Journal* 31 (1991), pp. 60–72.

Buchanan, Tom, 'Holding the Line: The Political Strategy of the International Brigade Association', *Labour History Review* 66(3) (2001), pp. 163–84.

Buxton, Neil K., 'Economic Growth in Scotland between the Wars: The Role of Production Structure and Rationalization', *Economic History Review* 33(4) (1980), pp. 538–55.

Caldwell, John T., 'The Battle for Glasgow Green', *Journal of the Scottish Labour History Society* 16 (1981), pp. 19–27.

Campbell, Alan, 'From Independent Collier to Militant Miner', *Scottish Labour History Society Journal* 24 (1989), pp. 8–23.

Campbell, Alan and John McIlroy, 'Reflections on the Communist Party's Third Period in Scotland: The Case of Willie Allan', *Scottish Labour History* 35 (2000), pp. 33–54.

Campbell, Alan and John McIlroy, 'A Reply to Critics', *Labour History Review* 69(3) (2004), pp. 373–80.

Campbell, Alan and John McIlroy, 'The Last Word on Communism', *Labour History Review* 70(1) (2005), pp. 97–101.

Campbell, Alan and John McIlroy, 'The National Unemployed Workers' Movement Revisited', *Labour History Review* 73(1) (2008), pp. 61–88.

Campbell, Roy H., 'The Scottish Office and the Special Areas in the 1930s', *Historical Journal* 22(1) (1979), pp. 167–83.

Childs, Michael, 'Labour Grows Up: The Electoral System, Political Generations, and British Politics, 1890–1929', *Twentieth Century British History* 6(2) (1995), pp. 123–44.

Clarke, Peter F., 'Electoral Sociology of Modern Britain', *History* 57 (1972), pp. 31–55.

Cohen, Gidon and Kevin Morgan, 'Stalin's Sausage Machine: British Students at the International Lenin School, 1926–1937', *Twentieth Century British History* 13(4) (2002), pp. 327–55.

Cohen, Gidon and Kevin Morgan, 'British Students at the International Lenin School, 1926–1937: A Reaffirmation of Methods, Results, and Conclusions', *Twentieth Century British History* 15(1) (2004), pp. 77–107.

Croucher, Richard, 'Shifting Sands: Changing Interpretations of German Communism', *Labour History Review* 68(1) (2003), pp. 11–31.

Cullen, Stephen M., 'The Fasces and the Saltire: The Failure of the British Union of Fascists in Scotland, 1932–1940', *Scottish Historical Review* 87(2) (2008), pp. 306–31.

Davies, Sam, 'The Membership of the National Unemployed Workers' Movement, 1923–1938', *Labour History Review* 57(1) (1992), pp. 29–36.

Dawson, Michael, 'Money and the Real Impact of the Fourth Reform Act', *Historical Journal* 35(2) (1992), pp. 369–81.

Deli, Peter, 'The Image of the Russian Purges in the Daily Herald and the New Statesman', *Journal of Contemporary History* 20(2) (1985), pp. 261–82.

Dickson, Tony, 'Marxism, Nationalism and Scottish History', *Journal of Contemporary History* 20(2) (1985), pp. 323–36.

Duncan, Robert, '"Motherwell for Moscow": Walton Newbold, Revolutionary Politics and the Labour Movement in a Lanarkshire Constituency, 1918–1922', *Scottish Labour History Society Journal* 28 (1993), pp. 47–69.

Durham, Martin, 'British Revolutionaries and the Suppression of the Left in Lenin's Russia, 1918–1924', *Journal of Contemporary History* 20(2) (1985), pp. 203–19.

Eatwell, Roger, 'Munich, Public Opinion and the Popular Front', *Journal of Contemporary History*, 6(3) (1971), pp. 122–39.

Epstein, James, 'Understanding the Cap of Liberty: Symbolic Practice and Social Conflict in Early Nineteenth-Century England', *Past and Present* 122 (1989), pp. 75–118.

Fielding, Steven, 'British Communism: Interesting but Irrelevant?', *Labour History Review* 60(2) (1995), pp. 120–3.

Fielding, Steven, 'Looking for the "New Political History"', *Journal of Contemporary History* 42(3) (2007), pp. 515–24.

Fishman, Nina, 'A First Revisionist Replies to Her Revisionists', *Labour History Review* 69(3) (2004), pp. 355–61.

Fishman, Nina, 'CPGB History at the Centre of Contemporary History: A Rejoinder to Alan Campbell and John McIlroy', *Labour History Review* 69(3) (2004), pp. 381–3.

Fleay, C. and M. L. Saunders, 'The Labour Spain Committee: Labour Party Policy and the Spanish Civil War', *Historical Journal* 28(1) (1985), pp. 187–97.

Flint, James, '"Must God Go Fascist?" English Catholic Opinion and the Spanish Civil War', *Church History* 56(3) (1987), pp. 364–74.

Foster, John, 'Scotland and the Russian Revolution', *Scottish Labour History Society Journal* 23 (1988), pp. 3–14.

Gallagher, Tom, 'Scottish Catholics and the British Left, 1918–1939', *Innes Review* 34(1) (1983), pp. 17–42.

Gallagher, Tom, 'Protestant Extremism in Urban Scotland, 1930–1939: Its Growth and Contraction', *Scottish Historical Review* 64(2) (1985), pp. 143–67.

Goebel, Stefan, 'Re-membered and Re-mobilized: The "Sleeping Dead" in Interwar Germany and Britain', *Journal of Contemporary History* 39(4) (2004), pp. 487–501.

Gordon, Eleanor, 'The Scottish Trade Union Movement, Class and Gender, 1850–1914', *Journal of the Scottish Labour History Society* 23 (1988), pp. 30–44.

Greene, Julia, 'The National Unemployed Workers' Movement and Popular Protest in Britain, 1920–1939', *International Labour and Working Class History* 30 (1986), pp. 94–102.

Harrison, Royden, 'Communist Party Affiliation to the Labour Party: Transcript of the Meeting of 29 December 1921', *Bulletin of the Society for the Study of Labour History* 29 (1974), pp. 16–34.

Harrison, Royden, 'Communists', *Labour History Review* 59(1) (1994), pp. 40–2.

Hatvany, Doris, 'The General Strike in Aberdeen', *Journal of the Scottish Labour History Society* 10 (1976), pp. 3–20.

Hobsbawm, Eric J., 'The British Communist Party', *Political Quarterly* 25 (1954), pp. 30–43.

Homberger, Eric, 'The Story of the Cenotaph', *Times Literary Supplement*, 12 November 1976, p. 1429.

Howell, David, 'Beyond the Stereotypes: The Independent Labour Party, 1922–1932', *Scottish Labour History Society Journal* 29 (1994), pp. 17–49.

Hunt, Karen and Matthew Worley, 'Rethinking British Communist Party Women in the 1920s', *Twentieth Century British History* 15(1) (2004), pp. 1–27.

Hyde, Samuel, '"Please, Sir, He Called Me 'Jimmy!'" Political Cartooning before the Law: "Black Friday", J. H. Thomas, and the Communist Party Libel Trial of 1921', *Contemporary British History* 25(4) (2011), pp. 521–50.

Jarvis, David, '"Mrs. Maggs and Betty": The Conservative Appeal to Women Voters in the 1920s', *Twentieth Century British History* 5(2) (1994), pp. 129–52.

Jarvis, David, 'British Conservatism and Class Politics in the 1920s', *English Historical Review* 111 (1996), pp. 59–84.

Johnstone, Monty, 'The Communist Party in the 1920s', *New Left Review* 41 (1967), pp. 47–63.

Kiernan, Victor, 'Labour and the War in Spain', *Journal of the Scottish Labour History Society* 11 (1977), pp. 4–16.

King, Frances, 'Archival Sources on the Communist Party of Great Britain', *Science and Society* 61 (1997), pp. 131–9.

Knox, William W. and Alan McKinlay, 'The Re-making of Scottish Labour in the 1930s', *Twentieth Century British History* 6(2) (1995), pp. 174–93.

Knox, William W., 'Religion and the Scottish Labour Movement c.1900–39', *Journal of Contemporary History* 23(4) (1988), pp. 609–30.

Kristjansdottir, Ragnheiur, 'Communists and the National Question in Scotland and Iceland, c.1930 to c.1940', *Historical Journal* 45(3) (2002), pp. 601–18.

LaPorte, Norman and Matthew Worley, 'Towards a Comparative History of Communism: The British and German Communist Parties to 1933', *Contemporary British History* 22(2) (2008), pp. 227–55.

Lawrence, Jon, 'The British Sense of Class', *Journal of Contemporary History* 35(2) (2000), pp. 307–18.

Lawrence, Jon, 'Fascist Violence and the Politics of Public Order in Inter-War Britain: The Olympia Debate Revisited', *Historical Research* 76 (2003), pp. 238–67.

Lawrence, Jon, 'Forging a Peaceable Kingdom: War, Violence, and Fear of Brutalization in Post-First World War Britain', *Journal of Modern History* 75(3) (2003), pp. 557–89.

Lawrence, Jon, 'Why Olympia Mattered', *Historical Research* 78 (2005), pp. 263–72.

Lawrence, Jon, 'The Transformation of British Public Politics after the First World War', *Past and Present* 190 (2006), pp. 185–216.

Lawson, Tom, '"The Free-Masonry of Sorrow"? English National Identities and the Memorialization of the Great War in Britain, 1919–1931', *History and Memory* 20(1) (2008), pp. 89–120.

Laybourn, Keith, 'The Rise of Labour and the Decline of Liberalism: The State of the Debate', *History* 80 (1995), pp. 207–26.

Long, Paul, 'Abe Moffat, the Fife Miners and the United Mineworkers of Scotland', *Journal of the Scottish Labour History Society* 17 (1982), pp. 5–18.

Macintyre, Stuart, 'British Labour, Marxism and Working Class Apathy in the Nineteen Twenties', *Historical Journal* 20(2) (1977), pp. 479–96.

McCarthy, Helen, 'Parties, Voluntary Associations, and Democratic Politics in Interwar Britain', *Historical Journal* 50(4) (2007), pp. 891–912.

McCarthy, Helen, 'The League of Nations, Public Ritual and National Identity in Britain, c.1919–1956', *History Workshop Journal* 70 (2010), pp. 108–32.

McCarthy, Helen, 'Whose Democracy? Histories of British Political Culture between the Wars', *Historical Journal* 55(1) (2012), pp. 221–38.

McIlroy, John and Alan Campbell, '"For a Revolutionary Workers' Government": Moscow, British Communism and Revisionist Interpretations of the Third Period, 1927–1934', *European History Quarterly* 32(4) (2002), pp. 535–69.

McIlroy, John and Alan Campbell, 'The Scots at the Lenin School: An Essay in Collective Biography', *Scottish Labour History* 37 (2002), pp. 50–71.

McIlroy, John and Alan Campbell, '"Nina Ponomareva's Hats": The New Revisionism, the Communist International, and the Communist Party of Great Britain, 1920–1930', *Labour/Le Travail* 49 (2002), pp. 147–87.

McIlroy, John and Alan Campbell, 'Histories of the Communist Party: A User's Guide', *Labour History Review* 68(1) (2003), pp. 33–59.

McIlroy, John, Barry McLoughlin, Alan Campbell and John Halsted, 'Forging the Faithful: The British at the International Lenin School, 1926–1937', *Labour History Review* 68(1) (2003), pp. 99–128.

McKibbin, Ross, 'Arthur Henderson as Labour Leader', *International Review of Social History* 23(1) (1978), pp. 79–101.

McKibbin, Ross, 'Why Was There No Marxism in Great Britain?', *English Historical Review* 99 (1984), pp. 297–331.

McLean, Iain, 'Red Clydeside After 25 Years', *Journal of the Scottish Labour History Society* 29 (1994), pp. 98–111.

Macleod, Jenny, '"By Scottish Hands, with Scottish Money, on Scottish Soil": The Scottish National War Memorial and National Identity', *Journal of British Studies* 49(1) (2010), pp. 73–96.

Macleod, Jenny, 'Memorials and Location: Local versus National Identity and the Scottish National War Memorial', *Scottish Historical Review* 89(1) (2010), pp. 73–95.

Macleod, Jenny, 'Britishness and Commemoration: National Memorials to the First World War in Britain and Ireland', *Journal of Contemporary History* 48(4) (2013), pp. 647–65.

Mah, Harold, 'Phantasies of the Public Sphere: Rethinking the Habermas of the Historians', *Journal of Modern History* 72(1) (2000), pp. 153–82.

Maitles, Henry, 'Fascism in the 1930s: The West of Scotland Context', *Journal of the Scottish Labour History Society* 27 (1992), pp. 7–22.

Maitles, Henry, 'Blackshirts across the Border: The British Union of Fascists in Scotland', *Scottish Historical Review* 82(1) (2003), pp. 92–100.

Matthew, H. C. G., Ross McKibbin and J. A. Kay, 'The Franchise Factor in the Rise of the Labour Party', *English Historical Review* 91 (1976), pp. 723–52.

Marwick, William H., 'Workers' Education in Early Twentieth Century Scotland', *Journal of the Scottish Labour History Society* 8 (1974), pp. 34–8.

Melling, Joseph, 'Whatever Happened to Red Clydeside?', *International Review of Social History* 35(1) (1990), pp. 3–32.

Miles, Andy, 'Workers' Education: The Communist Party and the Plebs League in the 1920s', *History Workshop Journal* 18 (1984), pp. 102–14.

Milligan, Tony, 'The British Union of Fascists' Policy in Relation to Scotland', *Scottish Economic and Social History* 19(1) (1999), pp. 1–17.

Millington, Chris, 'Street-fighting Men: Political Violence in Inter-war France', *English Historical Review* 129 (2014), pp. 606–38.

Morgan, Kevin, 'The Problem of the Epoch? Labour and Housing, 1918–1951', *Twentieth Century British History* 16(3) (2005), pp. 227–55.

Morgan, Kevin, 'Militarism and Anti-Militarism: Socialists, Communists and Conscription in France and Britain, 1900–1940', *Past and Present* 202 (2009), pp. 207–44.

Morgan, Kevin, 'The Trouble with Revisionism: or Communist History with the History Left In', *Labour/Le Travail* 63 (2009), pp. 131–55.

Morgan, Kevin, 'Socialists and "Mobility" in Twentieth-Century Britain: Images and Experiences in the Life Histories of British Communists', *Social History* 36(2) (2011), pp. 143–68.

Morris, Robert J., 'Skilled Workers and the Politics of the "Red" Clyde: A Discussion Paper', *Journal of the Scottish Labour History Society* 18 (1983), pp. 6–19.

Newman, Michael, 'Democracy versus Dictatorship: Labour's Role in the Struggle against British Fascism, 1933–1936', *History Workshop Journal* 5 (1978), pp. 67–88.

Nixon, Mark, Gordon Pentland and Matthew Roberts, 'The Material Culture of Scottish Reform Politics, c.1820–c.1884', *Journal of Scottish Historical Studies* 32(1) (2012), pp. 28–49.

O'Brien, Patrick K., 'Britain's Economy between the Wars: A Survey of a Counter-revolution in Economic History', *Past and Present* 115 (1987), pp. 107–30.

O'Gorman, Frank, 'Campaign Rituals and Ceremonies: The Social Meaning of Elections in England, 1780–1860', *Past and Present* 135 (1992), pp. 79–115.

Owen, Nicholas, 'MacDonald's Parties: The Labour Party and the "Aristocratic Embrace", 1922–31', *Twentieth Century British History* 18(1) (2007), pp. 1–53.

Pentland, Gordon, '"Betrayed by Infamous Spies?" The Commemoration of Scotland's "Radical War" of 1820', *Past and Present* 201 (2008), pp. 141–73.

Petrie, Malcolm R., 'Public Politics and Traditions of Popular Protest: Demonstrations of the Unemployed in Dundee and Edinburgh, c.1921–1939', *Contemporary British History* 27(4) (2013), pp. 490–513.

Petrie, Malcolm R., 'Unity from Below? The Impact of the Spanish Civil War on Labour and the Left in Aberdeen and Dundee, 1936–1939', *Labour History Review* 79(3) (2014), pp. 305–27.

Petrie, Malcolm R., '"Contests of Vital Importance": By-elections, the Labour Party, and the Reshaping of British Radicalism', *Historical Journal* 60(1) (2017), pp. 121–48.

Pickering, Paul A., 'Class without Words: Symbolic Communication in the Chartist Movement', *Past and Present* 112 (1986), pp. 144–62.

Price, Richard, 'Contextualising British syndicalism, c.1907–c.1920', *Labour History Review* 63(3) (1998), pp. 261–76.

Pugh, Martin, 'Popular Conservatism in Britain: Continuity and Change, 1880–1987', *Journal of British Studies* 27(3) (1988), pp. 254–82.

Pugh, Martin, 'The British Union of Fascists and the Olympia Debate', *Historical Journal* 41(2) (1998), pp. 529–42.

Pugh, Martin, 'The National Government, the British Union of Fascists and the Olympia Debate', *Historical Research* 78 (2005), pp. 253–62.

Rafeek, Neil, 'Rose Kerrigan, 1903–1995', *Journal of the Scottish Labour History Society* 31 (1996), pp. 72–84.

Reid, Fred, 'Socialist Sunday Schools in Britain, 1892–1939', *International Review of Social History* 11(1) (1966), pp. 18–47.

Roberts, J. M., 'Spatial Governance and Working Class Public Spheres: The Case of a Chartist Demonstration at Hyde Park', *Journal of Historical Sociology* 14(3) (2001), pp. 308–36.

Samuel, Raphael, 'British Marxist Historians, 1880–1980: Part One', *New Left Review* 120 (1980), pp. 21–96.

Samuel, Raphael, 'The Lost World of British Communism', *New Left Review* 154 (1986), pp. 3–53.

Samuel, Raphael, 'Staying Power: The Lost World of British Communism, Part Two', *New Left Review* 156 (1986), pp. 63–113.

Samuel, Raphael, 'Class Politics: The Lost World of British Communism, Part Three', *New Left Review* 165 (1987), pp. 52–91.

Samuel, Raphael, 'Reading the Signs', *History Workshop Journal* 32 (1991), pp. 88–109.

Samuel, Raphael, 'Reading the Signs: II. Fact-grubbers and Mind-readers', *History Workshop Journal* 33 (1992), pp. 220–51.

Savage, Michael, 'The Rise of the Labour Party in Local Perspective', *The Journal of Regional and Local Studies* 10(1) (1990), pp. 1–15.

Schwarz, Bill, 'The Language of Constitutionalism: Baldwinite Conservatism', *Formations: Of Nation and People* (1984), pp. 1–18.

Schwarz, Bill, 'Politics and Rhetoric in the Age of Mass Culture', *History Workshop Journal* 46 (1998), pp. 129–59.

Schwarz, Bill, '*Philosophes* of the Conservative Nation: Burke, Macaulay, Disraeli', *Journal of Historical Sociology* 12(3) (1999), pp. 183–217.

Smyth, J. J., 'Resisting Labour: Unionists, Liberals, and Moderates in Glasgow between the Wars', *Historical Journal* 46(2) (2003), pp. 375–401.

Tanner, Duncan, 'The Parliamentary Electoral System, the "Fourth" Reform Act and the Rise of Labour in England and Wales', *Bulletin of the Institute for Historical Research* 56 (1983), pp. 205–19.

Tanner, Duncan, 'Elections, Statistics, and the Rise of the Labour Party, 1906–1931', *Historical Journal* 34(4) (1991), pp. 893–908.

Taylor, Anthony, '"Commons-Stealers", "Land-Grabbers" and "Jerry-Builders": Space, Popular Radicalism and the Politics of Public Access in London, 1848–1880', *International Review of Social History* 40 (1995), pp. 383–407.

Thackeray, David, 'Building a Peaceable Party: Masculine Identities in British Conservative Politics, c. 1903–24', *Historical Research* 85 (2013), pp. 651–73.

Thane, Pat, 'What Difference Did the Vote Make? Women in Public and Private Life in Britain since 1918', *Historical Research* 76 (2003), pp. 268–85.

Thompson, James, '"Pictorial Lies"? Posters and Politics in Britain c. 1880–1914', *Past and Present* 197 (2007), pp. 177–210.

Thorpe, Andrew, 'Arthur Henderson and the British Political Crisis of 1931', *Historical Journal* 31(1) (1988), pp. 117–39.

Thorpe, Andrew, 'Comintern "control" of the Communist Party of Great Britain, 1920–1943', *English Historical Review* 113 (1998), pp. 637–62.

Thorpe, Andrew, 'Stalinism and British Politics', *History* 83 (1998), pp. 608–27.

Thorpe, Andrew, 'The Membership of the Communist Party of Great Britain, 1920–1945', *Historical Journal* 43(3) (2000), pp. 777–800.

Thorpe, Andrew, 'Communist Party History: A Reply to Campbell and McIlroy', *Labour History Review* 69(3) (2004), pp. 363–5.

Thorpe, Andrew, 'CPGB History at the Centre of Contemporary History 2002: A Rejoinder', *Labour History Review* 69(3) (2004), pp. 385–7.

Thorpe, Andrew, 'The Communist Party and the New Party', *Contemporary British History* 23(4) (2009), pp. 477–91.

Tomlinson, Jim, 'The Political Economy of Globalisation: The Genesis of Dundee's Two "United Fronts" in the 1930s', *Historical Journal* 57(1) (2014), pp. 225–45.

Toye, Richard, '"Perfectly Parliamentary"? The Labour Party and the House of Commons in the Inter-war Years', *Twentieth Century British History* 25(1) (2014), pp. 1–29.

Walker, William M., 'Dundee's Disenchantment with Churchill: A Comment on the Downfall of the Liberal Party', *Scottish Historical Review* 49(1) (1970), pp. 85–108.

Walker, William M., 'Irish immigrants in Scotland: Their Priests, Politics and Parochial Life', *Historical Journal* 15(4) (1972), pp. 649–77.

Walker, William M., 'The Scottish Prohibition Party and the Millennium', *International Review of Social History* 18(3) (1973), pp. 353–79.

Ward, Stephanie, 'The Means Test and the Unemployed in South Wales and the North-East of England, 1931–1939', *Labour History Review* 73(1) (2008), pp. 113–32.

Weitz, Eric D., 'Eve Rosenhaft's *Beating the Fascists*? An Appreciation', *Twentieth Century Communism* 2 (2010), pp. 169–79.

Williamson, Philip, '"Safety First": Baldwin, the Conservative Party and the 1929 General Election', *Historical Journal* 25(2) (1982), pp. 385–409.

Wirsching, Andreas, 'Violence as Discourse? For a "Linguistic Turn" in Communist History', *Twentieth Century Communism* 2 (2010), pp. 12–39.

Worley, Matthew, 'Left Turn: A Reassessment of the Communist Party of Great Britain in the Third Period, 1928–1933', *Twentieth Century British History,* 11(4) (2000), pp. 353–78.

Worley, Matthew, 'The Communist International, The Communist Party of Great Britain, and the Third Period, 1928–1932', *European History Quarterly* 30(2) (2000), pp. 185–208.

Worley, Matthew, 'Echoes from the Dustbin of History: A Reply to Campbell and McIlroy', *Labour History Review* 69(3) (2004), pp. 367–72.

Worley, Matthew, 'Introduction: Communism and Political Violence', *Twentieth Century Communism* 2 (2010), pp. 5–11.

Young, James D., 'Nationalism, "Marxism" and Scottish History', *Journal of Contemporary History* 20(2) (1985), pp. 337–55.

Zeitlin, Jonathan, '"Rank and Filism" in British Labour History: A Critique', *International Review of Social History* 34(1) (1989), pp. 42–61.

Unpublished theses

Brown, Gordon, 'The Labour Party and Political Change in Scotland, 1918–1929: The Politics of Five Elections' (unpublished PhD thesis, University of Edinburgh, 1982).

Cohen, Gidon, 'The Independent Labour Party, 1932–1939' (unpublished PhD thesis, University of York, 2000).

Kibblewhite, Elizabeth, 'The Impact of Unemployment on the Development of Trade Unionism in Scotland, 1918–1939' (unpublished PhD thesis, University of Aberdeen, 1979).

Phipps, C. W. M., 'Aberdeen Trades Council and Politics, 1900–1939: The Development of the Local Labour Party in Aberdeen' (unpublished MLitt dissertation, University of Aberdeen, 1980).

Tolland, Siobhan, '"Just Ae Wee Woman": Dundee, the Communist Party and the Feminisation of Socialism in the Life of Mary Brooksbank' (unpublished PhD thesis, University of Aberdeen, 2005).

Index